# Clinical Pharmacology of Learning and Memory

# Clinical Pharmacology of Learning and Memory

**Walter B. Essman, M.D., Ph.D.**
Department of Psychology
Queens College
Flushing, New York

**SP MEDICAL & SCIENTIFIC BOOKS**
a division of Spectrum Publications, Inc.
New York

SPECTRUM PUBLICATIONS, INC.
175-20 Wexford Terrace
Jamaica, NY 11432


Library of Congress Cataloging in Publication Data

Essman, Walter B.
   Clinical pharmacology of learning and memory.

   Includes index.
   1. Psychopharmacology. 2. Learning—Effect of drugs on.
3. Memory—Effect of drugs on. 4. Psychotropic drugs. I. Title.
[DNLM: 1. Learning—Drug effects. 2. Memory—Drug effects. 3. Psychotropic drugs—Pharmacodynamics. QV 77 E78c]
RM315.E77       615'.78       82-3321
ISBN 0-89335-167-9              AACR2


Printed in the United States of America

For
Shirley and Eric

# Preface

The search for drugs to alter learning and memory processes in animals and man has its roots in mythology as well as the history of medicine. The use of plant alkaloids to improve memory was a recommendation of Benjamin Rush in his "Diseases of the Mind" (1812, P. 284), and the mysterious contents of lethe, a liquid capable of causing the erasure of earthly memories is found in Egyptian and Greek mythology, as well as described by Dante, remains a still-sought amnesic molecule. The facilitation of learning or improvement of memory has been claimed for several plant-derived substances including coca, chat, caffeine, and nicotine. Hypotheses concerning substances found in the brain and their presumed significance for learning or memory led to the development and use of agents that contained such substances. For example, as observed by William James (1892, P. 132), the emphasis, in Germany during the 1860's, upon phosphorus in the brain for cognitive functions gave rise to the suggestion that foods high in phosphorus content, such as fish, were good for brain function. Phosphorus-containing preparations were advocated for use in cases of poor memory, exhaustion, etc., and though sometimes useful, probably were effective due to a non-specific stimulant effect. Whether the positive cognitive efficacy of non-specific CNS stimulants such as phosphorus, rosemary, lavender, cubeb berries, etc. were really very different from those investigated in animal experiments (Lashley, 1917) or those documented within recent decades remains to be explored.

In the light of more contemporary studies of drugs upon learning and memory, earlier animal investigations yielded results that were puzzling and in some instances contradictory to predicted CNS effects. For example, acquired maze behavior by rats was enhanced by treatment with methanol and belladonna alkaloids and disrupted by ethanol, nicotine, caffeine, morphine, and codeine (Macht, et al., 1920, 1921, 1922, 1923, 1924, 1925, 1932, 1935, 1938, 1939). Drugs have also been studied and found to alter bar-pressing rates in a Skinner box, with insulin and benzedrine producing marked rate increases (Wentink, 1938).

The present volume summarized both differences in theoretical and methodological approaches to learning and memory processes, but also considers those classes of drugs that have been employed to either evaluate basic conceptual issues or to explore their behavioral applications and clinical utilization.

Since the mechanisms of action for agents that influence learning and memory processes are frequently enlarged upon or change with new developments in neuropharmacology and neurochemistry, the direction of clinical utility for such agents is also sometimes changed. This may often explain that even though the basic premise for the use of a given drug, based upon its central effect, is a sound one, the effect itself is unimpressive. We have tried to balance both sides of the issues of controversy regarding theoretical issues and empirical findings and where possible, to suggest those areas where relevant answers may be found.

The present volume is intended as a reference guide for the researcher and clinician. The search for new drugs or new applications for existing agents to the processes of learning and memory is a continuing effort, as in such information of value to the clinician who seeks to apply such findings toward the treatment of disorders of learning and memory. It is our hope that this volume will provide the researcher as well as the clinician with something of value.

WALTER B. ESSMAN

Flushing, N.Y.
January, 1983

# Contents

# Introduction

Drugs affecting the performance of learned behavior or modifying the acquisition of new behaviors generally include agents which produce effects that may be considered as facilitative or disruptive. The nature of such facilitation or disruption may be considered at the level of the response itself (secondary action) or on the basis of the effect upon an underlying process of learning or memory (primary action). The former may include peripheral as well as central nervous system sites of drug action, and can involve motor, neuromuscular, vascular, endocrine, or indirect visceral effects, whereas the latter sites of drug action involve either perikaryal or synaptic effects which can be regional, cellular, or subcellular. To address oneself to primary actions of those agents, which modify learning and/or memory processes, one must necessarily formulate a series of relationships by which either the electrophysiological, the morphological, or the metabolic correlates of learning or memory are logically as well as empirically linked with parameters of change in behavior as mediated by drug action. The former two disciplines do not consistently succeed in satisfying such a stringent requirement, probably because of several limitations: (1) methodological limitations, (2) temporal variations, (3) limitations imposed by regional or cellular specificity, (4) the complexity of the learning situation or adequacy of response retrieval, (5) chronicity of the drug regimen required, and (6) the physiological approximation of drug dosage. Although not complete in the encompassment of all issues, empirical findings, and parameters of drug action (route, absorption, disposition, binding, metabolism, affinity, etc.), it appears that drug action, particularly as relevant for learning and memory, finds a more secure explanatory foundation in processes and events which can be correlated with metabolic effects and for which such metabolic changes also constitute issues for learning and memory mechanisms.

Of course, at some levels metabolic effects of drug action are reflected electrophysiologically and, to some degree, morphologically (e.g., mitochondrial swelling, membrane changes, cytoplasmic inclusion bodies, etc.), although such changes have limited significance for either the mechanisms which underlie or the response indices of learning and/or memory.

The clinical pharmacology of learning and memory is largely constituted of a framework provided by a more basic pharmacology based upon largely animal studies and, to a more limited degree, the application of derivative findings to studies in man. Obviously a pharmacology of facilitative agents has more direct clinical relevance than a pharmacology of disruptive agents, although the latter does provide for insight into such phenomena as amnesic processes, documentation of cognitoxic agents, and the potential prevalence of specific drug interactions.

A further distinction between behaviorally active drug effects may be made on a clinical level between the facilitative or disruptive effects of a given agent in a "normal" human population as contrasted with a population demonstrating a neurological, vascular, or metabolic lesion of the central nervous system. In the case of those agents for which facilitative effects are considered, there may well be differences in effect depending upon whether facilitation of learning or memory is defined as an improvement of normal performance, perception, or problem-solving ability, or as a reduced deficit in one or more responses from which learning or memory are inferred. The nature of the deficit as well as the mechanism of drug action are important in resolving such differences, particularly in those instances where a paradoxical effect of the drug may occur. For example, in children with so-called "minimal brain damage," barbiturates may act as stimulants and amphetamines as depressants; such effects can also be reflected in differences in drug effects in learning paradigms where motivation, attention, and comprehension are important, and in response-reflecting memory (stored information, based upon acquired responses) which is subject to retrieval and may be discriminated from nonrelevant, neutral, or other stimuli.

A problem, which further complicates the analysis of a relationship between metabolic factors in learning and memory processing and effects of drugs upon these same metabolic events and associated behavioral alterations, lies in separating the peripheral effects of drug action from central effects. Peripheral effects of parenterally administered drugs occur at muscle and glandular sites, the response of which provides feedback as well as direct input to the central nervous system. Of course such effects may also be secondary to direct central actions. These effects are not easily demonstratable in the clinical situation, but may be inferred from studies in which parenterally administered drugs which alter learning and/or memory are also agents that do not traverse the blood–brain barrier and therefore exert no direct central effect.

# Clinical
# Pharmacology
# of Learning
# and Memory

# 1

# Drug Interactions

The clinical pharmacology of drugs affecting learning and memory involves agents that may be classed as psychoactive in the sense of their usual clinical application, as well as compounds that may have no direct clinical utility in the treatment of behavior disorders or altered affective states. There are a wide range of agents in clinical use for the management of behavior disturbances, hypertension, endocrine dysfunction, cardiac rhythm disturbances, obesity, and so on, which are well known for their behavioral side effects, such as a disturbance of performance or motivation. These are important variables for learning ability or capacity and also for memory fixation, retrieval, and stability. They are not, however, agents the effects of which concern direct actions upon learning or memory processes or on the molecular bases upon which such processes are founded. Another aspect of this same issue is the interaction of both exogenous as well as endogenous molecules with drugs that may affect learning or memory processes. Previous or concurrent

1

administration of agents such as phenytoin, phenobarbital, or steroids — capable of inducing hepatic drug-metabolizing enzymes — may well shorten the duration of drug action, reduce its potency, or minimize the degree to which it becomes capable of exerting an effective central molecular effect.

In another case renal function, notably for those agents metabolized by this route, constitutes an endogenous basis for particular interactions. The elimination of drugs is, of course, altered by uremia in man, and several factors of peripheral significance for central drug effects may be modified under such circumstances. For example, vitamin D oxidation is prolonged (Avioli et al., 1968), cortisol reduction is prolonged (Englert et al., 1958), paminosalicylate acetylation is prolonged (Ogg et al., 1968), insulin hydrolysis is prolonged (O'Brien and Sharp, 1967), and cholinesterase activity is slowed (Holmes et al., 1958). Urinary excretion of drugs which affect learning- and memory-related behaviors can be directly affected by several factors, but one basic parameter is the pH of the urine. Enhanced renal excretion of some acids, such as salicylic acid and phenobarbital, occurs at high urinary pH, whereas at a low urinary pH the excretion of such bases as amphetamine and quinidine is increased.

Certainly a number of disease states also affect the disposition of several drugs, which may have a role in their application to the study of learning and/or memory. This is a particularly relevant consideration inasmuch as one area to which pharmacological facilitation of learning or memory may hold considerable clinical relevance and applicability is the geriatric population, in which age-related and/or cerebrovascular or cellular change in cognition and affect constitute consideration of altered learning or memory. Certainly in such a population disorders of learning and/or memory, even though separable from disorders of affect, both conceptually as well as therapeutically, are still subject to a number of coexisting disease states and their effect upon the disposition of potentially useful drugs. The development of an autonomic neuropathy in chronic renal failure reduces receptor sensitivity to atropine and related drugs (Lowenthal and Reidenberg, 1972), and in Bartter's syndrome there is an end-organ refractoriness to angiotensin (Bartter et al., 1962). Other alterations in drug disposition have also been described with renal dysfunction, and include for example vasopressin resistance (Tannen et al., 1959), carbohydrate dysmetabolism (Cerletty and Engbring, 1967), penicillin encephalopathy (Bloomer et al., 1967), increased barbiturate sensitivity and rise in free-drug level (Dundee and Richard, 1954), and increased erythropoesis with androgens (Parker et al., 1972).

There appear to be endogenous factors characterizing some disease states, which may interact directly with a drug or drugs being considered for study with learning or memory disorders. For example, in Down's syndrome the response of the autonomic nervous system to atropine is greatly exaggerated, and such hypersensitivity may reflect an endogenous alteration in the autonomic threshold (Harris and Goodman, 1968). An autonomic imbalance in bronchial asthma has also been indicated as a basis for an abnormal response to epinephrine (Grieco et al., 1968).

There are numerous other endogenous factors which may constitute issues of clinical relevance for their interaction with drugs that affect learning or memory. These may include endocrine factors such as altered thyroid activity (Doherty and Perkins, 1966), modified tissue response to drugs dependent upon parathormone (Schaaf and Payne, 1971), and modified drug metabolism through corticosteroids (Brooks et al., 1972). Such factors may involve plasma proteins which, when reduced, cause an elevation in the unbound fraction of most drugs, and when normal, may be competed for by concurrently administered drugs that are highly protein bound. On the other hand, the increased availability of degradation products from plasma proteins, such as from albumin can decrease the central stimulant effects of some classic centrally-active stimulants (Buczko and Tarasiewicz, 1976).

One final point concerning drug interactions of relevance to the clinical pharmacology of learning and memory deals with exogenous agents which may result in either a reduced or an increased availability of the drug of interest at its site of action. For example, blockade of the norepinephrine pump (by which norepinephrine is transported physiologically into the nerve ending) may be brought about by any of the tricyclic antidepressants (imipramine, desipramine, nortriptyline, amitriptyline, protriptyline, doxepin). Such a blockade can interfere with drugs that require access to the sympathetic nerve ending in order to effectively act. Guanethidine represents one such drug which, in the presence of a tricyclic antidepressant, cannot exert its blocking effect at the sympathetic nerve ending, and therefore fails to exert an effective antihypertensive action (Mitchell et al., 1970). Amphetamines, on the other hand, are transported by a norepinephrine pump into the nerve ending, where they force guanethidine molecules out of the ending, thereby reversing the clinical effect. An example of increased drug availability at the receptor site as a result of interaction may be found between warfarin and drugs that alter protein binding, such as phenylbutazone, which displaces warfarin from albumin (Aggeler et al., 1967), or chloral hydrate, the metabolite of which (trichloroacetic acid) displaces warfarin from albumin (Sellers and Koch-Weser, 1970). The clinical effects of warfarin under such circumstances would be enhanced and its action prolonged.

It thereby should be emphasized that drug interactions or factors arising from either exogenous or endogenous sources may modify the action of pharmacological agents which alter processes of learning or memory. Since such interactions, like the drugs themselves concerned, involve molecular events which can be related, at least indirectly, to similar effects upon learning and memory-related mechanisms that are altered by specific drugs, these are appropriate to consider in the present context. There is, of course, much more that needs to be known about drug interactions in learning and memory.

There are issues possibly related to the clinical pharmacology of learning and memory which are indirect or indistinct in present perspective. In any case, their clinical relevance may be in question. One such issue concerns so-called state-dependent learning, in which accurate performance of an acquired response is contingent upon the drug state that is present during acquisition of the behavior. Barbiturates and cholinergic drugs have frequently been utilized to demonstrate such state-dependent properties, but several other classes of drugs have also been implicated. It should be emphasized that state-dependent properties of drugs do not necessarily dispose their action to one of facilitation or impairment of either learning or memory.

Another issue concerns the controversial phenomenon of information transfer by extracts from the brain tissue of trained animals. The experiments concerned with this phenomenon have been carried out largely in mice and rats, and have been questioned by failure of replicability as well as by a lack of neurobiological mechanism by which the purported phenomenon may be explained. The molecular bases upon which such transfer of information studies have been founded rely upon ribonucleic acid (RNA) or proteins, or both, within the structure of which specific information may have been encoded. Indeed there are some firm bases upon which RNA and protein occupy prominent roles in the mechanisms regulating learning and memory. Direct or indirect inhibition of the synthesis of such macromolecules can impair learning or memory fixation, and facilitation of learning or memory has been related to the central effects of certain peptides and metabolites of nucleotides.

The ultimate significance of such issues for either learning or memory remains to be delineated on a much more detailed basis than presently available. There seems little doubt that the regional, perikaryal, and synaptic events of the central nervous system, which are involved in the mediation of acquired behavior and the consolidation of the memory trace, are also responsive to pharmacological agents which modify these processes.

# 2

# Macromolecules in Learning and Memory

The participation of macromolecular substrates in learning and memory processes has been based theoretically upon the view that frequency-modulated inputs to the central nervous system alter the ionic equilibrium of the cell cytoplasm and modify the stability of the nitrogenous bases of the RNA molecule (Hydén, 1959). Altered molecular structure through base modification leads to the synthesis of new RNA-dependent proteins capable of interacting with molecules of complementary structure. The release of transmitter molecules from their presynaptic vesicular storage could follow as a result of such an interaction. The theory does hold considerable promise, even currently, but fails to resolve a number of issues that appear critical to an understanding of how learning and memory are affected by specific drugs. Namely, (1) the relationship between nuclear changes and effects at the synapse remains unclear; (2) the protein interaction does not provide for a mechanism of reversibility to account for acquisition failure or retention deficits; (3) drug

7

effects would have to involve either cytoplasmic ionic changes or alteration of vesicular release processes to be consistent with the overall concept; and (4) there is no adequate means of accounting for memory consolidation—a process that occupies a central conceptual role in dealing with drug effects upon memory fixation. To clarify the latter point, the preservation–consolidation hypothesis of memory fixation (Müller and Pilzecker, 1900) stated that the memory trace, a neural representation of an acquired stimulus, was actively perseverated in the neuron for a brief period beyond its initiation by an acquired stimulus. It was considered that once this perseverative activity was terminated, the memory trace was consolidated, the acquired stimulus was reproduced, and its retrieval from storage was possible. An agent or event capable of interfering with the onset, or progress, of the perseveration phase (fixation) resulted in impairment in memory consolidation.

More recent experimental evidence has supported a memory consolidation process in both animals and man, and indeed the time-dependent nature of this process has made it a superb theoretical model by which drug effects upon memory have been evaluated.

The first suggestion that the interaction of an amnesic stimulus with a drug could be used to define the effect of the drug upon memory consolidation utilized electroconvulsive shock (ECS) as the amnesic stimulus and a malononitrile derivative as the drug studied (Essman, 1965). These studies were based upon the use of a single-trial conditioning paradigm initially developed to study the temporal characteristics of memory consolidation (Jarvik and Essman, 1960; Essman and Alpern, 1964). These issues will be dealt with again in later chapters.

Another theoretical view of historical interest for a molecular approach to learning and memory is the position that a nucleoprotein lattice of regionally and experientially specific molecules constituted the basis for memory traces (Katz and Halstead, 1960). This view also offers considerable applicability for later investigations, notably those concerned with the use of inhibitors of protein synthesis as tools to study the stability or molecular dependence of certain memories. For example, such antibiotics as puromycin, which inhibit protein synthesis (Flexner and Flexner, 1968), are behaviorally disruptive (Davis, 1968). Although some, but not all, inhibitors of cerebral protein synthesis disrupt learning or interfere with memory formation or response retrieval, the fact is that the same degree of inhibition can occur without behavioral impairment; this places into question the validity of cerebral protein synthesis as a generalized concept for learning and memory. The nature of specific proteins, their sites of activation and/or inhibition, and endogenous factors by which such loci and effects are physiologically mediated remain to be more precisely defined. Such a definition will have to be rather specific about the nature of those endogenous molecules which, when activated, bound, degraded, etc., either physiologically or pharmacologically, are capable of modifying the synthesis or disposition of proteins of possible significance for learning and memory.

A distinction should be made between macromolecular change as a dependent variable of learning and memory and macromolecular effect as a pharmacological variable in learning and memory. The former is highly relevant, conceptually and practically, to the latter, but it is the pharmacological aspect of this contingency that is of primary concern to this chapter. Macromolecular change, however, does deserve some comment. When rats were trained to reverse the use of their preferred forepaw to obtain food (reverse handedness), an increased incorporation of an amino acid precursor into hippocampal nerve cell protein fractions was demonstrated (Hydén and Lange, 1970). When malononitrile-treated patients (post lobotomy) were compared with untreated controls (accidental death), an increased production of nucleic acid and protein was measured (Hydén and Hartelius, 1948; Hartelius, 1950). This gave rise to other experiments in which the dimer of malononitrile, tricyanoaminopropene (TCAP), when parenterally administered, was shown to increase the RNA and nucleoprotein contents of single neurons in the rabbit brain (Egyhazi and Hydén, 1961). Rabbits injected with 20 mg/kg of TCAP showed a 27% increase in nuclear protein and a 26% increase in nuclear RNA in Dieter's nerve cell 1 hour later; RNA from adjacent glia was decreased by 45% (Hydén, 1962). Drug-treated animals showed a significant decrease in nerve cell cytosine, and glial cytosine was significantly increased. In contrast to this apparently reciprocal cellular base change following TCAP, a central nervous system stimulant, increased neuronal and glial cytosine occurred in the same region following the administration of tranylcypromine, a monoamine oxidase inhibitor which provides for the accumulation of biogenic amines.

Although somewhat preliminary to the issue of learning and memory, the molecular effects of the central nervous system stimulant TCAP and of tranylypromine do relate in several practical ways to learning and memory. Such relationships support not only a molecular relationship, but they also suggest a basis for an interdependent role for nucleic acids and biogenic amines in the central nervous system.

The malononitrile derivatives represent one class of psychoactive agent which relates not only to nucleic acid metabolism and synthesis in the brain, but also to learning and memory. Although malononitrile affects nucleic acid changes with reverse handedness, changes in the specific activity in two acidic protein fractions from the rat hippocampus (pyramidal cells from the CA3 region) also occurred when reverse handedness was compared with an equal number of preferred-handedness trials among control animals (Hydén and Lange, 1972). In highly inbred sublines of rats, which differed in the learning ability of an avoidance task, reversal of handedness training increased the labeling of acidic proteins from the sensory-motor cortex, visual cortex, hippocampus, and entorhinal cortex; this change occurred for high-score learners, but no differences were observed for low-score learners (Hydén et al., 1973). Changes in the base composition of brain RNA have also been shown to occur with the acquisition of new behavior (Hydén and Egyhazi, 1962, 1963, 1964), as well as significant changes in the base composition of RNA from nerve cells of the inferior temporal gyrus with a visual discrimination task in monkeys (Hydén et al., 1974); adenine was increased, and cytosine was decreased. With a delayed-alternation type of learning the nerve cells of the gyrus principalis showed RNA base changes.

The issue of RNA base changes, their bearing upon the proteins synthesized regionally in nerve cells and their adjacent glia, and those drugs that may alter learning or memory has received some, but notably sparse, attention in the experimental literature. It is interesting, however, that this issue was investigated experimentally after its rationale had been derived from some clinical observations. Malononitrile, a central nervous system stimulant, was initially reported as having some success in the treatment of psychiatric patients. Malononitrile and its derivatives are central stimulants, as defined by their electrophysiological activating effects, and increase in locomotor activity, they have an antithyroid effect which apparently is not manifested either neurochemically or behaviorally upon acute administration. The behavioral effects of TCAP were noted as facilitatory, inasmuch as its acute administration enhanced the retention of a conditioned avoidance response in rodents (Chamberlain et al., 1963). In the behavioral situation, emotionality and the acquisition of maze behavior were unaffected by the drug.

A relationship between malononitrile derivatives and memory has been formulated on the basis of the interaction between the drug effect and the effect of an amnesic stimulus. The amnesic stimulus chosen was posttraining ECS, which both in animals and in man acts to produce a temporal gradient of retrograde amnesia, that is as the interval between a learning experience and the administration of a single ECS (producing a full clonic–tonic convulsion with a postictal episode) is increased, the subsequent retrograde amnesia is less pronounced. In another respect, the shorter the time between behavioral acquisition and ECS, the greater the incidence of retrograde amnesia. The common denominator by which TCAP effects and ECS effects may be associated is that they affect the RNA content of cells in the brain. The RNA content of whole mouse brain was shown to be decreased by approximately 17% within 20 minutes after a single ECS. Under the same conditions, 72% of those mice trained to acquire a passive avoidance response and given ECS within 10 minutes after the training trial showed a retrograde amnesia for the avoidance response when they were tested 24 hours later. Mice treated with TCAP (20 mg/kg × 3 days) prior to training did not show any difference in acquisition or in susceptibility to ECS-induced convulsions, but only 27% of these animals showed a retrograde amnesia. The important point is that pretreatment with TCAP blocked the RNA-depleting effect of ECS (Essman, 1965). The fact that TCAP produced such an effect without any anticonvulsant properties is of some methodological significance for the selection of presumed memory-facilitative drugs through the use of the consolidation-amnesia paradigm provided with the ECS model. Drugs that alter an ECS-induced convulsion may appear to be facilitatory if the amnesia is seizure dependent. In this regard, then, drugs, such as phenobarbital, phenytoin, carbonic anhydrase inhibitors, some benzodiazepines, or some monoamine oxidase inhibitors, might be expected to benefit the memory consolidation process since they act to reduce the electrical manifestation of seizure activity produced by ECS. In fact, none of these agents facilitates consolidation or reduces the amnesic effect of ECS. Neither the amnesic nor the biochemical effects of ECS were altered when the convulsion was blocked by pretreatment with lidocaine hydrochloride. This local anesthetic, a monoamine oxidase inhibitor, acts as a most effective anticonvulsant, but not as an antiamnesic (Essman, 1968). A similar effect was also observed with 2,4-dichlorophenoxyacetic acid, a thermolytic drug which also acts as an anticonvulsant, but not as an antiamnesic.

The regional and cellular effects of TCAP are of interest and of possible relevance to a molecular view of memory consolidation. Those brain regions most apparently affected include the structures of the limbic region and the corpus callosum. While the former is richly endowed with mixed cell populations, the latter lacks nerve cell bodies and contains only axons and glia (Essman, 1966). It was shown (Essman, 1965) that ECS reduced nerve cell RNA and increased glial RNA in cells isolated from the hippocampal cortex; TCAP increased nerve cell RNA and decreased glial RNA contents for cells in this same region.

The enhancement of discrimination learning in rats (Daniels, 1967; Schmidt and Davenport, 1967) with TCAP has been reported, and the drug has also been shown to be without significant effect upon active avoidance and water maze learning (Brush et al., 1966), conditioned emotional response acquisition and extinction (Solyom and Galley, 1966), maze learning (McNutt, 1967), passive avoidance learning (Gurowitz et al., 1967), or response rates during continuous avoidance performance (Stern and Heise, 1970). No effect upon brain RNA content or metabolism or upon antagonism of ECS-induced amnesia was found in mice (Buckholtz and Bowman, 1970). Elimination of the motor learning component of an acquisition task prior to the administration of TCAP (10–60 mg/kg × 3 days) provided for enhanced maze learning and a dose-related increase in whole-brain RNA content (Lewis, 1967). The use of a trimer of malononitrile, tetracyanopropene (T4CAP), provided for facilitation of maze learning and habit reversal in mice (Lewis and

Essman, 1967), but this effect was limited by the toxicity of this compound at doses above 30 mg/kg.

Learning capacity and memory function were tested using TCAP in 23 senile patients given the drug (600 mg/day, p.o.) without any evidence of drug benefit over that of a placebo (Talland et al., 1965). If, as suggested, this drug acts upon the memory consolidation process, either by minimizing molecular changes attendant upon amnesic stimuli that interfere with consolidation, or by accelerating the consolidation time, thereby reducing the interval within which amnesic stimuli may be active, it is not surprising that TCAP is not effective for multiple-trial learning tasks or for memory and performance tasks in senile humans. The latter population, in particular, is one where pharmacological alteration of learning or memory becomes very difficult to define. It would appear more likely that a reduction of confusion and disorientation might be better achieved through the use of agents that favor increased attention and more consistent stimulation of the central nervous system. This topic is perhaps better relegated to a consideration of central nervous system stimulants and analeptics, which will be discussed in a later chapter.

A final word may be added regarding the antiamnesic properties of T4CAP, which has been shown to facilitate memory consolidation in a dose-related manner (Essman and Essman, 1969). The results of these studies have led to the suggestion that a drug-induced facilitation of memory consolidation represents an effect that involves the interaction of both RNA and other molecules, particularly putative neurotransmitters. Whereas a number of amnesic agents or events, such as ECS, audiogenic seizure, pentylenetetrazol convulsions, $CO_2$ inhalation, hypothermia, short-chain fatty-acid-induced coma, ether anesthesia, and so on, reduce the regional content and metabolism of brain RNA, they also exert effects upon the content or metabolism of such biogenic amines.

# 3

# The Cholinergic System in Learning and Memory

The effects of cholinergic drugs on learning and memory processes have been indicated in several studies (Pfeiffer and Jenney, 1957), where relatively small doses of scopolamine impaired acquisition in rats. Similarly, two different anticholinergic drugs, scopolamine and atropine, produced an acquisition deficit in an operant alternation task (Hearst, 1959). A role for acetylcholine (ACh) in learning and memory processes was further emphasized (Rosenzweig et al., 1960) in studies where ACh and acetylcholinesterase levels differed between strains of rats, and such differences were correlated with differences in learning.

Although the results of these early studies were neither conclusive nor methodologically sound, ACh had been implicated in learning and memory processes. It was postulated (Carlton, 1961) that an inhibitory cholinergic mechanism functioned to antagonize (or inhibit) an opposing system of activation of nonrewarded or punished behavior. The activating or excitatory system was believed to have a noradrenergic basis and was reciprocally related to the inhibitory cholinergic system.

The level of activation could be viewed as controlling the tendency for all responses to occur, whereas an inhibitory cholinergic system would act to antagonize this action as nonreinforced responses (Carlton, 1963). Thus whenever learning to discontinue or inhibit a response that was previously reinforced, the cholinergic mechanism would be responsible for the cessation of such responses. Accordingly, anticholinergic agents are believed to interfere or disrupt this cholinergic inhibitory system and produce disinhibition (loss of inhibition). Disinhibition could be manifested by a performance deficit on those tasks that require the inhibition of nonreinforced or punished response on succeeding trials. For instance, alternation and discrimination tasks all require that the subject inhibit a response previously reinforced. In addition, a lack of inhibition would be expected to facilitate two-way active avoidance training and have no effect on the performance of tasks in which inhibition is not involved, as with simple mazes. Finally it was suggested that this cholinergic inhibitory mechanism was a central phenomenon. Quaternary forms of the same cholinergic drugs did not affect these behaviors, presumably because they are unable to cross the blood–brain barrier.

As predicted by a cholinergic inhibitory mechanism, anticholinergic drugs, such as scopolamine (unlike its quaternary analogues, methylscopolamine or methscopolamine), impair acquisition of a step-down passive avoidance task (Mollenauer et al., 1976) and one-way avoidance procedure (Domino and Domino, 1976). In addition, cholinolytically induced performance decrements have been reported on a variety of tasks of alternation (White, 1974), complex mazes (Van der Poel, 1974), habituation (Anisman et al., 1976), and discrimination (Warburton and Brown, 1976). Anticholinergic agents also abolish spontaneous alternation behavior (Drew et al., 1973) and increase a variety of behaviors, such as resistance to extinction (McCoy, 1972) and general activity (Anisman and Kokkinidis, 1975). An inability to withhold responses occurs on a differential reinforcement.

The more recent research also confirms earlier reports of disinhibitory effects following localized administration of cholinergic drugs. That is, intrahippocampal injections have been found to impair extinction performance (Singh et al., 1974), DRL responding (Ross and Grossman, 1974), and general activity levels (Leaton and Rech, 1972). Similar deficits have been reported with intraseptal injections on DRL schedules (Ellen et al., 1975), activity measures (Leaton and Rech, 1972), and reversal learning (Hamilton, 1970). In addition, inappropriate DRL responding is also associated with intrahypothalamic (Ross et al., 1975) and intra-corpus-striatum injections (Haycock et al., 1973). Furthermore, intrahypothalamic injections have been found to decrease performance on a variety of operant tasks (Miczek and Grossman, 1972; Ross et al., 1975). Scopolamine administered to the corpus striatum has been found to suppress habituation (Haycock et al., 1973) and increase DRL responding, while physostigmine decreased it (Neill, 1976). Finally, intraventricular injections of pyrrolcholine (inhibits choline uptake) have been reported to impair passive avoidance behavior (Glick et al., 1975), to mention but a few.

Studies using lesions consistently showed that a destruction of "cholinergic areas" (as those mentioned above) produced learning impairments parallel to those observed after administration of anticholinergic drugs. In particular, disinhibition was most apparent following lesions of the septohippocampal pathway. This tract consists of cholinergic fibers originating in the medial septal nucleus and the nucleus of the diagonal band. These fibers synapse on cholinoceptive cells in the hippocampal formation (Lewis and Shute, 1967; Shute, 1975). Lesions affected differential responding for low rates (DRL) (Meyer et al., 1976), a differential reinforcement for other responses (DRO), and fixed-ratio schedules of reinforcement (Morley and Russin, 1978), following injections of scopolamine or mecamylamine. Finally scopolamine-treated rats showed facilitated two-way avoidance acquisition (Buxton et al., 1976), similar to the effects of mecamylamine (Driscoll and Battig, 1973).

Further support of a cholinergic inhibitory system derives from studies of behavioral effects from acetylcholinesterase inhibitors and cholinergic agonists. For instance, anticholinesterases (as physostigmine and DFP (diisopropylphosphofluorodate) and Phosdin or Mevinphos decrease such behaviors as operant responding (Lewis and Mertens, 1973; Overstreet et al., 1974), resistance to extinction (Heise 1970), and spontaneous activity levels (Hughes and Trowland, 1976). In addition, such drugs also enhance habituation (Overstreet, 1977), discrimination performance (Warburton and Brown, 1972), and passive avoidance (Baratti et al., 1979). Similarly, cholinergic agonists, such as arecoline and pilocarpine, reduce fixed-ratio responding and spontaneous activity (Pradhan and Dutta, 1970; Overstreet, 1974). In addition, nicotine has facilitated one-way avoidance performance (Evangelista and Izquierdo, 1972), as has oxotremorine with passive avoidance procedures (Baratti et al., 1979). (It should be noted that these drug-induced effects are dose dependent, while nicotine effects are also dependent upon strain, species, chronicity of treatment, and motivation.) of any of these areas produce a behavioral syndrome strikingly similar to that found after administration of anticholinergic drugs.

There is also a great deal of ontogenic research to demonstrate the close relationship between cholinergic activity and an inhibitory capacity. It appears that the functioning of the inhibitory mechanism coincides with the maturation of cholinergic neurons in the brain. Furthermore, it seems that inhibitory-dependent behaviors cannot be performed until differentiation of cholinergic neurons occurs. Thus immature rats have been found to perform in an analogous manner to anticholinergically treated adults on tasks involving response inhibition.

Spontaneous alternation behavior does not emerge until after 25–30 days in the altricial rat. However, the precocious guinea pig was found to alternate at 7–10 days postnatally (Eggar et al., 1973; Bronstein et al., 1974a,b). In addition, rat pups (10–25 days) were unable to respond appropriately on several other tasks involving response inhibition. For example, active and passive avoidance (Feigley and Spear, 1970; Schulenberg et al., 1971), conditioned suppression (Wilson and Riccio, 1973), and habituation in an open field (Bronstein et al., 1974a,b) and to a novel stimulus (Feigley et al., 1972) were all found to be absent or deficient.

In addition, Fibiger et al. (1970) reported that dose related activity increases and decreases did not appear until rats were approximately 25 days of age. Similarly, scopolamine-induced passive avoidance deficits did not occur until this age (Feigley, 1974).

Considering the vast amount of research on the role of cholinergic drugs on a variety of behavioral tasks, it is surprising that so few studies have combined pharmacological, behavioral, and biochemical approaches. The early studies, for the most part, employed indirect measures of ACh in the brain by correlating levels of acetylcholinesterase or cholinestarase activity (ACh's degradative enzymes) with performance on several tasks following injections of an anti cholinesterase. Such studies report that reduction of brain cholinesterase or acetylcholinesterase from 40 to 60% of its normal activity was found to have detrimental effects on performance requiring inhibition. However, more recent literature seems to suggest that the relationship between acetylcholinesterase and learning is not as obvious or consistent as originally conceived (Buxton et al., 1976; Will, 1977; Jaffard et al., 1979).

Giarman and Pepeu (1962) and Rosecrans et al., (1968) conducted some of the few studies to directly measure the total brain content of ACh and correlate it with a performance impairment following cholinergic blocking drugs. Domino and Domino (1976) have confirmed this relationship between the ACh content in the brain and performance in a one-way shuttle box. Subjects were given scopolamine hydrobromide (0.032, 0.10, 1.0 or 3.2 mg/kg), methscopolamine bromide (1.0 or 10.0 mg/kg), or NaBr (0.36 mg/kg). Only scopolamine produced a dose-related impairment during acquisition, and a smaller deficit emerged during retention tests. In addition, these effects were highly correlated with a dose-related decrease in brain ACh on both acquisition and retention measures.

These results are in agreement with Buxton et al. (1976). In this study a two-way avoidance task was used (a procedure in which disinhibition would be expected to facilitate learning). The acquisition rates, in addition to total brain acetylcholinesterase levels, of Roman high and low avoidance strains of rats were compared. It was found that while the two strains differed in ACh concentrations, these were independent of any alternations in acetylcholinesterase levels. In addition, a significant correlation emerged between performance abilities and ACh levels. That is, the poor avoidance rats (RLA) were found to have significantly greater amounts of ACh than the better avoidance strain (RHA). Unfortunately differences in regional variations of ACh, as well as regional turnover rates, were not examined in either of these studies.

Finally, biochemical studies have also attempted to correlate choline acetylase (ACh synthetic enzyme) activity to the acquisition of a black–white discrimination task. Izquierdo et al. (1973) reported that while physostigmine (0.25 mg/kg) treatment enhanced learning, the activity of choline acetylase (presumed to be an indirect index of ACh activity) in the dorsal hippocampus and frontal cortex was similar to that of saline-treated animals. However, the choline acetylase levels were found to be lower in the animals that failed to learn the discrimination. Thus it was suggested that a minimal level of brain choline acetylase (and probably ACh) is necessary for discrimination learning.

It seems that the cholinergic system is involved in the learning and retention of a variety of paradigms involving response suppression. This conclusion is based on behavioral ontogenic and biochemical data demonstrating that a disruption of cholinergic pathways produces a specific behavioral deficit on several procedures requiring the inhibition of a previously reinforced response. However, there is an equally extensive literature suggesting that the cholinergic inhibitory mechanism is not as easily characterized as originally conceived.

To begin with, the more recent ontogenic data seem to suggest that inhibitory-dependent behaviors emerge earlier than at 25–30 days of age in the rat. Wilson and Riccio (1976) studied the effects of anticholinergic-induced deficits on passive avoidance behavior as a function of age. Rats were tested at 15–16, 18–19, 21–22 or 30–32 days postnatally. Subjects were administered scopolamine (1.0 or 2.0 mg/kg, i.p.) or saline prior to training and retention sessions.

In contrast to the findings of Schulenberg et al. (1971) and Feigley (1974), animals were found capable of passive avoidance behavior from 15 days of age. In addition, scopolamine-induced adultlike performance deficits appeared from 18 to 19 days of age. In fact, a similar impairment could be demonstrated in weanlings as early as at 15–16 days with the higher dosage of scopolamine. Finally, retention tests 1 week later showed a significant retention deficit inversely related to the age of original training, regardless of drug state.

Wilson and Riccio (1976) used retention measures with

immature rats. Unfortunately these results are ambiguous, since they failed to control for age differences between the test and retest days. Therefore it is difficult to separate learning, memory, and/or performance effects of scopolamine.

The acquisition data, however, are confirmed by Blozouski et al. (1977), who tested rats from 14 to 28 days on a passive avoidance and extinction task following administration of atropine (5 mg/kg, i.p.) or saline. It was found that although subjects were slower to acquire both tasks, learning improved significantly from 17 to 21 days. In addition, this age coincided with drug-induced performance decrements.

In a more comprehensive study, Ray and Nagy (1978) studied the emergence of inhibitory-dependent behaviors in mice 7, 11, 15, 19, and 85–115 days of age. Several doses of scopolamine and methscopolamine were employed (0.5–8.0 mg/kg, i.p.). Passive avoidance measures and alternations in locomotor activity as a function of age and drug effects were studied.

Mice as young as 7 days were found capable of learning a step down (actually, roll-down) passive avoidance procedure. In addition, retention was demonstrated 1 hour later. However, 24-hour savings did not occur until subjects were 19 days of age. Furthermore, scopolamine was not found to impair passive avoidance behavior until 15 days of age. These findings are in contrast with activity measures in which scopolamine was found to have no effect prior to 19 days. At this time a dose-dependent increase was found that corresponds with adult rats. Thus consistent results between emerging capacity to learn the passive avoidance procedure (at 7 days) and the onset of drug-induced effects on passive avoidance (at 15 days), in addition to the inconsistent findings between the two behavioral measures, were found.

Based on these contrasting data, and similar results by Nagy et al. (1975), it was concluded that the cholinergic system may not be the sole mediator of response suppression until the second or third postnatal week. Furthermore, the cholinergic system may not uniformly control all inhibitory responses in all behavioral conditions. These results are further confirmed by Remington and Anisman (1976), who found scopolamine to differentially affect spontaneous alternation and locomotor activity in mice as a function of age and strain. Similarly, this relationship was nonlinear, thus further suggesting that these behaviors were not mediated solely by the cholinergic system.

The ontogenic findings are not the only data supporting a cholinergic inhibitory model which have been contradicted. There is extensive research suggesting that the conceptualization of a cholinergic system mediating inhibitory learning and memory processes is too narrow. In addition, much of the original data on which this formulation was based are questioned by more recent findings.

Ross et al. (1975) suggest that the present cholinergic model of inhibition may be too simplistic, and attempted to determine whether disruption of cholinergic pathways at different sites would produce a similar inhibitory deficit. Furthermore, they were interested in determining if the disinhibitory effects would be comparable with nonreinforced and punished trials. Atropine methylnitrate and mecamylamine hydrochloride were administered (1.0–5.0 $\mu$g) intrahippocampally or intrahypothalamically.

In contrast to earlier studies, it was found that both intrahippocampally administered anticholinergic agents increased signaled nonreinforcement responding but not punished responding. In addition, intrahypothalamic atropine increased nonreinforced responding, while mecamylamine did not increase punished responding and atropine actually decreased it. Thus it appears that interference of the cholinergic system at different loci does not produce a uniform effect. The two types of response suppression procedures do not appear to be mediated by the same underlying mechanism. That is, while cholinolytic agents consistently disrupt nonreinforced behavior, their effect on punished behavior was dependent on the specific type of drug (i.e., muscarinic versus nicotinic blocking agents) and site of location. The present study seems to suggest that the hippocampus and hypothalamus may be involved in two separate functional and anatomical cholinergic inhibitory systems.

The issue, however, is still unclear since Phillips and Lowe (1975) cite further support of response inhibition being mediated by both nonreinforcement and punishment. In this study rats were either shocked or left alone (nonreinforced) during preexposure in a test chamber. Saline-treated rats demonstrated a suppression of ambulation, rearing, and arm crossings regardless of whether response suppression was induced by nonreward or by punishment. Similarly, atropine (10 mg/kg, i.p.) blocked both types of induced suppression equally.

There are several other studies that seem to imply that although the initial concept of a cholinergic system mediating inhibition may be valid, it may also be too general. Mollenauer et al. (1976) report that scopolamine (1 mg/kg, i.p.) significantly impaired the performance of an olfactory discrimination task. A cholinergic inhibitory explanation would predict this finding due to an inability to withhold a previously reinforced response. However, an analysis of the data does not support this.

Results indicate that 95% of the errors of scopolamine-treated animals (as compared with saline) was due to their failure to initiate any response within the time limit. Furthermore, during the second half of each session their discrimination performance was perfect. In an operant task, scopolamine produced a similar delay in responding, such that once animals began to barpress, their rate of responding was unaffected by the drug (Plotnick et al., 1976). Thus these studies suggest that the scopolamine-induced discrimination deficit was not due to a lack of inhibition but to some delay of initial responding. Plotnick et al. suggest that this delay was due to a drug-induced delay in food-reinforcement behavior.

Such a drug-induced effect on food reinforcement is further supported by Morley and Russin (1978). In this study the effects of scopolamine, methscopolamine, and saline (0.5 and 1.0 mg/kg, i.p.) were compared when food or water was used as reinforcement during learning. It was found that scopolamine increased barpress responding during extinction and spontaneous recovery, as expected, but only with water reinforcement. Scopolamine had no effect on behavior when food was the reinforcement. It was concluded that the cholinergic system does not mediate all types of suppressed behaviors, but only those that were acquired with water reinforcement. However, a more parsimonious conclusion may be that, at least for extinction and response recovery performance, there appear to be differences in cholinergic mediation of food- and water-reinforced behavior.

It has often been presumed that all inhibitory-dependent behaviors are equally reliable indicators of cholinergic function and dysfunction. However, Anisman and Kokkinidis (1975) cite evidence of a differential scopolamine effect upon two separate inhibitory-dependent procedures. Several doses of scopolamine (0.1–1.0 mg/kg, i.p.) or saline were administered to three different strains of mice prior to testing for spontaneous alternation and locomotor activity. The drug decreased spontaneous alternation across strains, while a dose-dependent increase in activity was found with only two strains. Thus scopolamine disrupted one type of inhibitory behavior independent of another.

Waddington and Olley (1977) demonstrated that different types of passive avoidance tasks are identical only in theory. Therefore, in contradiction to Carlton's model (1963), anticholinergic agents would not necessarily be expected to produce a single acquisition and/or retention deficit. Two apparently similar step-down passive avoidance tasks were employed. Following injections of atropine (10 mg/kg, i.p.) or chlordiazepoxide (5 mg/kg, i.p.) rats were trained with either continuous or discrete trial training and tested for retention (4 days later) under saline.

Atropine differentially affected the performance on the two tasks; it impaired acquisition of the avoidance responses with both procedures. However, there was a significantly greater decrement on the continuous trial retention test. Thus apparently learning was similar across paradigms, while retention was not. It was therefore concluded that the acquisition deficit was a performance and not a learning deficit. Furthermore, since performance on the different tasks was selectively affected by atropine, it was speculated that the two behaviors were possibly mediated by different underlying cholinergic mechanisms.

Evidence also demonstrates that disruption of cholinergic pathways will produce disinhibition only on simple behavioral tasks. For instance, Stewart et al. (1974) reported differential drug effects on the performance of a geometric progressive ratio schedule. Subjects were administered scopolamine (0.05–2.0 mg/kg, i.p.), atropine methylnitrate (1.0–20.0 mg/kg, i.p.), or saline following training.

It was found that scopolamine produced an inverted U-shaped response curve. The total number of response reinforcements, postreinforcement pauses, regular responding, and final ratio levels attained were all varied in opposite directions between high and low dosages.

McKim (1974) showed that the effects of cholinergic drugs on operant learning may not produce results consistent with an inhibitory deficit explanation. Rats were administered scopolamine or methylscopolamine (3.2 mg/kg, i.p.) and/or physostigmine (0.02– 16 mg/kg, i.p.) during acquisition of a fixed interval schedule of 2 minutes. The curvature index, which is sensitive to changes in the response pattern but not the response rate, was measured. The curvature index is also more sensitive to drug-induced behavioral effects, since it is not influenced by most drugs as are response rate or extinction measures.

It was found that only scopolamine affected the curvature index. However, when physostigmine was administered in conjunction with scopolamine, it blocked the scopolamine-induced decline in performance. Therefore although scopolamine and physostigmine were not reported to produce opposite effects on responding, they did show an antagonistic effect. Such findings are consistent with data reported by Valliant (1967). On the other hand, several earlier studies have reported reverse effects following scopolamine and physostigmine treatments. In contradiction to these, McKim's data suggest that while response suppression may be cholinergically mediated, response increments may not. Furthermore, prior reports of reverse effects of these two drugs may be a result of using behavioral measures which are not adequately sensitive to the specific effects of different cholinergic drugs.

Warburton and Groves (1969) indicate that the habituation of a startle response was unaffected by scopolamine. Such a finding would appear to challenge the hypothesis (Carlton, 1963; Carlton & Markiewicz, 1971) that a cholinergic inhibitory mechanism regulates habituation responses. Therefore Williams et al. (1974) studied the effects of scopolamine and septal lesions on the habituation of an exploratory response (head poking) and a startle response (to a loud click).

Subjects were administered scopolamine (0.5–2.0 mg/kg, i.p.), scopolamine methylnitrate (0.5 and 2.0 mg/kg, i.p.), saline, medial septal lesions, or sham operations prior to testing. Results clearly indicate that habituation of a head-poke response and a startle response was not affected by scopolamine in an analogous manner. Scopolamine impaired habituation of the exploratory behavior, but had no effect on the startle response. Furthermore while scopolamine and septal lesions both suppressed habituation of the head-poking response, only septal lesions affected the startle response.

Exploratory behavior involves the emission of a response that is associated with response contingent feedback (which is often rewarding). The startle response is an elicited response, independent of response-contingent feedback. Thus it appears that while habituation of a head-poke response is mediated by a cholinergic system regulating inhibition of responses following nonreward, responses that are not associated with reinforcement are not a function of the cholinergic inhibitory mechanism.

In contrast to earlier suggestions, it was concluded that not all habituation responses are mediated by a cholinergic inhibitory process, but only those responses associated with previous reinforcement. In addition, scopolamine and septal lesions do not necessarily produce parallel effects on performance because it is unlikely that they are disrupting the same underlying inhibitory process, as originally contended.

These findings are further supported by Williams et al. (1975), who show the developmental emergence of habituation to an exploratory response and startle response. While habituation of the startle response was found in all rats (15–16 and 36–39 days), habituation of an exploratory response was not demonstrated by the younger rats. Thus it was concluded that habituation to a reflexive behavior, such as the startle response, develops earlier than more complex behaviors, such as exploration. In addition, Carlton and Adokat (1973) found that $p$chlorophenylalanine ($p$CPA) (which depletes brain serotonin) but not scopolamine, decreased startle responses. Similarly, serotonin, when compared with ACh, had no effect on exploratory behavior (Swonger and Rech, 1972).

Unfortunately the question of the cholinergic system mediating only the habituation of exploratory behavior and the serotonergic system regulating startle habituation is further clouded by other data (Overstreet, 1975). In this study both cholinergic and serotonergic drugs did not affect the habituation of the startle response. However, cholinergic drugs that increased cholinergic activity, decreased startle responding, while those that antagonized ACh, increased the response. Thus it appears that the cholinergic system may modulate the startle-response level but not its habituation, while serotonergic involvement is still unclear. It is possible that the lack of effect from the serotonergic drugs was a result of an inappropriate dose or other experimental conditions.

Graf (1974) also indicates that cholinergic drugs selectively suppress different types of habituation responses. The habituation of fear and several types of motor activities following scopolamine (0.25–1.0 mg/kg, i.p.) or saline was compared. Rats were tested in a free exploratory condition (where they had free access to a novel chamber) and a forced exploratory condition (where they were placed in a chamber and could not retreat).

Scopolamine did not suppress habituation of all responses equally (locomotor, scanning, object contact, fear, and general motor activity). The drug interfered with the inhibition of fear and general activity. This is consistent with Carlton's (1963) speculation that the cholinergic system inhibits a general excitatory system. However, no difference between drug and no-drug groups on other behavioral measures suggests that response inhibition was not affected by cholinergic impairment. Thus while fear and general activity habituation appear to be cholinergically mediated, inhibition of behavioral response habituation appears to be regulated by noncholinergic processes.

Stewart et al. (1974) studied the effects of scopolamine (0.25–4.0 mg/kg, i.p.) and physostigmine (0.01–0.1 mg/kg, i.p.) or saline on ambulation, rearing activity, and grooming behavior. Stewart and Blain (1975) found that increasing doses of scopolamine produced an inverted U-shaped response curve for ambulation, increased rearing activity, and had no effect on grooming behavior. Further, while scopolamine may influence measures of habituation (as frequency of ambulation, rearing, and grooming), it did not affect the rate of habituation (time or duration).

These results are contrary to those of Worsham and Hamilton (1976), who also reported that scopolamine (1.0 mg/kg, i.p.) affected the frequency of a head-poke response in a manner similar to that produced by septal lesions or saline. However, while the latter two treatments did not influence the duration of the response, scopolamine increased response duration over time.

Stewart et al. (1974) and Stewart and Blain (1975) also found scopolamine to produce opposite effects as a function of the habituation procedures employed, that is, open field versus exploratory box. In addition, scopolamine effects were influenced by preexposure, the size of the test environment, and the behavioral measures used (Stewart, 1977). Similar factors influenced habituation under physostigmine (Hughes and Trowland, 1976; Stewart and Stewart, 1977). The work of Stewart et al. further demonstrates that the habituation of different behaviors (ambulation, rearing, grooming, and reaction to novelty) may not all be regulated by the same underlying cholinergic system, as originally presumed.

Green and Summerfield (1977) found that a variety of cholinergic agonists and antagonists influenced head poking and locomotor activity in an unexpected direction. Habituation of a head-poke response was found following scopolamine (0.5 and 1.0 mg/kg, i.p.), arecoline (2.0 and 4.0 mg/kg, i.p.), and nicotine (0.15 and 0.30 mg/kg, i.p.). In addition, a similar decrease in responding, though to a lesser extent, was reported with peripherally acting cholinergic drugs at the higher dose. That is, methscopolamine (1.0 but not 0.5 mg/kg, i.p.) and carbamylcholine (0.15 and 0.30 mg/kg, i.p.) also modified habituation behavior. A similar trend occurred for locomotor activity.

All of the drugs, when compared to saline treatment, produced a decrease in behavior, although there was a difference in the degree of the decrement. Thus it was concluded that head-poke responding and locomotor activity involve a major central component (although not necessarily cholinergic), since the behaviors were more sensitive to the centrally acting drugs.

There are some criticisms of the present study. Scopolamine increased locomotor activity in one experiment and significantly decreased it in another. Green and Summerfield suggested that this failure to replicate their own scopolamine-induced effects was possibly due to differences in body weight, housing conditions, or basal activity levels which were not appropriately controlled. It is feasible to extend this interpretation to explain their other inconsistent drug effects. Thus it is possible that the similarity between agonists and antagonist drugs was due to these same inadequate controls.

Another potential flaw is that the dose range used was too high. For instance, several studies, such as that by Pradhan and Dutta

(1970), found that doses of arecoline (greater and less than 0.5 mg/kg) have the opposite effects on barpressing. Similarly, Morrison and Armitage (1967) found lower doses of nicotine (0.05 and 0.10 mg/kg) increased responding, while higher doses (0.2 and 0.4 mg/kg) produced an initial decrease followed by an increase in responding 20 minutes later. Such findings may explain Green and Summerfield's unexpected results.

A further point about the results of Green and Summerfield (1977) is that subjects were injected 10 minutes prior to testing, and the session only lasted 20 minutes. It is possible that the testing period was too short for the drugs to exert maximal effects. This is based on findings that drugs, such as scopolamine, have their greatest effect in producing an avoidance deficit and in reducing total brain levels of ACh (Giarman and Pepeu, 1962; Pazzagli and Pepeu, 1964) between 30 and 90 minutes after injection.

In addition, other studies (Graf, 1974) reported significant differences in behavior from the first and second halves of 14 minute testing sessions with a 20 minute delay after injection. It is possible that certain drug-induced effects are more sensitive to ACh levels. Perhaps arecoline and methscopolamine would have produced their expected results if the observation period had been extended or if the postinjection time was increased.

A final point is the failure to use apropriate quaternary controls. That is scopolamine was compared to methylscopolamine (in which some differences were observed), and arecoline and nicotine were compared to carbamylcholine. More appropriate comparisons may have produced results more consistent with the drugs' known effects.

Based on several studies, Warburton and Brown (1971) and Brown and Warburton (1971) postulated that learning impairments following disruption of the cholinergic pathways are not the result of an inability to withhold responses. Accordingly, the resulting performance deficits are due to an impairment of stimulus inhibition processes and not response inhibition. In order to extend their original findings, Warburton and Brown (1972) compared the effects of physostigmine (0.05–0.20 mg/kg, i.p.), scopolamine (0.0625–0.25 mg/kg, i.p.), or saline on a simple discrimination task. Rats were trained to respond only in the presence of a cue light and not during the 9-second intertrial interval period. The number of responses, reinforcements, and interresponse times were analyzed within the theoretical framework of signal detection. Results indicated that the lower doses of physostigmine (0.05 and 0.10 mg/kg, i.p.) improved discrimination, while all doses of scopolamine impaired performance. The higher doses of physostigmine, however, decreased learning similar to that of the scopolamine.

Since physostigmine at lower doses increased stimulus sensitivity indices independent of response bias indices, it was suggested that physostigmine improved "attention" to the stimulus rather than response inhibition. Furthermore, biochemical data further support these results. Following lower doses of physostigmine there was an inhibition of cholinesterase by 35–55%. This range has been found to be associated with neural facilitation. In addition, the highest dose produced an inhibition of 75%, a level that has been found to correspond with performance deficits (Russell and Warburton, 1971).

Ksir (1974, 1975) studied the effects of scopolamine on the performance of a two-lever alternation task as a function of stimulus control. In the earlier study a correct alternation response on the first trial was indicated by either a simple stimulus discrimination (illumination of a cue light over correct lever or no cue light over incorrect lever) or a more difficult discrimination (steady or flashing light). The intertrial interval was randomly varied (2.5, 5, 10, 20, or 40 seconds).

After training was completed, subjects were administered either scopolamine (0.25–1.0 mg/kg, i.p.), methyscopolamine (0.50 mg/kg, i.p.), or saline. With the more difficult discrimination, flashing–steady light, scopolamine-treated rats demonstrated a significantly greater number of incorrect responses. In addition, increasing doses of scopolamine increased errors in the weak stimulus control condition only. The intertrial interval had no effect.

These results are further supported by Ksir (1975) in a study in which a two-lever simultaneous brightness discrimination task was employed. In this case the difference in brightness between the two cue lights (differences ranged from 20 to 90 V) interacted with the effects of scopolamine. When the difference between the lights was smallest (20 V), scopolamine produced a dose-related increase in errors. Consistent with these studies, Warburton and Brown (1976) found that scopolamine (0.0625, 0.125, and 0.25 mg/kg, i.p.) produced a greater performance deficit in rats previously trained to barpress to a single stimulus (cue light) as opposed to a double stimulus (light and tone). Thus it appears that scopolamine-induced deficits may be a function of stimulus characteristics.

There are several other studies which support anticholinergic drugs as disrupting discrimination processes and not response suppression. Heise et al. (1975) trained rats on two similar operant tasks. For one, subjects were trained on a discrete two-lever alternation task in which the correct lever was indicated on each trial by a cue light over it. For the other, a centrally located cue light indicated onset of the trial; thus subjects had to alternate responses based on their memory of the previous trial. In both procedures, the intertrial interval was randomly varied (2.5, 5, 10, 20, or 40 seconds).

For the alternation discrimination task (first procedure above), prior administration of scopolamine (0.25 mg/kg, i.p.) and increasing intertrial-interval durations decreased response occurrence comparable to saline-treated rats. However, scopolamine and intertrial-interval duration had no effect on response accuracy. Even higher doses of scopolamine (0.5 and 1.0 mg/kg, i.p.) reduced response occurrence but not response accuracy.

On a second procedure with variable intertrial-interval spatial alternation, the effects of intertrial-interval duration and scopolamine on the response occurrence were similar to those in the first procedure. However, it was found that with increasing intertrial-interval durations the accuracy decreased for all groups in a parallel manner. Further, scopolamine reduced the accuracy in proportion to dosage. However, each dose had a consistent effect across all intertrial intervals (except 40 seconds).

Since all drug and nondrug groups demonstrated a decrease in accuracy as a function of increasing intertrial intervals, any conclusion based on a time-dependent process (such as memory) being disrupted by scopolamine is disconfirmed. It was concluded that anticholinergic drugs produce a stimulus discrimination deficit during learning.

More recently Gonzalez and Altshuler (1979) compared the effects of scopolamine (0.4 mg/kg, i.p.) and saline on the acquisition of three separate operant tasks requiring response suppression. Disruption of response suppression by scopolamine would be expected to increase responding and thus impair performance. However, the drug failed to increase a variable interval (VI)-60 seconds, modified DRL 15 seconds or modify the development of a conditioned emotional response.

Furthermore, performance on the modified DRL procedure supports a cholinergic stimulus discrimination deficit. The modification required subjects to alternate responses between trials. The correct response was indicated by the presence of a light or tone. It was found that scopolamine did not produce an increase in the total responding rate, but rather it increased responses to the incorrect lever. These results were confirmed by Handley and Calhoun (1977) on a serial discrimination reversal task. In this case scopolamine increased responses to the discriminative stimulus, while the total number of responses were equivalent to those of saline subjects. Thus it appears that scopolamine interfered with a cholinergic system mediating stimulus discrimination and not response inhibition.

One of the few studies to simultaneously test both explanations of a cholinergic system mediating response or sensory inhibition (Rasmussen and Szerb, 1975) utilized a cortical cup implantation to measure ACh release from visual and sensorimotor cortices. The quantity of the ACh release was compared in rabbits after learning one of four operant reinforcement schedules. Subjects were tested on a DRL and VI schedule, with or without a cue light.

Although ACh release increased during stimulus discrimination trials from both sites, the increase was only significant for the somatosensory cortex. According to Carlton's theory (1963), a significant difference in responding should be demonstrated between the VI and DRL schedules as a function of the ACh levels. For instance, a low ACh release would be expected to be associated with an increase in DRL responding due to disinhibition. However, no significant difference was found. Similarly, a sensory discrimination model as proposed by Warburton would predict that the visual cortex would have an increase in ACh release since a visual cue was employed; this was not found either. There was, however, an effect of the cue light which would tend to support the findings of Warburton et al. However, the data of Rasmussen and Szerb lack strong support for either a cholinergic response or a sensory inhibitory mechanism.

Alpern and his collaborators took the idea of a cholinergically mediated sensory discrimination process one step further. In several reports they studied its involvement in short-term memory (STM) processes. Stripling and Alpern (1976) employed a delayed reversal discrimination task in which scopolamine- (0.5 or 2.0 mg/kg, i.p.) or physostigmine- (0.05 or 0.20 mg/kg, i.p.) treated animals were trained in a T maze on successive days to avoid shock. Between the first trial when the correct arm was indicated (sign trial) and the second (test trial) there was either a 5- or, 20-minute delay (correlating with differences in the strength of STM). During the delay, sensory stimulation was varied.

Scopolamine produced impairment on two measures of STM with the 5-minute delay and normal sensory conditions. However, scopolamine improved performance at the same delay with a lower sensory stimulation. A dose-dependent relationship was also reported. These results were consistent with earlier findings (Alpern and Marriott, 1973; Marriott and Alpern, 1973).

On the other hand, measures of long-term memory (LTM) were unaffected by scopolamine. Furthermore, the anticipated facilitative effect of physostigmine was not found. However, Alpern and Marriott (1973) reported physostigmine and scopolamine to have opposite effects within a 5-minute delay (STM). Thus it seems that scopolamine interferes with STM processing of relevant stimuli (on sign trials) and irrelevant stimuli (during intertrial intervals) as indicated by poor test trial performance.

Alpern and Jackson (1978) extended their findings to determine if STM processes are selectively sensitive to only cholinergic drugs. By using a similar delayed discrimination procedure it was found that while cholinolytic drugs impaired performance, catecholaminergic and serotonergic agents had no consistent effect on delayed responding. While several others have reported LTM and consolidation processes to be influenced by all of these, STM was not. Thus STM appears to have a more selective substrate than the other memory process, and therefore it seems possible that STM and LTM are morphologically distinct.

An earlier study by Singh et al (1974) partially confirms the results of Alpern and co-workers Singh et al. employed a Y-maze discrimination task and administered atropine intrahippocampally

(0.5 $\mu$g) at different times during learning (1 minute prior to training, posttraining, or prior to 24 hour retention test). Atropine was found to impair acquisition by disrupting STM processing (similar to Alpern and co-workers) and to facilitate LTM and consolidation processes. Thus it seems that normal STM and LTM processes are dependent on an intact cholinergic system.

Further evidence in support of cholinergic involvement in STM and LTM processes is reported by Jaffard and his collaborators (1976, 1977, 1979). By using a different approach, they studied the effects of choline acetyltransferase levels (ChAc, or CAT, the synthetic enzyme of ACh) on acquisition and retention measures. ChAc activity was genetically lower in certain strains of mice, and furthermore these differences were correlated with learning ability on inhibitory-dependent tasks (Ebel et al., 1973; Mandel et al., 1974). In addition it was found that 24-hour posttrial stimulation at subseizure threshold to the hippocampus decreased ChAc activity (Jaffard et al., 1976, 1977).

Jaffard et al. (1979) studied the relationship between ChAc levels and the acquisition and retention of a CRF barpress response. Changes in the ChAc levels were induced genetically (using strains with different amounts of ChAc) or experimentally (prestimulation of the hippocampus 24 hours before training). It was found that rats with genetically high ChAc levels performed better on retention tests 24 hours later (LTM). However, strains with low ChAc activity performed significantly better on the immediate retention tests (STM). In addition, when rats with high ChAc levels were given prestimulation 24 hours prior to training, their performance was similar to the low ChAc strains. Furthermore, biochemical assays of each group confirm the behavioral data.

In a second series of experiments posttraining (30 seconds) stimulation facilitated the performance of high ChAc strains during LTM tests. However, when ChAc was reduced by pretraining, the posttraining stimulation facilitation was suppressed. It was assumed that the ChAc levels are correlated with the ACh levels. Thus Jaffard et al. (1979) concluded that high ChAc activity (and presumably ACh levels) during learning blocks STM. Over time, these levels dissipate and thereby facilitate LTM.

As Jaffard et al. (1976, 1977, 1979) note, their conclusion was, to a great extent, dependent on the fact that their behavioral task was cholinergically mediated. Therefore it is unclear why they chose a CRF reinforcement procedure in which cholinergic involvement has not been reported. In fact, Jaffard et al. (1977) employed a passive avoidance task and a CRF procedure. However, results of the passive avoidance task were reported as not easily interpretable. In addition, their study relies on the assumption that ChAc levels are an accurate indication of ACh activity. However, Glick et al. (1973) demonstrated that a behaviorally effective dose of ChAc inhibitors (NVP methiodide and NVP hydroxyethyl bromide) significantly reduced hippocampal ChAc activity. However, these ChAc inhibitors failed to have any influence on hippocampal ACh levels for at least 5 hours.

Deutsch (1971) proposed that the degree of retention was a function of changes in the sensitivity of the cholinergic synapse over time. Deutsch and his collaborators found that the same dose of anticholinesterase (physostigmine or DFP) would produce either a facilitation or an impairment in performance, depending on the time of injection and the retention test from original learning. For the most part, rats were tested on a discriminated avoidance task in a Y maze.

Performance was impaired by prior anticholinesterase injections (intrahippocampally or intraperitoneally) when retested 30 minutes or 7–14 days after initial training. At 24–48 hours and at 1–4 days posttraining the drug produced no effect. However, performance improved at 28 days after training with the same dosage (Deutsch et al., 1966; Hamburg, 1967). Furthermore, scopolamine produced a mirror-image effect from the anticholinesterase drugs (Weiner and Deutsch, 1968). In addition, the strength of original learning (Deutsch and Leibowitz, 1966) and time of reversal training (Deutsch and Weiner, 1969) were also found to affect the rate of memory decay.

These relationships have also been established on an appetitively reinforced task (Deutsch and Weiner, 1969; Weiner and Deutsch, 1968). Stanes and Brown (1976) attempt to extend Deutsch's cholinergic theory of memory decay to include a broader drug dose range and to account for individual differences in learning ability.

Stanes and Brown trained and retested rats on an appetitively motivated Y-maze discrimination task within the framework of

Deutsch's model. Retention scores were compared at 1, 4, 7, and 28 days after acquisition, following 0.1 or 0.2 mg/kg, i.p., of physostigmine or saline. Contrary to the findings of Deutsch, it was found that retention was significantly better at 4 days than at 7 days, and there was no performance difference on days 7 and 28 for control subjects. An unexpected finding was that the lower dose had no significant effect. Finally neither dose had any effect on days 1 or 28, posttraining. In addition, neither individual learning ability nor drug dose (0.05–0.20 mg/kg, i.p.) alone affected retention. However, there was a significant interaction such that physostigmine facilitated retention for slow learners and impaired retention for fast learners at 4 days, but not at 7 or 35 days posttraining.

Stanes and Brown (1976) disconfirmed several of Deutsch's findings. However, some of these differences can be explained by changes in methodologies. In general the results are consistent and suggest that the modification of a cholinergic theory of memory decay is necessary to account for such variables as a greater drug dose range and individual learning capacity.

George and Mellanby (1974) also attempted the replication of several studies of Deutsch et al. Their data seriously question Deutsch's theory. Using a similar procedure, they found that after 30 days the control subjects were still able to perform on a Y-maze avoidance task; Stanes and Brown (1976) made similar observations. This is contrary to Deutsch's postulation that after 30 days untreated animals should demonstrate a performance decrement. In addition, hippocampal injections of peanut oil, 24 hours prior to retraining, produced a performance deficit at 7 and 30 days. This is in contrast to a group given no treatment or sham operants who performed equally well at 7 and 28 days posttraining. Thus it seems that the peanut oil itself, the vehicle that Deutsch used for DFP administration, caused performance decrements.

Signorelli (1976) injected rats with physostigmine (0.4 mg/kg, i.p.) and retested them at 3, 4, 12, 13, or 14 days after training for retention of a Y-maze discrimination problem. In contrast to Deutsch et al. (1966), control rats showed good retention on days 3 and 4, and no retention on days 12–14. In addition, physostigmine produced an impairment on day 3 and a facilitation on day 12. However, both of these effects were not apparent on days 4 or 13 and 14, when retested in a no-drug state. If physostigmine affects consolidation processes, as Deutsch proposed, then a performance deficit or facilitation should persist on successive test days. Thus it seems that the drug affects performance only, on the day of its administration, and not memory processes.

George et al. (1977) replicated the Deutsch and Leibowitz (1966) study employing a similar shock-escape and shock-avoidance procedure. At 7 and 21 days after training, physostigmine (0.4 mg/kg, i.p.) induced only a slight transitory amnesic effect, in addition to causing a slowing effect upon movement. This effect did not vary as a function of the posttraining interval. Finally brain inhibition of acetycholinesterase by physostigmine indicated that the dosage used had effectively reduced acetycholinesterase AChE levels.

Additional criticism of Deutsch's research has been reported by others such as Cox (1974). Contrary data were found with rats given physostigmine, prior to the retention of a Y-maze avoidance task, at different intervals of time. Gadusek and Kalat (1975) also report that they were unable to extend Deutsch's cholinergic memory decay model to a learned aversion paradigm.

There is an abundance of more general criticisms which can be levied not only against Duetsch's, but also against Warburton's and Carlton's proposed involvement of the cholinergic system in learning and memory processes. The obvious flaw is that they are all too simplistic to account for such complex processes. In addition, several studies demonstrate a close interaction between the cholinergic and adrenergic systems (Singer et al., 1971), the cholinergic and serotonergic systems (Aprison, 1962), and the cholinergic and dopaminergic systems (Neill, 1976) on several tests of learning and memory. Such studies seem to indicate that cholinergic drugs may produce behavioral effects by direct and/or indirect effects on other neurotransmitter systems.

In studying the role of the cholinergic system and the effects of cholinergic drugs on acquisition and retention, researchers have often lost sight of (or chose to ignore) the fact that cholinergic receptors can be differentiated. An abundance of electrophysiological and electrophoretic evidence demonstrates a need to further classify cholinergic receptors as muscarinic and nicotinic. Inconsistencies in the behavioral literature would also seem to support such a classification system. However, few studies have systematically examined the possibility of differential effects of muscarinic and nicotinic drugs in the same learning paradigm.

Glick and Greenstein (1972) considered the differential effects of muscarinic (scopolamine) and nicotinic (mecamylamine) blocking agents. The selective effects of these two drugs were studied during the acquisition and retention of a passive avoidance procedure. Subjects were administered (1.0 or 3.0 mg/kg, i.p.) scopolamine, mecamylamine, or saline prior to training, 4 hours after training, or immediately prior to a retention test 24 hours later. In addition, since both drugs have been known to produce state-dependent effects, cross-dependent effects were also examined.

The two types of cholinergic drugs were differentially affected by the time of administration. In addition, simultaneous injection produced a synergistic effect or an antagonistic effect (the effect was neutralized), depending on whether injections were given prior to or immediately following training. And finally, a lack of a cross-dependent effects was reported. Therefore it was concluded that there are two separate cholinergic systems that impair acquisition and retention of a passive avoidance task.

It should be noted, however, that Glick and Greenstein's results are questionable, since group comparisons were made across experiments. That is, not all control subjects were run in each experiment so that drug performance in one experiment was compared with another drug group's performance from a preceding experiment. Nonetheless more recent research seems to support their idea of the differential effects of muscarinic and nicotinic receptors.

Ross and Grossman (1974) studied the effects of muscarinic agonists (acetyl-$\beta$-methylcholine chloride, 1 $\mu g/\mu l$) and antagonists (scopolamine methylnitrate, 10 $\mu g/\mu l$), in addition to nicotinic agonists (nicotine, 0.1$\mu g/\mu l$) and antagonist (mecamylamine hydrochloride, 10 $\mu g/\mu l$). Drugs were administered intrahippocampally before training on two different tasks, dependent on the cholinergic system (Sidman avoidance and DRL-30). In general it was found that scopolamine impaired performance of the avoidance task, while methylcholine facilitated performance as compared with predrug states. In addition, the nicotinic agent was found to produce the opposite effect, mecamylamine-enhanced acquisition, while nicotine hindered it. Furthermore, on the DRL procedure a similar relationship was found for anticipatory responding measures. Thus it seems that while muscarinic and nicotinic receptors are involved in an aversively and appetitively motivated task, their effects are antagonistic. However, few other studies have found such a clear antagonistic effect of muscarinic and nicotinic drugs across learning tasks.

The effects of scopolamine and mecamylamine were compared on other tasks previously found to be disrupted with antimuscarinic drugs. For instance, Avis and Pert (1974) tested rats in a novel situation for habituation differences and in a conditioned emotional response paradigm. Subjects were given either scopolamine (1 mg/kg, i.p.), methscopolamine (1 mg/kg, i.p.), mecamylamine (1, 5, 15, or 30 mg/kg, i.p.), hexamethonium (5 mg/kg, i.p.), or saline prior to initial testing and then were retested under saline. Only scopolamine suppressed habituation rates. However, both scopolamine and mecamylamine disrupted the learning of a conditioned fear response. These results are further confirmed by Pert and Avis (1974).

In conclusion, while both mecamylamine and scopolamine produced a dissociation of learning states, only scopolamine suppressed habituation. Thus scopolamine's suppression of habituation is the result of disrupting underlying muscarinic activity and not a state-dependent effect. Further, since scopolamine and mecamylamine disrupted fear conditioning in a similar manner, it is believed that both nicotinic and muscarinic receptors are involved in this behavior, unlike habituation.

The above studies suggest that muscarinic involvement in learning tasks is more extensive than that of nicotinic receptors. Moss and Rogers (1975) cite evidence which further supports this notion. Intracranial injections of cobra neurotoxin (a specific irreversible nicotinic blocking agent) did not impair the retention of a Y-maze discrimination task. Several doses were administered (10 $\mu$g to 45 $\mu$g) over various training intervals (immediate, 24 and 48 hours) and tested on different retention periods (1–6 days). All groups, regardless of the injection dose or interval, performed as well as controls in spite of obvious motor deficits. Therefore it seems that nicotinic receptors (or at least those that are sensitive to cobra neurotoxin) are not involved in the retention of a Y-maze discrimination task.

Unfortunately much of the research in this area has not been conducted in a systematic fashion. As a result, comparisons had to be made between studies whose methodologies vary widely. Thus differences in experimental results may be merely due to differences in methodological procedures. However, in spite of the diversity in techniques employed (and each with its own inherent limitations) and the broad range of behavioral paradigms incorporated, a few generalizations can be drawn. The cholinergic system is involved in a variety of learning and memory processes as acquisition, STM, LTM, and possibly consolidation. Furthermore its involvement in these processes seems to be that of mediating inhibition, more likely sensory than response inhibition, although it is difficult to separate the two. Finally, the probably most important, an abundance of research seems to suggest that one should no longer assume that there is a unitary functional and anatomical cholinergic system which mediates performance behavior independently of the other neurotransmitter systems.

In humans a somewhat similar relationship between drugs affecting the cholinergic system has emerged. A dose-dependent effect of physostigmine has been demonstrated, particularly in relation to memory storage processes (David and Yamamura, 1978). Although physostigmine does not affect the cognitive function level (Drachman and Leavitt, 1974), it has been shown to antagonize the cognitive impairment induced by scopolamine (Ghoneim and Mewaldt, 1977). An interesting effect of physostigmine and scopolamine has been observed in trained chess players (Liljequist and Mattila, 1979). Physostigmine (20 mg/kg, i.v.) impaired the performance of good players, but there was improved solution to chess problems in players with low performance levels. On the other hand, scopolamine (6 $\mu$g/kg, i.v.) impaired the performance of all players, and when combined, the two drugs appeared to cancel out each other's effects.

The use of the acetylcholine precursor choline, and the choline precursor lecithin, has represented a rather controversial subject. There is little substantive evidence to support either dietary agent as a successful treatment modality in the senile dementias, and equivocal results have emerged when such dietary regimens have been attempted in normal human subjects. In both instances, improved cognitive performance has been questionable (Hier and Caplan, 1980). Both LTM and STM functions (digit span, retrieval, and selective reminding storage) were evaluated in young subjects given 15 g of choline chloride (Davis et al., 1980); no significant effects were observed. No significant beneficial effects of choline chloride upon memory functions were observed in patients with mild memory dysfunction (Mohs et al., 1979), with 35 weeks of treatment given (4 g of choline chloride, four times a day). One study in which some beneficial cognitive effects of oral choline chloride have been noted concerned the short-term effect of this agent in young adults (Sitarem et al., 1978). Acquisition of numbered unrelated word sequences 90 minutes following ingestion of 10 g of choline produced an improved recall of word sequences, especially those containing abstract words.

# 4

# Serotonin in
# Learning and Memory

A serotonin-related basis for learning, memory consolidation, or amnesia has been derived, not only from a correlation between brain changes is this amine and in amnesic agents or events, but also from pharmacological studies. An early study (Woolley, 1965) found that mice with an elevated brain serotonin level produced with a combination of 5-hydroxytryptophan (60 mg/kg) and benzlmethoxytryptamine (15 mg/kg) had a 13% reduction in the average number of correct maze responses performed. A decrease in brain serotonin with either reserpine (1.2 mg/kg) or oral DL-phenylalanine combined with L-tyrosine increased correct maze responses by 7 and 9% respectively.

A reduction in the brain serotonin content with the tryptophan hydroxylase inhibitor pCPA reduced emotional reactivity in rats, increased reactivity to painful stimuli, and increased the acquisition of a conditioned avoidance response (Tenen, 1967). The facilitation of a brightness discrimination response by rats, but not a position discrimination or reversal, was caused by $p$CPA (Stevens et al., 1967). In mice $p$CPA did not facilitate passive avoidance response acquisition or reduce ECS-induced retrograde amnesia. (It may be observed, however, that the maximum reduction in brain serotonin) achieved with a 300-mg/kg dose of $p$CPA in mice was only 39%, as contrasted with the approximate 90% depletion accomplished with a comparable dose of this drug in rats.)

The clinical use of $p$CPA has been limited to experimental conditions, not so much related to learning or memory, but to circumstances where tissue or blood levels of serotonin are elevated and the drug has been utilized in an attempt to lower concentrations of this indole. This had found some limited usefulness in such conditions as carcinoid syndrome, medullary carcinoma of the thyroid, and mastocytosis, where some, but not all, of the serotoninemia-related symptoms, such as diarrhea, pigmentation changes, and pruritus, have been attenuated. The course of the clinical disorder, however, appears little benefited from this agent. In such conditions there is little evidence of a central serotonin excess or any changes in learning and memory, probably related to the blood–brain barrier to serotonin and the increased rate of peripheral catabolism and excretion.

In previous studies it has been noted that the reduction of brain serotonin by $p$CPA could provide for better learning behavior and improved memory, as measured by a reduced susceptibility to the retrograde amnesic effects of disruptive stimuli. The reduction of brain serotonin may be brought about regionally even hours after $p$CPA administration to mice (Essman, 1975), as exemplified in the data summarized in Table 1. Further examination of this effect indicated that there were diurnal differences in the serotonin-

**Table 1.   Mean ($\pm\sigma$) Regional Concentration of Serotonin Measured 3 Hours Following $p$-Chlorophenylalanine or Saline Injection in Mice**

| Brain Region | Treatment Condition | |
|---|---|---|
| | NaCl | $p$CPA |
| Cerebral cortex | 0.28 (0.09) | 0.10 (0.03) |
| Limbic area | 0.46 (0.10) | 0.15 (0.04) |
| Diencephalon | 0.16 (0.08) | 0.09 (0.06) |

depleting effect of *p*CPA, probably residing in diurnal differences in the extent to which *p*CPA inhibited tryptophan hydroxylase activity. For several regions of the mouse brain the differences between control and *p*CPA-treated animals are shown, with treatment given either in the AM (0800) or in the PM (2000); these results are given in Figure 1. It was apparent that for the cerebral and the cerebellar

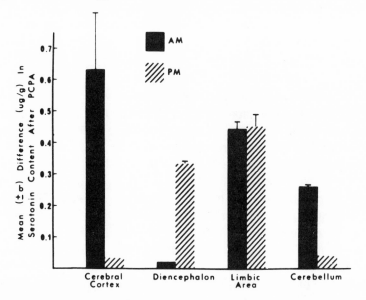

**Figure 1.** Diurnal Differences in the Serotonin-Depleting Effect of *p*-Chlorophenylalanine

cortices a greater reduction in serotonin content resulted from *p*CPA administration in the AM, although basal serotonin levels were lower in the PM. In order to assess the effects of *p*CPA on learning, specifically for diurnal differences in the basal level as well as the reduced level after *p*CPA, mice were trained for the acquisition and reversal of an escape response from a single-choice water maze. Maze trials were given 3 hours after either saline of *p*CPA treatment at either 0800 or 2000 hours. The frequency of errors committed in escaping from the maze was measured for each condition, and these results are summarized in Table 2. As previously noted, there were fewer PM errors, and, furthermore, reduction of forebrain serotonin content after *p*CPA favored a greater reduction in maze errors for the AM conditions.

Table 2.    Mean ($\pm\sigma$) Incidence of Water Maze Errors
by Mice During Acquisition and Reversal. Effect of
p-Chlorophenylalanine at 0800 and 2000 Hours

| | AM | | PM | |
|---|---|---|---|---|
| Treatment | Acquisition | Reversal | Acquisition | Reversal |
| NaCl | 12 | 9 | 6 | 4 |
| | (2.6) | (1.9) | (2.1) | (1.0) |
| pCPA | 5 | 4 | 3 | 3 |
| | (1.3) | (1.2) | (1.1) | (0.6) |

On the basis that PM serotonin levels were lower than AM levels, learning was more efficient in the PM than in the AM , and serotonin reduction was of a greater magnitude under AM conditions following pCPA, both endogenous and drug-related microsomal protein synthesis might be appropriately correlated. The incorporation of $C^{14}$-leucine into microsomal proteins of the cerebral cortex was determined for mice treated with either saline or pCPA under either AM or PM conditions. The results shown in Table 3 indicate that microsomal protein synthesis in the cerebral cortex was somewhat greater in the PM under control conditions and was increased after forebrain serotonin was decreased by pCPA. The magnitude of the increment in protein synthesis was greater for AM conditions (39%), where serotonin reduction after pCPA was greater, than for PM conditions (9%).

Table 3.    Incorporation of $C_{14}$-Leucine into Microsomal
Proteins (cpm/mg Protein) Following
p-Chlorophenylalanine at Different Times

| Treatment | AM | PM |
|---|---|---|
| NaCl | 227 | 275 |
| pCPA | 316 | 298 |

Another pharmacological relationship between brain serotonin and the processes of learning and memory may be found in the use of 6-methoxy-$\beta$-carboline, which has been shown to provide for a marked increase in forebrain serotonin concentration (Ho et al., 1969) (Table 4). Except in the case of the cerebral cortex, there were

**Table 4.  Percent Increase in Regional Serotonin Concentration
1 Hour Following 6-Methoxy-$\beta$-Carboline Injection**

| Brain Region | AM | PM |
|---|---|---|
| Cerebral cortex | 95 | 700 |
| Diencephalon | 50 | 50 |
| Limbic area | 180 | 110 |
| Cerebellum | 270 | 170 |

generally greater serotonin increases when the drug was given in the
AM. When given 1 hour prior to passive avoidance conditioning,
less than 20% of the mice tested showed acquisition under AM or PM
conditions. Microsomal protein synthesis for all brain areas was
reduced in the AM (30%) and PM (13%), with the limbic area and
cerebellum contributing largely to the greater reduction in protein
synthesis for AM conditions (16 and 18%, respectively). It thus
appears that increased brain serotonin effected with 6-
methoxy-$\beta$-carboline occurs differentially under AM or PM
conditions, and this differential change appears well correlated with
the magnitude of inhibition for regional microsomal protein
synthesis. The observed impairment of avoidance acquisition could
not be discriminatively differentiated on an AM–PM basis, since at
both times after serotonin elevation (0900 and 2100 hours) learning
did not exceed 20%.

The tyrosine hydroxylase inhibitor $\alpha$-methyl-$p$-tyrosine provides for a reduction in the levels of brain dopamine and
norepinephrine, but also bears upon the brain serotonin response to
ECS (Essman, 1970c). The percent elevation in brain serotonin,
measured 15 minutes after a single ECS given to mice, has been
shown as a function of time after $\alpha$-methyl-$p$-tyrosine treatment
(Figure 2). It is apparent that for those times when brain
catecholamines are reduced, serotonin is not elevated by ECS. The
behavioral corollary of this observation is that mice trained to
acquire a passive avoidance response after $\alpha$-methyl-$p$-tyrosine
showed reduced acquisition at the point of peak catecholamine
depletion (4 hours), but ECS immediately after training did not
further decrease retention of the avoidance response. The interesting
point here is that catecholamine depletion before a serotonin-
elevating stimulus blocked the elevation and partially prevented the

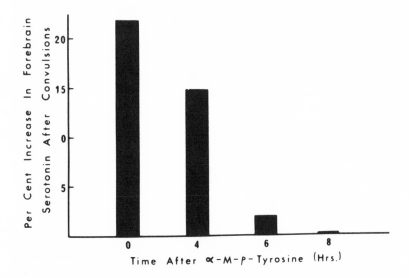

**Figure 2.** Elevation of Brain Serotonin after Convulsion. Effects of $\alpha$-Methyl-*p*-tyrosine

amnesic effect of this stimulus. With intracranial injection of serotonin, as previously noted, tissue serotonin is elevated, regional protein synthesis is inhibited, and a temporally dependent retrograde amnesia is effected. Intraventricular injection of norepinephrine was given 10 minutes prior to the avoidance conditioning and posttrial intrahippocampal injection of serotonin to mice. Other pretraining treatments consisted of intraventricular injection of either an equivalent volume of 0.9% NaCl or an equimolar concentration of tyrosine, dopamine, or epinephrine. When all mice were tested for retention of the avoidance response 24 hours later, the amnesic effects of serotonin treatment were apparent. As shown in Figure 3, pretreatment with norepinephrine blocked the retrograde amnesic effect of serotonin, but the other catecholamines had no appreciable antiamnesic effect.

A similar relationship has been developed for the effects of norepinephrine on the behavioral and biochemical effects of ECS (Essman, 1973C). Intracranially administered norepinephrine given 10 minutes prior to ECS blocked the ECS-induced reduction in protein synthesis by the forebrain. Normetanephrine exerted a similar effect. The behavioral effect of pretreatment of mice with norepinephrine or normetanephrine prior to avoidance conditioning

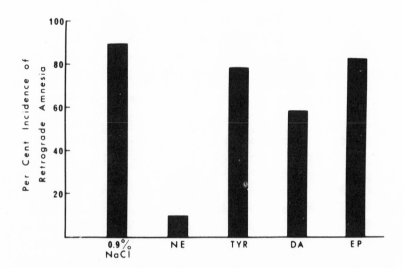

**Figure 3.** Effects of Intraventricular Norepinephrine upon the Amnesic Effect of Intrahippocampal Serotonin

and ECS has been summarized in Table 5. Both norepinephrine and normetanephrine produced significant attenuation of the retrograde amnesic effect of ECS. The basis for this effect appears related to both of the interdependent mechanisms that have been under discussion—changes in serotonin metabolism and resulting alterations in protein synthesis. It was previously shown (Essman, 1973c) that norepinephrine and noremetanephrine reversed the inhibition of mitochondrial and cell sap protein in the cerebral cortex of mice after a single ECS. The effects upon ECS-induced forebrain serotonin elevation are shown in Table 6. It is apparent that norepinephrine or normetanephrine given intraventricularly 10 minutes prior to ECS blocked the elevation of brain serotonin which occurs within 15 minutes after such treatment.

**Table 5.  Percent Incidence of Conditioned Response Retention for Mice 24 Hours after Avoidance Training**

| | Posttraining Treatment | |
|---|---|---|
| Pretraining Treatment | ECS | ECS |
| 0.9% NaCl | 20 | 90 |
| Norepinephrine | 80 | 90 |
| Normetanephrine | 75 | 85 |

Table 6.  Forebrain Serotonin Concentration ($\mu$g/g)
before ECS and after ECS

| Pretreatment | ECS | ECS |
| --- | --- | --- |
| 0.9% NaCl | 0.96 | 0.82 |
| Norepinephrine | 0.78 | 0.76 |
| Normetanephrine | 0.78 | 0.77 |

There is some question as to whether the antiamnesic and antiserotonin effects of norepinephrine reside in its properties as a receptor antagonist or as an independent stimulus to protein synthesis. The use of serotonin receptor antagonists generally has not found extensive applicability in studies of learning or memory, and almost none of these agents alters the tissue content of serotonin. Perhaps one reason for such limited use is the question of central versus peripheral serotonin antagonism or the difficulty in separating these effects. Agents such as methysergide, cyproheptadine, and mianserin have been used only to a limited extent in relating learning or memory to serotonin receptor antagonism. The latter compound, a tetracyclic antidepressant, has been shown to attenuate the amnesic effect of ECS in mice, but this effect is difficult to separate clearly from the changes in sensory threshold to foot shock or in seizure threshold to ECS also attributed to this agent. Another serotonin receptor antagonist, cinanserin, has been shown to affect the performance of hungry rats responding to a food reward in a straight alley (Rosen and Cohen, 1973). The drug produced lower levels of initial responding and reduced performance. It is quite likely that, like cyproheptadine, cinanserin may stimulate appetite under non-food-deprived conditions and thereby confer altered motivational properties upon the food reward for a hungry rat. In rats which were trained by shock reinforcement to suppress a reinforced lever-pressing response to a tone, cinanserin reduced the conflict behavior (Geller and Hartmann, 1973). The attenuating effect of cinanserin was reduced in rats that were treated with either $\alpha$-methyltryptamine or 5-hydroxytryptophan, suggesting that competition for molecular antagonism may be the basis for the effect of this agent upon learned behavior.

Another drug which provides a basis for the relationship between brain serotonin metabolism and learning and memory is

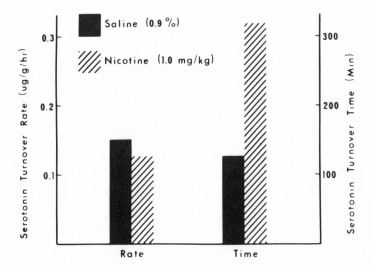

**Figure 4.**  Effects of Nicotine upon Forebrain Serotonin Metabolism

nicotine (Essman, 1973b). In mice, nicotine alters forebrain turnover of serotonin (Figure 4) such that there is a slight reduction (20%) in the serotonin turnover rate, and turnover time is increased (200%) by 45 minutes following nicotine injection. It was shown that the injected nicotine was maximally concentrated in the hippocampus and basal ganglia 45 minutes after intraperitoneal injection. The effects of nicotine upon the regional content of serotonin and 5-hydroxyindoleacetic acid (5-HIAA) may be observed in Table 7. Differences in the effect of nicotine upon serotonin and 5-HIAA concentration, and in the effect of the nicotine metabolite cotinine, may be observed at 15 minutes as compared to 45 minutes after injection. The content of both serotonin and 5-HIAA was elevated by nicotine but normalized by 45 minutes after cotinine, which, based upon previous observations, is accumulated as a nicotine metabolite in the cerebral cortex and basal ganglia by 45 minutes after nicotine treatment. On the basis of these observed effects of nicotine and cotinine upon the brain serotonin metabolism, differences in the behavioral effect of the drug may be time related. For mice given nicotine and then trained for a single-trial passive avoidance response either 15 or 45 minutes later, followed by a single ECS, differences in the amnesic effect of

**Table 7.  Mean (±$\sigma$) Regional Concentration ($\mu$g/g) of Serotonin and 5-Hydroxyindoleacetric Acid Following Saline or Drug Treatment**

| Brain Area | Posttreatment Time | | | | | |
| --- | --- | --- | --- | --- | --- | --- |
| | 15 Minutes | | | 45 Minutes | | |
| | Saline | Nicotine | Cotinine | Saline | Nicotine | Cotinine |
| Cerebral cortex | | | | | | |
| Serotonin | 0.38(0.06) | 0.42(0.01) | 0.33(0.04) | 0.39(0.04) | 0.66(0.04) | 0.28(0.03) |
| 5-HIAA | 0.52(0.19) | 0.55(0.06) | 0.43(0.05) | 0.12(0.02) | 0.37(0.02) | 0.36(0.04) |
| Mesencephalon | | | | | | |
| Serotonin | 0.33(0.04) | 0.82(0.02) | 0.83(0.05) | 0.33(0.04) | 0.64(0.06) | 0.33(0.05) |
| 5-HIAA | 0.21(0.02) | 0.45(0.02) | 0.36(0.04) | 0.18(0.03) | 0.35(0.06) | 1.00(0.12) |
| Diencephalon | | | | | | |
| Serotonin | 0.33(0.04) | 0.96(0.20) | 0.56(0.04) | 0.33(0.05) | 0.90(0.15) | 0.28(0.05) |
| 5-HIAA | 0.15(0.03) | 0.45(0.09) | 0.29(0.04) | 0.14(0.03) | 0.45(0.18) | 1.07(0.11) |

the ECS were observed. Unshocked nicotine-treated mice showed an equivalent incidence of conditioned response retention (80%), regardless of whether they were trained 15 or 45 minutes after drug administration. Mice trained and shocked 15 minutes after drug treatment showed a higher incidence of amnesia (95%) than non-drug-treated shocked mice (80%). Those animals trained and shocked 45 minutes after nicotine showed a reduced incidence of ECS-induced amnesia (60%). A related observation is that regional protein synthesis, while reduced at 15 minutes after nicotine injection, was increased at 45 minutes after treatment. *In vivo* assessment of protein synthesis for several subcellular fractions from the mouse cerebral cortex has been carried out for mice 45 minutes after they were treated with nicotine. These results have been summarized in Figure 5. Significantly increased microsomal protein synthesis could be related to the effects of nicotine, which altered the serotonin metabolism at this same point in time.

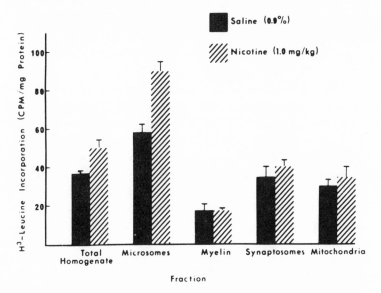

**Figure 5.** Effects of Nicotine upon Protein Synthesis among Several Subcellular Fractions of the Cerebral Cortex Obtained after Convulsion

In a previous communication (Essman, 1970c) the effects of uric acid upon several aspects of learning and memory were

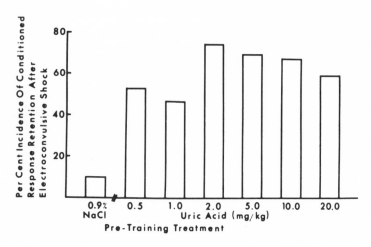

**Figure 6.**   Effects of Uric Acid on the Amnesic Efficacy of ECS

reviewed. As a metabolite of the purine bases of RNA there appear to be a number of circumstances where its concentration may be endogenously decreased or increased through exogenous means. As such this methylxanthine appears significantly interrelated to brain serotonin metabolism and the regulation of learning and memory. In mice pretreated with either saline or varying doses of uric acid, the latter afforded significant attenuation of the retrograde amnesic effect of a posttraining ECS. These results are shown in Figure 6. Within a dose range of 0.5–20.0 mg/kg, uric acid given 60 minutes prior to a training trial-ECS sequence reduced the amnesic effect of the otherwise disruptive stimulus. Uric acid did not affect the acquisition of the avoidance response in these experiments and did not modify the convulsive episode precipitated by ECS.

In mice pretreated with uric acid (1.0 mg/kg, i.p.) or saline 1 hour prior to being convulsed with a single ECS, changes in brain serotonin metabolism were measured 20 minutes later. In Figure 6 it is apparent that the effects of a single convulsion produced by ECS were reversed in mice pretreated with uric acid. These findings suggested that the uric-acid-induced antagonism of an ECS retrograde amnesia may reside in the attenuation and/or reversal of the serotoninergic changes that appear requisite for such an amnesia to occur. As discussed previously in this chapter, the age-related susceptibility or resistance of mice to amnesic stimuli was examined and related to (1) the ability of such stimuli to modify the brain serotonin metabolism and (2) the extent to which a serotonin related inhibition of protein synthesis occurred as a function of time after learning. In that context, the uric acid treatment in mice of different ages was examined in terms of its effect upon the susceptibility of such animals to an ECS-induced retrograde amnesia. Mice given 1.0 mg/kg or uric acid 60 minutes prior to avoidance conditioning and immediate posttraining ECS were compared with saline-treated mice for the retention of the conditioned avoidance response measured 24 hours later. The results, shown in Figure 7, agree well with previous findings that the 17-day-old CF-Is strain mouse is least susceptible to the amnesic effects of ECS. Furthermore, uric acid uniformly reduced the susceptibility to amnesia at all ages.

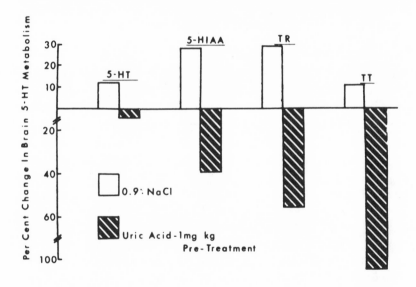

**Figure 7.**    Effects of Uric Acid upon Changes in Serotonin Metabolism by ECS

The susceptibility to the amnesic effects of several posttraining stimuli has been related not only to age but also to the ability of such stimuli to alter the brain serotonin metabolism, and thereby to reduce the rate of regional cerebral protein synthesis. The effects of ECS upon cerebral protein synthesis among mice at different ages was studied after uric-acid treatment under the same conditions as described for the behavioral studies. A comparison between the effects of uric acid and those of saline is presented in Figure 8. It is apparent that a reduced degree of inhibition, by ECS, of cerebral protein synthesis occurred for mice that were pretreated with uric acid. As before, 17-day-old mice showed a reduced susceptibility to the effect of ECS upon protein synthesis.

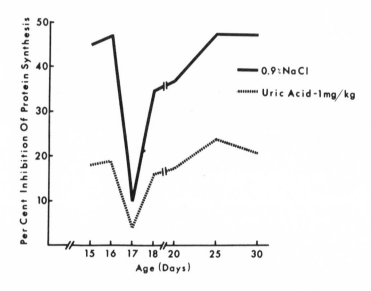

**Figure 8.**  Effects of Uric Acid on Age-Related Changes in ECS-Induced Inhibition of Cerebral Protein Synthesis

Another corollary of the effect of amnesic stimuli is the reduced regional synaptosomal uptake of serotonin (Essman, 1974). The *in vitro* uptake of serotonin was determined for synaptosomes derived from the cerebral cortex, midbrain, and cerebellum of mice convulsed with ECS or sham treated. The synaptosome preparations for each condition were incubated with either saline or uric acid ($10^{-5}M$), and the uptake of $C^{14}$-serotonin was measured. Figure 9 shows the reduction in the synaptosomal uptake of serotonin, *in vitro*, after *in vivo* ECS, for uric acid and control conditions. In synaptosomes from the cerebral cortex and midbrain, uric acid attenuated the ECS-induced reduction in serotonin uptake. These data again support the view that attenuation of the serotonin changes

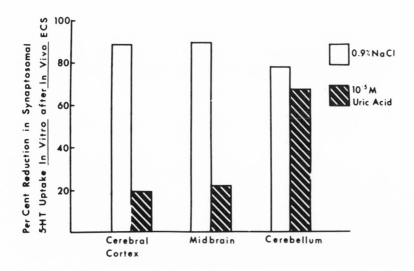

**Figure 9.**   Effects of Uric Acid upon ECS-Induced Changes in Synaptosomal Serotonin Uptake

by ECS at the nerve ending may be provided by uric acid, both through systemic action *in vivo* and through direct action, *in vitro*, upon the synaptosome. In addition to considering the uptake changes at the nerve ending, serotonin uptake by neurons and glia isolated by separatory methods (Essman and Essman, 1977) from several brain regions was also investigated.

Neurons isolated from the cerebral cortex, basal ganglia, diencephalon, and cerebellum of convulsed and control mice were incubated with $C^{14}$-serotonin in the presence of either saline or uric acid. Differences between the convulsed and control conditions and the effects of uric acid upon serotonin uptake by these isolated neurons have been summarized in Figure 10. It is apparent that uric acid either reversed or, in fact, increased the cell body uptake of serotonin. Neuronal cell bodies from the basal ganglia and cerebellum showed the greatest and most significant reduction of serotonin uptake after the convulsion, but these effects were attenuated or reversed by uric acid.

A similar experiment was performed for astrocytes isolated from several brain regions from convulsed and control mice. The effect of uric acid on the glial uptake of serotonin is shown in Figure 11, where differences between convulsed and control animals are

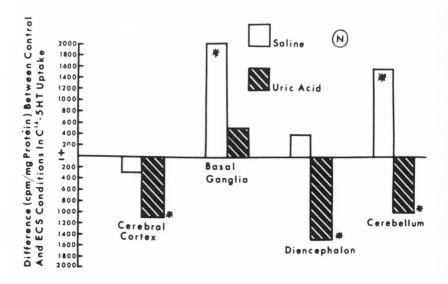

**Figure 10.** *In Vitro* Effects of Uric Acid upon Serotonin Uptake by Isolated Neurons from Several Brain Regions of Convulsed Mice

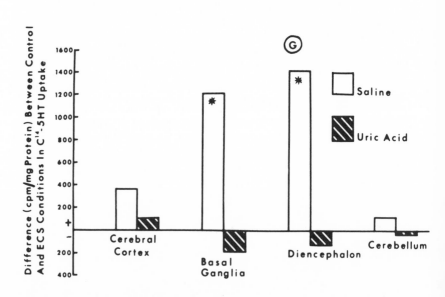

**Figure 11.** Effects of Uric Acid upon Serotonin Uptake by Glia Isolated from Several Brain Regions of Convulsed Mice

given. The significant decrease in serotonin uptake by glia from the basal ganglia and diencephalon produced by ECS was completely attenuated *in vitro* by uric acid. Thus, as will neuronal cell body fractions, an astrocyte-enriched fraction also showed a uric-acid-mediated reversal of the convulsion-induced reduction in serotonin uptake.

As has been previously indicated, the serotonin change incurred by ECS-induced convulsion produces an inhibition of cerebral protein synthesis. The foregoing effects of uric acid—(1) reversing the amnesic effect of ECS, (2) reversing the ECS-induced changes in brain serotonin metabolism, (3) reducing ECS-induced inhibition of protein synthesis, and (4) attenuating the ECS-induced reduction in synaptosomal, neuronal, and glial serotonin uptake—have warranted studies concerned with the *in vitro* synthesis of proteins by neuronal and glial fractions from convulsed mice.

Neuronal cell body fractions from several brain regions were compared between convulsed and nonconvulsed mice for the incorporation of $C^{14}$-leucine into proteins. Figure 12 shows the changes in regional brain protein synthesis by neurons as affected by

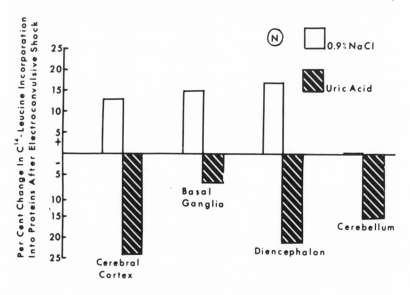

**Figure 12.**   Effects of Uric Acid upon Neuronal Protein Synthesis after Convulsion

the *in vitro* addition of uric acid. The decreased protein synthesis by neurons of the cerebral cortex, basal ganglia, and diencephalon produced by ECS was reversed by uric acid.

In a preparation of fractions of astrocytes from the brain regions of ECS-convulsed and control mice, the effects of uric acid upon protein synthesis were determined (Figure 13). The effect of ECS was to significantly increase glial protein synthesis in the diencephalon, with increases that were statistically insignificant for glia from the cerebral cortex, diencephalon, and cerebellum. The *in vitro* effect of uric acid was to reverse these ECS-induced changes, notably such that a significant decrement in glial protein synthesis for the diencephalic fraction occurred. It is therefore apparent that ECS, and its concurrent elevation of regional serotonin, can inhibit neuronal and increase glial protein synthesis. Such altered protein synthesis can be reversed for both systems by uric acid.

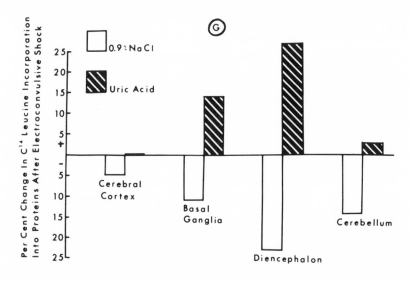

**Figure 13.** Effects of Convulsion upon Glial Protein Synthesis. Effects of Uric Acid

Previous mention has been made of butyric acid as an amnesic stimulus. This short-chain fatty acid, capable of mimicking hepatic coma (Zieve, 1966; Walker and Schenker, 1970), may complex with serotonin (Rizzoli and Galzinga, 1970), releasing it synaptically and elevating the brain level of this amine (Baldessarini and Fisher, 1973). The temporal gradient for the retrograde amnesic effect of systemically administered butyric acid (22.5 $\mu M$, i.p.) after a single-trial avoidance training session in mice is shown in Figure 14. The animals were tested for conditioned response retention 24 hours after training. Saline injection, as expected, did

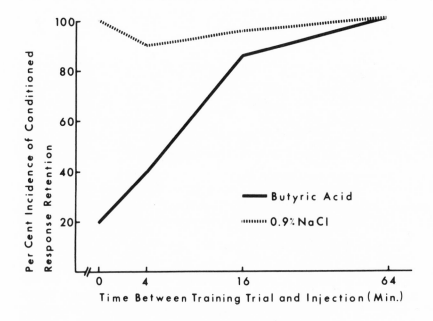

**Figure 14.**   Retrograde Amnesic Effect of Posttraining Butyric Acid

not alter the retention of the conditioned passive avoidance response, but butyric acid, producing the rapid onset of coma lasting $68.5 \pm 3.5$ minutes, produced a retrograde amnesia as a function of the interval between training and its administration. Significant amnesia occurred when butyric acid was given up to 4 minutes after training. The effect of the same dose of butyric acid upon regional serotonin concentration is shown in Figure 15. Although no serotonin concentration changes occurred in the cerebellar cortex, the other areas showed an appreciable increment by 16 minutes after treatment (approximately 8 minutes after the onset of coma), and sizable increments were still notable by 64 minutes when most of the animals had recovered from the coma.

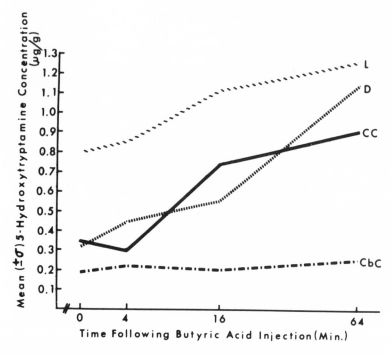

**Figure 15.** Effects of Butyric Acid upon Regional Serotonin Concentrations in the Brain

A remaining issue is cerebral protein synthesis. As previously observed, those agents or events that provide a retrograde amnesic effect in animals and produce an elevation in brain serotonin concentration also effect an inhibition in regional protein synthesis. If the two metabolic events were again correlated over time, one might anticipate that butyric acid treatment would also produce an inhibition of regional brain protein synthesis, with the greatest extent of inhibition coincident with the greatest extent of regional serotonin increase after butyric acid injection; this should be within the first 16 minutes after treatment. As may be observed in Figure 16, protein synthesis in the cerebral cortex, basal ganglia and diencephalon, and midbrain was inhibited over the first 16 minutes following butyric acid injection; but the greatest magnitude of inhibition was within the first 4 minutes. Thus butyric acid given shortly after training had a retrograde amnesic effect which was temporally related to its elevation of brain serotonin and inhibition of cerebral protein synthesis.

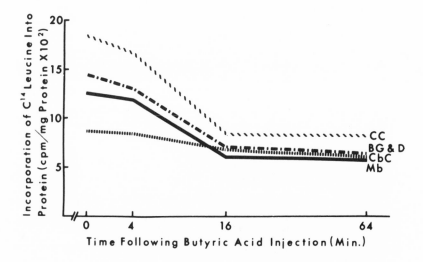

**Figure 16.** Effects of Butyric Acid upon Regional Protein Synthesis in the Brain

As with other amnesic stimuli, the protective and/or attenuating effects of uric acid pretreatment were studied with butyric acid. In mice pretreated with either uric acid (2 mg/kg) or saline, either butyric acid or saline was given 60 minutes later, immediately following a single training trial for conditioning of a passive avoidance response. Pretreatment with uric acid did not alter the onset or duration of the coma that was produced by butyric acid. The behavioral data, summarized in Table 8, indicate that uric acid pretreatment significantly reduced the incidence of butyric-acid-induced retrograde amnesia in mice. If the mechanism by which uric acid spares animals from the retrograde amnesic effect of butyric acid were consistent with the hypothesis advocated in this chapter, one might then expect that uric acid was capable of blocking those butyric-acid-induced changes that appear to account for amnesia—elevation of serotonin and inhibition of protein synthesis.

The results of experiments in which mice pretreated with uric acid and, 60 minutes later, given butyric acid, had regional serotonin concentrations and amino acid incorporation into protein measured are summarized in Table 9. In all regions sampled, except for the cerebellum, uric acid pretreatment significantly blocked butyric-acid-induced serotonin elevation and inhibition of protein

Table 8. Median Response Latency (Training and Testing) and Incidence of Conditioned Avoicance Response Retention in Mice Pretreated with Saline or Uric Acid Given Posttraining or Butyric Acid

| Condition | | Conditioned Avoidance Response Retention | | |
|---|---|---|---|---|
| Pretreatment | Posttraining Treatment | Median Response Training | Latency Testing | % Conditioned Response Retention |
| 0.9% NaCl | 0.9% NaCl | 10.2 | 86.7 | 100 |
| 0.9% NaCl | Butyric acid | 7.9 | 61.5 | 20[a] |
| Uric acid | 0.9% NaCl | 9.4 | 85.5 | 100 |
| Uric acid | Butyric acid | 8.6 | 83.5 | 70[a] |

[a] $X_2 = 13.60$; $p < 0.005$.

**Table 9.  Mean ($\pm\sigma$) Regional Serotonin Concentration and
C$^{14}$-Leucine Incorporation into Protein Measured in Saline- or
Uric-Acid-Treated Mice 60 Minutes Following Butyric Acid Injection**

| Brain Region | Serotonin Concentration | | C$^{14}$-Leucine (cpm/mg Protein) Incorporation | |
|---|---|---|---|---|
| | NaCl | Uric Acid | NaCl | Uric Acid |
| Cerebral cortex | 0.92 | 0.30[a] | 820 | 1660[a] |
| | (0.18) | (0.07) | | |
| Diencephalon | 1.26 | 0.45[a] | 640 | 1330[b] |
| | (0.27) | (0.11) | | |
| Limbic area | 1.28 | 0.86[b] | 865 | 1180[b] |
| | (0.12) | (0.09) | | |
| Cerebellum | 0.26 | 0.22 | 600 | 840 |
| | (0.04) | (0.04) | | |

[a]$p < 0.01$.
[b]$p < 0.05$.

synthesis. Therefore, as previously observed with other retrograde amnesic stimuli, uric acid reduces the amnesic effect by blocking the change in serotonin concentration and reducing regional protein synthesis—the metabolic changes that appear requisite for a reduction in learning or memory to occur.

The relationship of serotonin to the processes of learning and memory has been considered in the present discussion largely in terms of serotonin changes as being a negative influence upon the acquisition or processing of information by the central nervous system. We have attempted to show that a variety of agents or events, which interfere with learning or exert a retroactive effect upon memory, presumably by interrupting the consolidation process by which the memory trace is incorporated into longer term storage, have in common their potential for (1) changing the concentration, availability, turnover, or cellular uptake of serotonin, and (2) altering the synthesis of site-specific proteins. A number of variables, such as age, strain, diurnal changes, social-housing conditions, and drugs that are capable of altering the brain serotonin content or metabolism and protein synthesis at respective sites, also affect the processes of learning and memory, or modify the effects of conditions which change the learning ability or retention. The specificity, time course, and interaction of serotonin for those acquired behaviors and retained responses that have been considered in animal experiments have somewhat limited but perhaps relevant applications in man. Since it is not the purpose of this chapter to explore the role of serotonin in human learning or memory, owing to inherent problems in the measurement of tissue or fluid contents, only suggestive relationships will be observed with the hope that these may be further explored in the laboratory or clinic.

Several observations in man relate to the general theme and findings in the experimental studies documented. For example, a rise in brain serotonin after rapid-eye-movement (REM) sleep episodes can eliminate retention of the dream content occurring during the REM phase, unless wakening occurs before the serotonin rise, and dream retention remains intact. Another example may be found in systemic disorders where circulating levels of serotonin are sufficiently high to permit blood–brain barrier transport to this amine, as suggested by elevated cerebrospinal fluid levels of 5-HIAA. This is the case with the carcinoid syndrome and medullary carcinoma of the thyroid in which disturbances of recent memory and novel performance task disruption, in the absence of any cerebral metastatic process, have been described. The measurement of increased 5-HIAA in the spinal fluid of patients with senile psychoses, senile or presenile dementias, or viral infections may, in small part, also relate to the theme under discussion. Perhaps if a more definite relationship between serotonin and the processes of learning and memory is to be documented in man, the area in which such documentation may best begin is clinical pharmacology. There are at present numerous agents in the pharmacopeia which alter the synthesis, metabolism, availability, receptor action, and re-uptake of serotonin in man. Although there are few data concerning the effects of such agents on specific learned the retained behaviors, a consideration of such may constitute an important beginning for the documentation of altered serotonin and modified human cognitive behavior.

One route through which the role of serotonin in human memory and learning may be approached is the use of non toxic inhibitors or mediators or serotonin synthesis. One such agent is pyridoxine (Sourkes and Missala, 1969). As a requisite coenzyme for the enzymatic regulation of amino acid metabolism, the agent could be expected to affect serotonin metabolism in the brain, so as to provide for increased concentrations. In one study (Molimard et al., 1980) memorization of a digit coding task was impaired at doses of pyridoxine of 500 mg per day. At a dose of 1 g, subjects also showed lower word recognition performance and impaired visual retention. Although this study does not directly implicate only brain serotonin in the effects of pyridoxine, it does point to a possible relationship.

# 5

# Neuropharmacology
# in the Dysmnesias

A relationship may be sought between the neurochemical substrates of learning and memory and the neuroanatomical sites to which such systems are related, based upon pharmacological response. One basis through which such interactions may be further applied and from which clinical significance emerges, relates to the dysmnestic syndromes.

The two major brain regions that have been generally implicated in human memory dysfunction include the diencephalon and the hippocampi. The dysmnestic syndromes which involve these structures include impairment of long-term data storage, disruption of the encoding of short-term into long-term storage, or a loss of decoding or access to the long-term data storage. This concerns the latter two problems. *Dysmnesia* is the preferred term describing a partial memory loss, in contrast to the term *amnesia* which implies a total memory loss. Amnesia may be viewed as an extreme on a broad continuum of dysmnestic syndromes, where mild dysmnestic illnesses occur more commonly than total amnesia.

There are several complex biochemical systems, involving several putative neurotransmitters, which subserve human information storage. These are apparently arranged in both parallel and serial processing frameworks which make research difficult because of several confounding experimental factors. Organic dysmnesia and amnesia can present either acutely or chronically as a result of lesions of a degenerative, space-occupying, traumatic, vascular, infectious, anoxic, metabolic, epileptic, nutritionally induced, endocrinological, or other nature, with varying degrees of reversibility. Diffuse central nervous system damage is associated with widespread cognitive impairment. In contrast, focal damage to some of the discrete regions considered in this chapter can produce a very specific type of memory loss with maintenance of other intellectual functions.

The dysmnesias found in both Korsakoff's and bilateral hippocampal syndromes have general similarities. Memory for any new data inputs is absent or deficient. Immediate memory, also termed ultra-short-term memory, is unimpaired so that the patient is able to recall brief series of digits within the limits of focused attention due to constant verbal rehearsal. Data storage is absent, and memory is lost after several minutes due to an attention decrement. Perception, alertness, mood, social appropriateness, and affect may all appear to be perfectly normal.

The most prominent deficit in the dysmnestic syndromes is anterograde dysmnesia. This is characterized by severe impairment of new learning with its onset at the time of the original attack of illness, such as an episode of hypothiaminemia (Korsakoff's) or bilateral temporal herpes simplex encephalitis (hippocampal). The ability to place new data into information storage from the time of this illness is severely compromised. One result is the production of severe disturbances in orientation, especially for time.

It is important to distinguish recent memory loss from immediate memory preservation because the identification of dysmnesia could otherwise be missed. An alert, affable, friendly patient may perform completely normally on a standard digit span task. With bilateral hippocampal damage it has been shown (Drachman and Arbit, 1966) that verbal rehearsal may permit the recall of memory task material for quite a few minutes, and longer than observed for patients with Korsakoff's syndrome. As soon as distraction occurs, however, the memory trace is lost. Also, severe impairment of recall can occur for tasks that require the learning of lists longer than the digit span. Some degree of recall recovery is possible for Korsakoff patients, but is less likely to be observed for hippocampal patients.

Memory loss for events prior to the onset of illness, termed retrograde dysmnesia, exists to varying degrees of severity for all patients. The severity of the retrograde memory problem decreases as a function of the time since the onset of physical illness. The most severe degree of dysmnesia occurs for those events that are within the limits of the retrograde dysfunction, with a disorganization in the recall sequence (Lishman, 1978).

Anterograde time sense is also distorted, particularly for Korsakoff patients. Long periods of time may be subjectively experienced as condensed. Events that occur over short time periods may be recalled as having occurred over many years. The sequence of events is also disturbed. Events occurring at different times may be recalled as a single episode. The dysmnestic or amnesic patient may then be described as being, in effect, lost in time. It has been suggested (Sanders and Warrington, 1971) that when time-related stimuli are of equal difficulty, the temporal gradient for retention loss disappears. The temporal gradient of retrograde amnesia was studied in alcoholic Korsakoff patients to indicate a steep gradient; this was independent of task difficulty, and memory impairment occurred for all time sequences tested (Albert et al., 1979).

Coherent, orderly, but entirely falsified or confabulated histories can occasionally be obtained from nonmalingering Korsakoff patients, but not from hippocampal patients. This symptom appears to be a function of a number of factors, including loss of time sense and premorbid alcoholic personality disorder.

The mammillary bodies of the hypothalamus, the nucleus medialis dorsalis of the thalamus, and other gray matter surrounding the third ventricle appear to be critical sites of the lesions which produce the Korsakoff syndrome; such lesions are symmetrical. Other regions may also be involved, but to a lesser degree; these include the terminal portions of the fornices (near the mammillary bodies) and gray matter surrounding the aqueduct and fourth ventricle. Lesions of the ventricular surface portion of the nucleus medalis dorsalis invariably occur in Korsakoff's syndrome. Korsakoff's syndrome often involves other thalamic regions, expecially the pulvinar and nucleus anteromedialis. Damage only rarely occurs in the cerebral cortex, cingulate gyri, hippocampi, and other regions (Victor et al., 1971).

Korsakoff's syndrome often follows an attack of Wernicke's encephalopathy, and several investigators view the disorders as a unitary Wernicke–Korsakoff syndrome. Careful neuropathological studies have correlated the Wernicke symptoms of opthalmoplegia with lesions of the third and sixth cranial nerve nuclei, ataxia from cerebellar lesions, and nystagmus from lesions of the medial vestibular nuclei.

Alcoholics in general are at risk for cerebellar degeneration, central pontine myelinosis, and lesions of the corpus callosum (the latter in the Marchiafava–Bignami syndrome). These disorders and Korsakoff's amnesic syndrome relate to nutritional factors, notably a reduced blood level of thiamine (hypothiaminemia). Thiamine or its phosphorylated form are requisites for the coenzyme for pyruvate decarboxylation and also for the enzymes $\alpha$-ketoglutarate decarboxylase and transketolase. Thiamine deficiency therefore leads to increased blood and tissue levels of pyruvate and decreased activity of enzymes, reflecting an impairment in both the tricarboxylic acid cycle and the pentose phosphate pathway (Brin et al., 1960; Dreyfus, 1962). Neural tissue surrounding the third and fourth ventricles and aqueduct are particularly prone to lesions in thiamine depletion states, possibly as a result of a transketolase deficiency. Blass and Gibson (1977) have reported a transketolase defect (a thiamine-dependent enzyme) in fibroblasts from skin biopsy cultured from patients with Korsakoff's syndrome. These investigators suggested that those individuals who develop Korsakoff's syndrome possess an abnormality in the kinetics of the enzyme. Since the alteration in the fibroblasts persisted for more than 20 generations of culture, the authors suggested a genetic factor and a genetic variation in the susceptibility to thiamine deficiency.

Conditions other than alcoholism can also produce dysmnesia as a result of lesions from hypothiaminemia. These include debilitated infectious states, intestinal obstruction, pernicious anemia, starvation, and other forms of malnutrition. Deficiencies of the other B vitamins may also contribute to the state. Some authors have reserved the term *Korsakoff* to refer only to the dysmnestic syndrome found in chronic alcoholics, although most workers use the term for any nutritionally derived illness with the characteristic memory disturbance.

There is some controversy as to the precise site of hypothiaminemia-induced lesions. Classically most reports have documented characteristic bilateral lesions of the mammillary bodies. In one series Victor and colleagues (1971) noted that symmetrical mammillary damage was localized to the medial and central regions. While these authors confirmed the well-known invariable appearance of mammillary lesions in Korsakoff patients, they also reported data from five patients with bilateral mammillary lesions and no memory disturbance. Their neuropathological data were highly consistent for a relationship between amnesia and lesions of the magnocellular part of the nucleus medialis dorsalis of the thalamus. A good, but not perfectly consistent, relationship was found between memory disruption and lesions of the mammillary bodies and pulvinar.

The nucleus medialis dorsalis and the mammillary bodies constitute portions of the diencephalon in which the latter consist mainly of the spherical medial mammillary nuclei which form the characteristic two bulges at the base of the brain posterior to the pituitary body. These medial nuclei consist of small cells surrounded by a capsule of myelinated fibers. A rather small intermediate (also termed intercalated) mammillary nucleus is encountered upon outward extension. Some histologists have described the cells as larger in the intermediate than in the medial nucleus, while others have described completely the opposite. More laterally a larger lateral mammillary nucleus occurs, which in spite of its size, does not significantly contribute to the bulge of the mammillary body. The large cells of the lateral nucleus are identical with the merge with the structure of the posterior hypothalamic region, the latter being associated with sympathetic nervous system control.

Intraconnections within the mammillary bodies and between them and nearby other hypothalamic regions may exist but have not been clearly defined. Fibers of the medial forebrain bundle pass in close proximity with the mammillary bodies and may provide bidirectional interconnections with diverse regions extending from the forebrain through the preoptic and hypothalamic regions and into the midbrain. An important point to be given later consideration concerns possible connections between the mammillary bodies and the supraoptic nuclei.

The hippocampus and mammillary area are uniquely interconnected by hippocampohypothalamic fibers which mainly trvel through the fornix. A flow of information is probably unidirectional and terminates in the mammillary regions (the interconnections through the fornix, on the other hand, are largely bidirectional). This specific pathway is also a portion of Papez's limbic system circuit, the proposed physiological substrate for emotional behavior.

The fibers of the fornix are separated into pre- and postcommissural division, depending upon their relationship to the anterior commissure. The fornix will be discussed in greater depth later, but the postcommissural portion is of particular relevance for the present issue. The greatest number of afferent fibers to the medial mammillary nucleus derive from the postcommissural fornix. Lesions of this nucleus occur most frequently in Korsakoff's syndrome, although five cases of severe destruction in the absence of memory disturbance were reported, as noted previously. Lesions of the terminal portions of the postcommissural fornix have also often been observed in the spectrum of Korsakoff pathology. Fibers from the postcommissural fornix are also distributed to the thalamus, mainly to the anterior and intralaminar nuclei. The anterior nuclei receive as many direct fibers from the fornix as from the mammillothalamic tract (Powell et al., 1957). Postcommissural fibers also descend adjacent to the mammillary bodies and then join nearby fiber bundles which enter the midbrain (Naunta, 1958).

Amygdalo-hypothalamic fibers travel to the hypothalamus via the stria terminalis and the ventral amygdalofugal pathway. While clearly distributing to other regions of the hypothalamus, it is not known if these fibers provide any mammillary afferents.

Afferents from the brain stem and the reticular activating system are also relevant. The mammillary peduncles provide for fibers from the dorsal and ventral tegmental nuclei of the midbrain which terminate mainly in the lateral mammillary nucleus.

Fibers within the dorsal longitudinal fasciculus extend from the central gray of the midbrain to the periventricular gray matter near the mammillary complex. This fiber bundle relays impulses both rostrally and caudally. Those regions served by this fiber bundle are all highly sensitive to thiamine and may be involved in the lesions of Korsakoff's syndrome. In addition there is evidence that the gray matter surrounding the third ventricle, where the fasciculus terminates, contains vasopressin receptors. This finding bears upon another aspect of memory functions which will be considered in this chapter.

Mammillary efferent fibers arise mainly from the medial mammillary nucleus, but there are some efferents that derive from the intermediate and lateral nuclei. The efferents briefly travel together dorsally as the fasciculus mammillaris princeps and then divide into the mammillothalamic and mammillotegmental tracts. The mammillothalamic tract, another element of the Papez circuit, provides fibers from the medial mammillary nucleus which extend to the ipsilateral anteroventral and anteromedial thalamic nuclei. The mammillothalamic tract also provides fibers bilaterally from the lateral mammillary nucleus to both anterodorsal thalamic nuclei (Fry et al., 1963). Hippocampal fibers from the fornix join the mammillothalamic tract and project directly to the thalamus (Valenstein and Nauta, 1959).

As noted earlier, recent import has been given to the nucleus medialis dorsalis of the thalamus, particularly the magnocellular portion, as the critical site for the memory-disruptive lesions of Korsakoff's syndrome. The magnocellular portion of this thalamic nucleus lies most medially along the surface of the third ventricle, a region of interest for the possible locus of receptor sites for vasopressin, a functionally relevant neuropeptide with a role in memory processes to be discussed later.

The nucleus medialis dorsalis occupies much of the region between the internal medullary laminar and the periventricular gray matter just discussed. The magnocellular portion contains fairly large, deeply straining polygonal cells, and lies dorsomedially and rostrally. The larger parvocellular region contains clusters of small pale-staining cells. The medialis dorsalis has connections with the centromedianus, other intralaminar nuclei, and the lateral nuclei. The nucleus medialis dorsalis is thought to be involved in the integration of complex somatic and visceral inputs, aside from its role in memory. This region also represents a site where psychosurgery is believed to alter affective states through the interruption of diverse projections to the frontal lobes. The parvocellular portion of the nucleus medialis dorsalis projects in an organized distribution to the entire frontal cortex rostral to Brodmann areas 6 and 32. The magnocellular portion of the nucleus medialis dorsalis receives inputs, via the inferior thalamic peduncle, from the amygdala, temporal neocortex, orbital frontal cortex, and possibly the substantia innominata. The inferior thalamic peduncle with fibers interconnecting the amygdala and preoptic regions constitutes the ansa peduncularis (Carpenter, 1976). There are presumably interconnections between the magnocellular and parvocellular portions of the nucleus medialis dorsalis with considerable transmission of impulses likely from the magnocellular into the parvocellular regions.

It is relevant that vasopressin is capable of exerting trophic effects other than its more familiar properties as a neurohormone with antidiuretic and pressor activities. Data suggest that vasopressin has a role in memory processes through secretion into the third ventricle with receptors in the periventricular gray matter (the same highly thiamine-dependent tissue that is damaged in Korsakoff's syndrome). Exogenous vasopressin and its analogues, when injected intraventricularly, facilitate the consolidation of learned responses. Vasopressin antibodies, which biologically inactivate vasopressin, block memory consolidation when injected into the third ventricle, thus approximating a memory defect resembling that of Korsakoff's syndrome. The memory consolidation process usually refers to the transfer of information from short-term rehearsal (a period during which the, as yet unstable, memory trace is vulnerable to the disruptive effects of several agents or events) into long-term storage.

Vasopressin has been used in a number of animal studies in which it presumably facilitates the consolidation of the memory trace for simple avoidance tasks in rats (de Wied et al., 1975a). The application of vasopressin to studies of memory function in man, without clinical or measured biochemical changes, has suggested that intranasal installation of 16 IU of lysine-8-vasopressin significantly improved the performance of 12 patients on attention tasks, motor performance, and visual retention, recognition, and recall (Legros et al., 1978). Vasopressin has also been used with some success in the treatment of alcoholic as well as posttraumatic amnesias (Oliveros et al., 1978).

Vasopressin has been used with reported success in the treatment of Korsakoff's syndrome (Le Boeuf et al., 1978). The treatment involves nasal spray administration of the vasopressin three times per day. Replication of these reports would be extremely important. In animal studies vasopressin has been shown to facilitate memory consolidation, presumably through its selective action upon the hippocampus (Van Wilmersma-Greidanus and de Wied, 1977) and the suggestion for its application as a therapeutic medium in memory dysfunction in humans has been made (Legros et al., 1978; Oliveros et al., 1978). This research approach has provided for a "vasopressin" theory of Korsakoff's syndrome where the dysmnesia results from levels of exogenous vasopressin due to periventricular tissue damage. Both effector as well as some receptor gray matter are destroyed, to varying degrees, by the characteristic lesions of Korsakoff's syndrome, thereby influencing the potential responsibility of such sites to therapeutic vasopressin. Dysmnestic syndromes, so common in older adults, seems correlated with lowered blood levels of vasopressin in men and women over 50 years of age.

In addition to the studies with vasopressin, a "noradrenergic" theory of Korsakoff's syndrome has been proposed. It has been noted that the Korsakoff lesions lie along monoaminergic pathways that have been carefully delineated in histofluorescence studies. In one systematic study (McEntee and Mair, 1978) cerebrospinal fluid (CSF) metabolites of serotonin, dopamine, and norepinephrine were measured in Korsakoff patients. The concentration of methoxy hydroxyphenylglycol (MHPG), the primary metabolite of norepinephrine, was decreased in Korsakoff patients as compared with controls. The concentration of MHPG in the CSF was also correlated with psychometric measures of memory impairment, such that individuals with the lowest concentration of the norepinephrine metabolite showed the greatest degree of memory impairment. More recent data favoring a noradrenergic deficit in Korsakoff's syndrome have emerged in a study of eight patients in which significant improvement on memory tests occurred after 2 weeks of treatment with the $\alpha$-noradrenergic agonist clonidine (McEntee and Mair, 1980). These findings have been viewed as a

Korsakoff-selective diminished presynaptic effect of clonidine (favoring enhanced learning and memory), providing for unopposed postsynaptic $\alpha$-adrenergic receptor effect.

Animal experiments support this relationship between the noradrenergic system and memory functions. Lesions of the locus ceruleus in rats are associated with the impairment of subsequent learning and decreased cortical levels of norepinephrine (Anzelark et al., 1973). Agents which decrease the brain norepinephrine level produce amnesia for well-learned tasks; such impairment is reversible by the administration of drugs which elevate norepinephrine levels (Roberts et al., 1970). One cannot ignore several complex interactions between the noradrenergic and vasopressin systems.

Bilateral lesions of the hippocampus produce a dysmnestic syndrome symptomatologically quite similar to Korsakoff's syndrome. Unilateral hippocampal lesions do not produce such cognitive changes. Even though this structure–function relationship exists, the hippocampus is only rarely affected in Korsakoff's syndrome. The production of dysmnesia by bilateral hippocampal lesions was initially observed as an iatrogenic effect of surgical ablation of the temporal lobe for intractable epilepsy (Scoville and Milner, 1957). The critical lesions are those that bilaterally affect the hippocampi, on the medial surfaces of the temporal lobes. Damages to the temporal neocortex, amygdala, and uncus have no effect upon memory. Other causes of such bilateral hippocampal damage include cerebrovascular accidents and encephalitis, especially herpes simplex. The proportion of hippocampal tissue damage is roughly proportional to the severity of the dysmnestic syndrome produced (Milner, 1966). Hippocampal damage also produces a deficit in spatial orientation.

The hippocampal formation (also called Ammon's horn) includes the hippocampus proper, the dentate gyrus, and, according to many authors, the subiculum. The lips of the hippocampal fissure are formed respectively by the dentate gyrus and the hippocampus. The ventricular (lateral) surface of the hippocampus is covered by the alveus which is white matter composed of axons from the hippocampus. These fibers eventually enter the fiber bundle of the fornix.

The parahippocampal gyrus is demarcated by the hippocampal fissure and the collateral sulcus. The sequence of transition between the six-layered parahippocampal cortex and the three-layered hippocampus is: parahippocampal cortex, presubiculum, subiculum, prosubiculum, and hippocampus. The pre- and prosubiculum areas represent zones of transition.

The anterior portion of the parahippocampal gyrus, the uncus, and the lateral olfactory atria form the pyriform lobe. The rhinal sulcus, a rostral continuation of the collateral sulcus, separates the parahippocampal gyrus from the more lateral neocortex. The pyriform cortex can be divided into the prepyriform, periamygdaloid, and entorhinal regions. The prepyriform cortex (also called the lateral olfactory gyrus) can be viewed as an extention of the lateral olfactory stria, and is regarded as an olfactory relay center. The periamygdaloid region is a small dorsal region rostrally overlying the amygdala, and has many connections with the prepyriform zone. All of these regions are anterior to the hippocampus. The most posterior portion of the pyriform lobe is the entorhinal lobe which corresponds histologically to Brodmann area 28. The entorhinal cortex does not receive fibers from the olfactory bulb. The prepyriform cortex projects to the entorhinal region as well as to the nucleus medialis dorsalis of the thalamus. The entorhinal cortex, but not the periamygdaloid and prepyriform zones, projects to the hippocampus. The more intrinsic features of the hippocampus consist of three fundamental layers: the polymorphic, pyramidal, and molecular (the latter has also been termed the external plexiform layer). A second nomenclature is based upon the arrangements of neurons and their processes. From the superficial to the deep layers, these include (1) stratum moleculare, (2) stratum lacunosum (which both contain afferent fibers from the entorhinal area and terminal branches of pyramidal apical dendrites), (3) stratum radiatum, (4) stratum pyramidale, and (5) stratum oriens.

The stratum radiatum contains afferent fibers (including commissural fibers from the other hippocampus) and shafts of pyramidal apical dendrites. The prominent stratum pyramidale contains Golgi type II cells (short axon) as well as large and small pyramidal cells. Some of the pyramidal cells are termed *double pyramids* because of dense dendritic plexuses arising from both poles. Basket cells are found near the border between the stratum oriens but still within the stratum pyramidale. Their axons loop back through the stratum radiatum to form a basket plexus around pyramidal cells. The stratum oriens contains polymorphic cells and pyramidal cell dendrites and afferent fibers which enter from the entorhinal cortex or from the fornix.

On the basis of intrinsic structural differences, the hippocampus is divided into several subzones: CA 1, CA 2, CA 3, and CA 4. The CA subdivision are along the "surface" of the hippocampus and can be viewed as analogous to Brodmann areas. CA 4 lies within the hilus of the dentate gyrus, while at the other end of the hippocampus, CA 1 is continuous with the subiculum region. The smallest pyramidal cells are found in CA 1, while the largest are in CA 4.

The dentate gyrus also consists of three layers: molecular, granular, and polymorphic. The molecular layer of the dentate is continuous with the hippocampal molecular layer, that is, continuous with the strata radiatum, lacunosum, and moleculare. The granular layer consists of small round cells which give rise to axons which pass through the polymorphic layer to terminate in CA 3 near the roots of pyramidal cell apical dendrites. These granule cell derived processes are termed *mossy fibers*, which are part of a recurrent excitation network. The endings of such mossy fibers are mainly cholinergic.

The major inputs into the dentate and hippocampus derive from the lateral entorhinal area (Brodmann area 28) through the perforant or direct path. Perforant path fibers traverse the subiculum, then traverse the lower lip of the hippocampal fissure and terminate in the stratum moleculare of CA 1, CA 2, CA 3, and the dentate. Synapses are made with apical dendrites of the pyramidal cells and dendrites of the granule cells.

The medial entorhinal area serves as the origin of the alvear (or temporoalvear) path. These fibers pass through and distribute themselves in the deep layers of the subiculum. The remnant fibers then pass along the ventricular or alvear surface of the hippocampus, sending fibers along the way deeply to terminate in CA 1.

A crossed temporoammonic path from the contralateral entorhinal area terminates in the subiculum after traveling through the fornix and its commissure, the psalterium. The hippocampal commissure tends to be less distinct and less developed in man than in many lower species. The medial forebrain bundle and septal area send fibers to the hippocampal formation through the fornix. The medial septal nucleus projects to the dentate, CA 3, and CA 4. The majority of fibers passing through the psalterium terminate in all regions of the contralateral hippocampus and dentate. Some commissural fibers, after decussating, eventually enter the perforant path to terminate in apical dendrites of the pyramidal cells. Commissural fibers to the dentate end on the inner portion of the granule cell dendritic tree, in contrast to the perforant path terminations which occur on the outer portion of the dendrites.

Other inputs into the hippocampal region come from the cingulum, a large fiber bundle which travels through the core of the cingulate gyrus. The temporal continuations of the cingulum terminate in the presubiculum and entorhinal areas to form a key link in the Papez circuit. The supracallosal gyrus (or indusium griseum) is embryologically related to and sends fibers to the hippocampus. The axons of CA 3 pyramidal cells project to CA 2 and especially CA 1 pyramidal all apical dendrites through what are termed Schäffer collaterals, an important functional arrangement system with the mossy fibers for recurrent excitation. System complexity is enhanced by other pyramidal cell collaterals which synapse with basket cells to recurrently inhibit other pyramidal cells.

Efferent fibers from pyramidal cell neurons exit chiefly through the fornix. As the fornix passes under the splenium and body of the corpus callosum, the hippocampal commissure occurs. Further forward the body of the anterior commissure passes orthogonally through the now descending fornix, producing a division into the precommissural and postcommissural fornix with approximately half of all fibers going into each division. The anterior commissure is a structure largely unrelated to the fornix with importance for olfactory and cortical interconnections. Precommissural fibers distribute to the septal nuclei, the lateral portion of the preoptic region, the anterior hypothalamus, and the nucleus of the diagonal band of Broca. The remaining fibers are joined by septal efferents to form Zuckerkandl's bundle, a major component of the medial forebrain bundle, to distribute to central gray matter in the brain stem. It is relevant that regions associated with the production of vasopressin (the anterior hypothalamus) and norepinephrine (the locus ceruleus) appear to receive precommissural fibers from the hippocampus. The anterior commissure interconnects the amygdala and entorhinal and pyriform cortices, but not the hippocampi.

Approximately one third to one half of the postcommissural output projects to the mammillary bodies, chiefly to the medial mammillary nuclei. Many, if not the majority, of postcommissural fibers project to the thalamus, chiefly to the anterior group, intralaminar nuclei, and lateralis dorsalis. An interesting modification of the Papez circuit theory lies in the observation that as many fibers from the hippocampi may project directly to the anterior thalamic nuclei as come from the mammillary bodies. Postcommissural fibers also join the medial forebrain bundle to descend and distribute widely.

Studies by Raisman et al (1965, 1966) have clarified the relation of the hippocampus to other regions. Postcommissural efferents arise from CA 1 (anterior part) and CA 2 to terminate in thalamic and mammillary regions. Precommissural fibers arise from CA 1 (posterior part), CA 3, and CA 4 to terminate bilaterally to the diagonal band and lateral septum, and unilaterally to the medial septum. Further complex interrelationships have been observed. The dentate projects via mossy fibers to CA 3 pyramidal cells which, in turn, project to the septum and diagonal band, and then project back to CA 3. Schäffer collaterals from CA 3 excite CA 1, and connect to the prosubiculum, which in turn projects to the suprachiasmatic and arcuate nuclei of the hypothalamus.

Through these complex efferent systems the hippocampus can influence cortical activity and sensation. For example, hippocampal stimulation can inhibit cortical evoked responses from sensory inputs. Electrical stimulation of the hippocampus in man is capable of evoking autonomic functions, such as salivation, pupillary dilation, and the release of Thyroid Stimulating hormone (TSH) and Adrenocorticotropic hormone (ACTH). Increased voltage and reduced frequency in the ipsilateral frontal cortex are produced by electrical stimulation of the hippocampus.

The theta wave of the electroencephalogram is hippocampal in origin and is produced by visual, auditory, somatosensory, or olfactory stimulation. This 4–7-Hz wave can also be elicited by stimulation of the medial septal region, the lateral hypothalamus (sites of norepinephrine fiber tracts), the anterior hypothalamus (site of vasopressin production), and the reticular activating system. When the theta wave is recorded from the hippocampus, the neocortex shows fast low-voltage arousal activity. The inverse relationship between theta wave hippocampal activity and alpha wave neocortical activity may be due to inhibitory control of the hippocampus by periaqueductal and medial tegmental gray matter (Peele, 1977). These latter regions are affected in Korsakoff's disease. Further data are necesary to define the inhibitory functions of norepinephrine pathways to the hippocampus; this would provide a critical link in a more unified concept of memory mechanisms.

Loss of hippocampal theta wave rhythm through medial septal lesions in rats produced dysmnestic syndromes with prominent spatial memory deficits (Winson, 1978). In rabbits hippocampal electroencephalogram data taken before the onset of training predict subsequent learning rates even over a period of several days. The higher the proportion of pretraining theta wave activity, the better the memory for a learned task. Conversely, the greater the proportion of high-frequency (8–22 Hz) activity, the slower the rate of learning. The amount of theta activity determines the capacity for memory consolidation (Berry and Thompson, 1978).

Injection of moderate doses of eserine produces enhanced theta activity, which is dependent upon the septohippocampal-fornix pathway with the pacemaker in the septal region. Both ACh transferase and ChAc activity are dramatically reduced in the hippocampus following section of the septohippocampal pathways. Acetylcholinesterase accumulates on the septal side of this lesion (Shute and Lewis, 1963). In the hippocampus, there is a laminar distribution pattern of acetylcholinesterase. The septum appears to regulate the theta activity through a cholinergic septohippocampal excitatory pathway.

Glutamic acid is the most significant and powerful hippocampal excitatory putative neurotransmitter having its effect on the dendritic tree, but not the cell bodies of pyramidal cells on proximal dendritic regions (Schwartzkrain and Anderson, 1975). The most significant inhibitory hippocampal neurotransmitter is gamma-aminobutyric acid, which acts upon pyramidal cell soma receptors to inhibit both induced and spontaneous hippocampal pyramidal activity. Recurrent excitatory mechanisms previously discussed, such as mossy fiber and Schäffer collateral systems, appear to utilize glutamic acid, while recurrent inhibition mechanisms, such as the basket cell system, appear to involve gamma-aminobutyric acid. Complex interaction between septal pacemaker, recurrent inhibition, and recurrent excitation are probably responsible for spontaneous hippocampal electrical activity.

Other neurotransmitters found in high concentration in the hippocampus include serotonin, norepinephrine, and epinephrine. Unlike the other putative neurotransmitters mentioned, these substances do not show characteristic patterns of structural neuropharmacology and are found diffusely in high concentration throughout the hippocampus (Anderson, 1975). Norepinephrine probably has an important function in the memory functions of the hippocampus due to its concentration and wide distribution. The neuropharmacology and neurophysiology of norepinephrine-dependent limbic systems may be the key to a unified theory of memory consolidation.

One of the dysmnestic syndromes involving the hippocampi, but sparing the mammillary complex or nucleus medialis dorsalis, is Alzheimer's disease. Aside from the well-documented clinical picture of this disorder, the major gross pathological characteristic is atrophy, although this finding is a normal accompaniment of aging. The dysmnestic disorder is more directly associated with the development of neurofibrillary tangles; these are paired helically arranged filamentous structures (Kidd, 1963; Wiśniewski et al., 1976), which are believed to result from modified protein synthesis (Iqbal et al., 1975) or as a reaction from neuronal cell body injury (Torack, 1979). Neurons of the hippocampus containing neurofibrillary tangles from patients with Alzheimer's dementia have been shown to contain a high aluminum content in the nuclear region (Perl and Brody, 1980). In the cytoplasm of neurofibrillary tangle containing neurons from demented patients there was almost a 30% incidence of aluminum presence, as compared with only 11% in nondemented elderly patients. Other pathological findings in Alzheimer's disease include senile plaques and granulovacuolar degeneration. Plaques identical with those found in Alzheimer's disease have been studied in senile monkeys (Wiśniewski et al., 1973). Several abnormalities were noted, including scattered neurites, fibrillar material, vascular amyloidosis, lipofuscin accumulation, dark neurons undergoing phagocytosis, enlarged mitochondria, myelin remodeling, viruslike particles, electron-dense droplets, and paracrystalline mitochondrial inclusions. In patients with Alzheimer's disease, electron microscopic examination of biopsy material has revealed enlarged axons, presynaptic axon terminals, and probably dendrites, containing fibrils, branching vesicular profiles, and multilaminar bodies (Gonatas et al., 1967). The enlarged axon terminals seen in Alzheimer's disease resemble those seen in some retardation syndromes. A reduction of the number of presynaptic terminal vesicles very likely is a reflection of an altered disposition for neurotransmitters, which undoubtedly function to mediate memory functions.

Biochemical changes associated with dementia have been documented for the frontal gray matter (Bowen et al., 1973); these include a pronounced decrease in a neuronal-type protein, neuronin S-6, and a slightly increased concentration of the glia-associated protein S-100. These changes may reflect neuronal loss and glial hypertrophy, as observed in the Alzheimer-type dementia. Releated enzymatic findings in senile dementia (Bowen et al., 1974; Bowen and Davidson, 1975) have documented a pronounced depletion of glutamic acid decarboxylase in the frontal and temporal cortices. A lower activity of ChAc transferase was also observed in the cerebral cortex and caudate of patients with senile dementia (Bowen et al., 1976). The activity of ChAc was reduced in several brain regions of patients with dementia (Perry et al., 1977), and for several of such areas, enzyme activity was significantly lower in the Alzheimer-type dementia, as compared with multiinfarct demintia. These areas included the temporal cortex, parietal cortex, and the hippocampus — all interestingly bearing upon the general issue of memory function and amnesia. Because of the obvious role of neurotransmitter synthesizing enzymes in determining the disposition of specific amines and the suggested relationship of some of these substances to memory functions, there have been several bases for a neurotransmitter role in memory dysfunction.

A summary of the putative neurotransmitter changes, which have been measured in Alzheimer's disease and in animal models, is

**Table 10.    Putative Neurotransmitter and Related Metabolic Changes in Patients with Alzheimer's Disease or Senile Dementia**

| | |
|---|---|
| Acetylcholine | |
| Reduced cholinergic neurons in temporal lobe (35%) | Bowen et al., 1979 |
| Reduced choline acetyltransferase | |
|     Frontal cortex | Bowen et al., 1976 |
|     Hippocampus | Perry et al., 1977 |
| Reduced acetylcholinesterase activity | Davies and Maloney, 1976 |
| | Davies, 1979 |
| Hippocampal muscarinic cholinergic receptors | |
|     Decreased | Reisine et al., 1978 |
|     No change | White et al., 1977 |
| | Davies and Verth, 1978 |
| Dopamine | |
| Reduced dopamine | |
|     Striatum | Finch, 1972 |
|     Median eminence | |
|     Posterior pituitary | Finch, 1978 |
|     Thalamus | |
|     Pons | Adolfson et al., 1978 |
| Reduced dopaminergic cells | |
| Reduced homovanillic acid | |
|     Corpus striatum | Gottfries et al., 1969, 1970 |
| Norepinephrine | |
| Reduced norepinephrine | Winblad et al., 1978 |
|     Putamen | |
|     Frontal cortex | |
|     Hypothalamus | Finch, 1972 |
| Serotonin | |
| Reduced serotonin | |
|     Brain stem | |
|     Cortex | |
|     Hippocampus | Meek et al., 1977 |
| Reduced serotonin receptor activity | |
|     Temporal lobe | Bowen et al., 1979 |
|     No change in neocortex | Reisine et al., 1978 |
| Gamma-Aminobutyric Acid | |
| Reduced glutamate decarboxylase activity | |
|     Neocortex | Bowen et al., 1976 |
| Reduced gamma-aminobutyric acid | Perry et al., 1977 |
| | Reisine et al.,1978 |

References cited in this table agree with text citations or are referred to in appropriate text citations.

given in Tables 10 and 11. Several of these changes may have a bearing upon suggested aminergic substrates for memory consolidation — the stage of the memory process that appears to be principally impaired in the amnesic component of Alzheimer's dementia. A potential role for catecholamines (Kety, 1967), serotonin (Essman, 1978), and ACh (Drachman, 1977) in memory functions has been suggested, and simple neurotransmitter concentration status changes *per se* may not be adequate to describe the mechanism by which memory dysfunction in aging or dementia occurs. For example, changes in concentration, turnover, or effects at specific receptor sites may depend upon specific triggering events, an interaction with nutritional factors. Preliminary reports of the potential application of dietary cholinergic replacement regimens (lecithin, choline) for the treatment of memory dysfunction associated with Alzheimer's and other dementias have appeared (Wurtman, 1980). Certainly this approach appears somewhat promising in view of animal studies showing increased brain ACh content in animal treated with dietary lecithin (Hirsch and Wurtman, 1978; Wurtman et al., 1977) or choline (Cohen and Wurtman, 1976). Dietary choline may also act to stimulate cholinergic receptors (Karczmar, 1979; Karczmar and Dun, 1978). In several studies with oral choline therapy for memory dysfunction in presenile dementia, variable results have emerged. Some reduced confusional behavior in approximately one third of the patients receiving choline (9 g/day × 2 weeks) was observed, but no changes in memory tests were noted (Smith et al., 1978). Little cognitive benefit was observed from oral choline (5 g/day × 2 weeks + 10 g/day × 2 weeks) in elderly patients (Boyd et al., 1977), but some improvement in younger patients with a shorter history of Alzheimer's disease was noted after 3 weeks of choline treatment (9 g/day), when memory tests were given (Signoret et al., 1978). Although no memory testing changes were noted in patients with Alzheimer's disease treated with lecithin (25 g/day + additional 25 g/week × 4 weeks) learning scores and visual retention scores did improve (Etienne et al., 1978). Choline chloride (2 g, four times a day) given to elderly subjects for 21 days had no effect upon performance on memory storage tasks, retrieval tasks, or digit-symbol substitution (Mohs et al., 1980). The failure of choline to consistently improve memory functions in elderly

**Table 11.   Neurotransmitter and Enzyme Changes in the
Aging Brain and Dementia**

| | |
|---|---|
| Tyrosine hydroxylase | McGeer and McGeer, 1976 |
| DOPA decarboxylase | McGeer and McGeer, 1976 |
| Catechol-O-methyl transferese (hippocampus) | Robinson et al., 1977 |
| Monoamine oxidase | Cote and Kremzner, 1974 |
| | Grote et al., 1974 |
| | Robinson et al., 1972 |
| Monoamine oxidase, type B | Gottfries et al., 1975 |
| Dopamine | Carlsson and Winblad, 1976 |
| Norepinephrine | Robinson et al., 1972, 1977 |
| Homonanillic acid HVA (CSF) | Gottfries et al., 1969, 1970, 1974 |
| 5-HIAA (CSF) | Gottfries et al., 1969, 1970 |
| Glutamic acid decarboxylase | Bowen et al., 1974 |
| Choline acetyltransferase | McGeer and McGeer, 1976 |
| | Perry et al., 1977 |
| | Spillane, et al., 1977 |

References cited in this table agree with text citations or are referred to in appropriate text citations.

patients with memory dysfunction or Alzheimer's disease may reside in the weak cholinergic agonist activity of this agent, or in the failure of choline *per se* to effect nerve ending ACh release. Finally, choline as an ACh precursor does not provide for increased hippocampal ACh (Jenden, 1979)—a site-specific referent to the memory dysfunction to which a cholinergic hypothesis has been applied.

A possible parallel to the effects of oral cholinergic precursors or receptor agonists in memory functions may reside in clinical studies utilizing cholinergic drugs to study a variety of memory deficits. A summary of such studies may be found in Table 12.

The similar clinical manifestations of the Korsakoff and hippocampal syndromes have complex underlying structural and neuropharmacological substrates. The fornix is the fiber bundle that interconnects the two regions that are neuropathologically correlated with these dysmnestic syndromes. One would expect, on theoretical grounds, that lesions of the fornix would produce a dysmnestic syndrome. However, the evidence has been inconsistent (Brierly, 1977; Lishman, 1978; Peele, 1977). While there are cases where discrete fornical damage is indeed associated with amnesia, there are also patients with total fornical section who show no associated memory deficit. These latter cases represent an extremely puzzling neuropsychological finding. One conclusion that might be drawn is that there are at least two separate subsystems essential for memory consolidation.

**Table 12.  Cholinergic Agents and Memory Effects in Man**

| | |
|---|---|
| Physostigmine | |
| improvement of memory in normal volunteers | Davis et al., 1978a |
| Reversal of anticholinergic-induced memory impairment | Ghoneim and Mewaldt, 1977 |
| Antagonism of scopolamine-induced memory dysfunction | Drachman, 1978 |
| Scopolamine | |
| Memory impairment in normal subjects | Drachman and Leavitt, 1974 Drachman, 1978 |

Pribam (1971) has proposed a provocative holographic theory of human memory which deserves discussion. Holography, although popularized as three-dimensional photography, is actually a much more general process which can be applied in any media, including biological systems. The critical feature of holography is the ability to utilize Fourier mathematical spatial transformations as stored representations of information. Pribam presents a variety of neurophysiological data to support his contention that the human central nervous system does indeed operate using a Fourier transform mode to store memory. The hologram produced would be the broad expanse of neocortical tissue. The hippocampal and diencephalic systems discussed earlier would function in encoding and might also have a role in the decoding of holographically stored data. Holograms have the property of equipotentiality. In the case of the cerebral cortex, data are stored throughout all constituent gray matter, and all portions of the cortex have an equal capacity to store information. Long-term memories are therefore never destroyed completely by focal lesions, but only more diffuse. The law of mass action is also obeyed by holograms with the clarity of stored information directly proportional to the amount (mass) of the hologram available for decoding from the Fourier transform mode. RNA-dependent conformational changes in protein molecules of the cerebral cortex would play a role in information storage analogous to the photographic silver nitrate emulsion crystals in optic holograms. Anterograde dysmnesia is represented by a loss of encoding capacity, while dysfunctional decoding is retrograde dysmnesia. The loss of cerebral cortical tissue is associated with a reduction in the clarity of long-term memory storage. Lashley's laws of mass action and equipotentiality as well as clinical features of the Korsakoff and hippocampal syndromes can be explained in terms of the holographic theory.

Research on the neuropharmacology of dysmnesia must take structural considerations such as holographic theory into account. Studies of noradrenergic, cholinergic, glutaminergic, GABA-ergic, serotonergic, dopaminergic, and vasopressin-dependent limbic neurotransmitter systems should help clarify encoding and decoding mechanisms of human memory. In another respect, research concerned with RNA-dependent protein synthesis and conformational changes could probably be useful as a basis for understanding the nature of long-term storage. The complex interactions between these subsystems remains to be further clarified to provide structural neuropharmacology research with methods of clarifying the unknowns and complexities of the human dysmnesia syndromes.

# 6

# Major Tranquilizers

The more potent of the so-called major tranquilizers include a variety of agents of the phenothiazine, butyrophenone, and rauwolfia alkaloid classes. The limitations upon the accurate assessment that such agents play in learning and memory processes concern their sedative, motor, and peripheral side effects. Perhaps as a prototype of this group of agents, reserpine represents one drug that bears some consideration—much of which finds applicability for many of the other drugs in this broad category.

The reduced level of brain serotonin resulting from reserpine (Pletscher et al., 1955) is difficult to be related directly to learning or memory in view of the multiple effects of this agent and its duration of action. In general, pharmacological doses of this rauwolfia alkaloid impair performance and require the distinction between performance measures and those of learning or memory. There is a bearing of the serotonin-depleting effects of reserpine upon the action and effects of other agents, which does relate to some of the methodological issues that concern learning and memory. For example, there is an interaction between reserpine and morphine (Shin and Cheon, 1973), such that the analgesic effects of morphine are eliminated, the hyperglycemic effects of morphine are augmented, and the serum transaminase activities induced by morphine (SGOT, SGPT) are inhibited by reserpine. These findings strongly suggest that central as well as peripheral effects of other agents or the sites at which environmental stimuli act to produce such changes may be modified by reserpine. They also suggest, of course, that the central and peripheral effect of morphine may be serotonin dependent in view of the serotonin-depleting effect of reserpine. This, although not the direct concern of this chapter, has been treated elsewhere, particularly as it concerns the analgesic effects of this narcotic (Samanin et al., 1970) and the effects of morphine upon myocardial metabolism (Essman, 1978b). Aside from its clinical utility as an antihypertensive agent, the cardiovascular effects of reserpine cannot be overlooked (Luckens and Malone, 1973). Tachycardia produced by direct myocardial action is not blocked by reserpine, which only blocks catecholamine action at adrenergic receptors (Teoh and Cheah, 1973). These peripheral effects of reserpine are complex and may themselves contribute to altered performance in tests of learning and memory. Low doses of reserpine (0.05 mg/kg) facilitated avoidance learning in rats; at a higher dose (0.25 mg/kg) the drug reduced pattern discrimination learning, and at a still higher dose (0.40 mg/kg) it impaired exploratory behavior (Walk et al., 1961).

Varied effects of reserpine upon avoidance learning and the consolidation of such responses have been observed. Conditioning of an emotional response was unaffected by reserpine (0.50 mg/kg) (Stein, 1956), but the performance of established conditioned emotional responses could be impaired with reserpine (Brady, 1956). Reserpine also significantly attenuated the amnesic effects of ECS in mice (Essman, 1970c). This latter effect might again be related to the serotonin-depleting effect of the drug and the failure of ECS to elevate brain serotonin in reserpine-treated animals. This finding holds some further significance in that reserpine acts as a proconvulsive agent; that is, it potentiates the seizure-producing effects of ECS and increases the intensity of the resulting convulsion. Again, as noted previously, there does not appear to be a relationship of amnesia to the absence of a convulsion, or of the reduction in the amnesic potential of a convulsant to the intensity of the convulsion.

The phenothiazines, as psychoactive agents, are probably best characterized by chlorpromazine, which was the first of this class of compounds to be applied in a psychiatric setting. Historically the phenothiazines, as therapeutic agents, derive from methylene blue, which was utilized as an antimalarial agent by Ehrlich in 1891 and had received occasional, but only minor, attention in 1899 for its sedative effects. It would be unfair to attribute such casual clinical observation to any central effect of this compound, inasmuch as even small doses can lead to cardiovascular changes and thermolytic effects, while mental confusion in experimental animals and man can result from higher doses. Chlorpromazine was synthesized by Carpentier in 1950 as a result of searching for phenothiazine derivatives which had both anesthetic potentiating activity as well as central effects. The "tranquilizerlike" effect of this compound was observed when it was used by Laborit and co-workers; Laborit recognized the unique capacity of chlorpromazine to abolish anxiety and excitement in surgical patients. Through subsequently favorable reports of the clinical psychiatric efficacy of the compound (Delay et al. 1952; Lehmann and Hanrahan, 1954) it gradually became accepted for treating a wide spectrum of behavior pathologies, ranging from mild anxiety and psychomotor excitation to psychotic disorders of varied etiology.

Chlorpromazine, in animals, results in decreased cardiac output and a fall in blood pressure, probably related to one of this compound's characteristic effects — adrenergic blocking action. By virtue of its autonomic action, chlorpromazine can lead to an inhibition of gastrointestinal motility. Several of these extrabehavioral effects may become relevant in evaluating the presumed, more direct, behavioral effects of this drug.

The phenothiazine derivatives, as a class of compounds with which central depressant action can be associated, has often found the referent "tranquilizer" used descriptively. The "tranquilization" that attends initial doses of 50–100 mg in man, or the sedative effect characterized as the "neuroleptic syndrome" by Delay (Delay and Deniker, 1952) hardly seem applicable to the nature of the improvement shown by psychiatric patients who benefit from chlorpromazine treatment specifically, or phenothiazine therapy more generally. When behavioral changes resulting from 12 weeks of phenothiazine treatment were assessed with the use of the multidimensional scale for rating psychiatric patients (MSRPP), those variables sensitive to improvement were (1) restlessness, (2) belligerence, (3) thinking disturbance, (4) perceptual disturbance, (5) mannerisms, and (6) paranoid projection (Casey et al., 1960). It is apparent that the term *tranquilizer* does not adequately describe the behavioral effect of these compounds when the therapeutic effect is considered.

Chlorpromazine was the earliest phenothiazine to be used experimentally and clinically, and has probably been studied more extensively than any of the other compounds in this class. It is probably one of the most extensively used clinical drugs, and for this reason it will be treated here as a model of the phenothiazines, to the extent that specific distinctions between chlorpromazine and other phenothiazines, where relevant, will be considered and, in addition, any directly relevant considerations for other derivatives.

The effects of chlorpromazine on brain biogenic amines are somewhat confused. Some investigators have reported no effect (Ehringer et al., 1960; Pletscher and Gey, 1960), whereas slight elevations in both serotonin and norepinephrine have been reported by others (Bartlet, 1960; Costa et al., 1960). It is clear, though, that an elevation in brain serotonin produced by iproniazid (monoamine oxidase inhibition) can be blocked by chlorpromazine (Ehringer et al., 1960; Pletscher and Gey, 1960; Bartlet, 1960). In general the effects of chlorpromazine on biogenic amines in brain are: (1) inhibition of serotonin and norepinephrine increments following treatment with either monoamine oxidase inhibitors or amino acid precursors, (2) inhibition of the reserpine-induced monoamine decrease, and (3) an increase in the proportion of serotonin association with the ''free'' brain tissue fraction. These effects may possibly support the view (Gey and Pletscher, 1961) that the passage of monoamines to and from their brain storage depots can be inhibited by chlorpromazine through a decrease in the permeability of either an intracellular membrane or storage organelles.

Other metabolic effects observed experimentally with chlorpromazine include: (1) inhibition of both cerebral tissue respiration and the increase in such tissue respiration induced by electrical or electrolyte stimulation (Lindan et al., 1957, (2) uncoupling of oxidative phosphorylation (Abood, 1955), (3) decreasing the synthesis of some brain phospholipids and stimulating the synthesis of certain other phospholipids in brain (Strickland and Noble, 1961), and (4) possibly, affecting membrane permeability (Ernsting et al., 1960).

It has been shown more recently (Roth et al., 1979) that chlorpromazine, as well as its metabolites, are capable of inhibiting human monoamine oxidase. Such inhibition, although relevant for both types of the enzyme, type A and type B, was greater for type A for which serotonin is a substrate. The tricyclic antidepressants, which also inhibit monoamine oxidase, exert a preferred effect upon type B.

In general, clinically effective doses of chlorpromazine lead to a reduced activity level associated with increased unresponsiveness, passivity, and motivational decrement.

A reduction in spontaneous locomotor activity was produced in mice given oral or subcutaneous chlorpromazine, ranging from 1 to 5 mg/kg; the activity reduction was dose dependent. Complete suppression of locomotor activity occurred at 5 mg/kg, although ataxia was not apparent and coordinated responses could be elicited (Cook and Weidley, 1957). The proportionality of locomotor suppression and chlorpromazine level can be accounted for by brain concentration. Whereas quite small doses of chlorpromazine can lead to measurable changes in spontaneous locomotor activity in a variety of animal species, even doses as large as 365 mg/kg, i.p., did not induce sleep in mice (Brown, 1960). This type of behavioral finding draws a sharp contrast between the phenothiazines and the barbiturates.

A reduction, by chlorpromazine, in both nocturnal and diurnal activity has been observed; however, under these conditions no effect was exerted on the circadian rhythm (Sandberg, 1959; Schallek et al., 1956; Stone et al., 1960).

Exploratory behavior of rodents has been modified by chlorpromazine in a number of varying experimental situations. The exploratory behavior of mice was abolished at a dose lower than that required to inhibit motor activity (Buchel et al., 1962). Mice, exploring holes in a vertical panel, reduced the number of such explorations as a function of dose, where the latter was varied from 0.25 to 2.00 mg/kg, i.p. In a multiple T maze the reduction in exploratory activity of chlorpromazine was similarly dose dependent (Boissier and Simon, 1964; Boissier et al., 1964; Blogovski, 1959). Mice show a predictable tendency to climb inclined planes when provided with a ladder, screening, mesh, or wire. Escape behavior, by means of a wire-mesh ladder or screen, to an exit from a jar or cage was inhibited in mice by 1.9–4.2 mg/kg, s.c., or 5.6 mg/kg, i.p. ($ED_{50}$) (Boissier et al., 1961; Kneip, 1960; Sandberg, 1959).

When the motor activity of animals was elicited, using rotorod performance, the effective dosage to interfere with performance closely paralleled the effective dosage needed to disrupt spontaneous locomotor activity. Other tests in rodents, such as sloping planes to test for maintenance of position, activity wheel performance, pole climbing, backward tube climbing, rolling dowel traversal, wire clinging, and tube traversal, have all been sensitive to the effects of chlorpromazine.

Another interesting chlorpromazine-induced alteration in motor activity of a specific type may be found in experiments in which chlorpromazine solutions given to spiders caused a marked cessation of web spinning, lasting from 1 to 3 days after drug administration; any completed webs were still characteristic of normal webs (Witt, 1955). In contrast to these findings, oral doses of 50 $\mu$g/day for 10 successive days led to the construction of smaller webs with decreased radii in *Aranea sericata* (Groh and Lemieux, 1964). These effects were irreversible, and persisted beyond the cessation of drug treatment. The spiders showed slowed reflexes, and the quality of the web silk decreased.

The maze performance of rodents treated with chlorpromazine has been extensively investigated, with a variety of maze tasks. The general finding which has emerged from such studies is similar to what was observed for locomotor behavior, the latency to complete a successful maze response and the time spent in the maze were increased by drug treatment; this finding appears consistent with both positively as well as negatively reinforcing stimuli (Courvoisier et al., 1958; Herr et al., 1961; Latz, 1964). Utilizing multiple T-maze performance, error frequency was not affected at low doses of the drug (1.0–6.0 mg/kg) (Domer and Schueler,

1960), but at higher doses (10.0–20.0 mg/kg, s.c. and p.o.) error incidence was increased (Courvoisier et al., 1958). The use of a water maze to test the hypothesis that stereotyped behavior caused by pretrial water submersion could be eliminated by chlorpromazine-induced reduction in motivational strength yielded results suggesting impairment of acquisition and retention of stereotyped and nonstereotyped responses (Mitchel and King, 1960). In studies of this type it is difficult to separate the thermolytic effects of the phenothiazines from their direct behavioral effects. Whereas water temperature under normal circumstances serves as a basis for introducing differences in the motivational level, drug-treated rodents, under these conditions, can become moderately hypothermic and show impaired maze performance as a result (Essman and Sudak, 1962). A possible exception to the behavioral effects of chlorpromazine-induced hypothermia in cold water derived from findings that indicate that the rate of core temperature reduction in cold (19 °C) water for chlorpromazine- and saline-treated rats forced to swim was the same, whereas at higher water temperature (32 °C) the drug-treated rats showed a more rapid rate of temperature loss (LeBlanc, 1958). At the low water temperature 10 mg/kg, i.p., of chlorpromazine decreased endurance time by 50%, whereas the same dose at the higher temperature has no apparent effect.

Conditioned responses, as affected by chlorpromazine, have been extensively studied. Climbing by rats to avoid food-shock onset signaled by an auditory stimulus was impaired (Courvoisier et al., 1953). At reduced drug dosage (1.0 mg/kg), although avoidance of shock was still impaired, escape from shock onset was not affected. The use of a pole-climbing technique in rats permitted the study of the relationships between unconditioned and conditioned responses (escape and avoidance). Selective impairment of avoidance was obtained at doses of 10.5 mg/kg, p.o., 2–3 hours following treatment, and the escape behavior was impaired at higher doses (Cook and Weidley, 1957; Cook et al., 1953). The locomotor and avoidance-suppressant properties of eight phenothiazines were compared (Irwin, 1961) with results suggesting that there was a comparable degree of potency in suppressant effect. Avoidance behavior in rats appears to be selectively affected by chlorpromazine within rather consistent dose ranges, regardless of the conditioned avoidance task specifically utilized to test such behavior. These doses ($ED_{50}$) are approximately 5–12 mg/kg, p.o., 1.2–7.0 mg/kg, s.c., and 2–5 mg/kg, i.p. These dose ranges derive from studies in which rats have been tested: rope climbing, pole climbing, lever-pressing avoidance, shuttle box, hurdle box, and hole jumping.

Barpressing behavior by rats has also been affected by chlorpromazine, where continuous reinforcement with food, water, or heat was given to maintain the behavior. The dose required to initiate such decreased barpressing in motivated rats was somewhat lower than that previously indicated for the abolition of conditioned avoidance (1–4 mg/kg, i.p.). In pigeons a discriminative response, based on stimulus-specific fixed-ratio or fixed-interval acquisition, was not altered by 1.7–3.0 mg/kg, i.m., of chlorpromazine (Dews, 1956). The effect on the response rate appears to be dose dependent.

Dissociation of responses, as affected by chlorpromazine, has been demonstrated in rats trained after drug treatment and tested for followine saline treatment, or with a training–testing sequence in the reverse order (Otis, 1964). Rats that were trained under chlorpromazine (1.25 mg/kg) and tested under saline in an avoidance situation, or trained under saline and tested under chlorpromazine, showed less recovery of the avoidance response than rats trained and tested under both conditions with either chlorpromazine or saline. These results are interpreted as a drug-induced internal state that serves as a stimulus, while in a learning situation it may acquire associative connections with a response. A similar study (Stewart, 1962) where rats were given a somewhat higher drug dose (3–4 mg/kg, i.p.) demonstrated dissociative learning in animals trained under the drug to choose one colored goal box and, under saline, to choose another of a different color. These observations have led to the speculation that the therapeutic gains of hospitalized patients maintained on drugs may be drug dependent and may not survive discontinuance of drug therapy (Otis, 1964). These studies have a possible bearing on others that have investigated the effect of chlorpromazine on extinction. Rats trained to acquire a conditioned emotional response (CER) in a grill box, either with or without chlorpromazine, and then tested under saline for extinction differed in that drug-treated rats showed a weaker CER and extinguished more rapidly. Rats trained for a CER under saline conditions and given extinction trials under chlorpromazine showed CER behavior for 2 days after the completion of the extinction series (Hunt, 1956). The effect of chlorpromazine on extinction appears dependent on the acquisition conditions, the complexity of the response, and the possible relationship between the drug-induced diminution of fear responses and/or pain. A relevant consideration in this latter regard is the possible analgesic property of the drug. In rats and mice, chlorpromazine-induced analgesia has been noted (Maxwell et al., 1961; Barkov, 1961a,b). Rats given 5 mg/kg, s.c., of chlorpromazine showed a significant increase in the reaction time to thermal pain by 60–90 minutes after injection. An increase in reaction time to pain induced by infrared rays was observed at even lower doses (Barkov, 1961a). These effects were attributed to the action of the drug on the spinal cord. The analgesic effect of 5 mg/kg of chlorpromazine in rats was determined as equivalent to the effect of a comparable dose of morphine (Barkov, 1961b), and combined treatment with 5 mg/kg of chlorpromazine and 5 mg/kg of morphine exceeded the analgesic potency of 10 mg/kg of morphine. Studies of this nature point toward an important consideration in evaluating the results of studies utilizing aversive reinforcement, and offer a possible alternative to some of the rather broadly stated and usually generally accepted conclusions that derive from such investigations.

In a comparative study of several phenothiazines it was shown that conditioned avoidance behavior provided by auditory stimulation preceding pole climbing was inhibited by chlor-promazine, but was blocked to a greater degree by prochlorperazine (2–3 times) and perphenazine (10 times). Thioridazine was less effective in its inhibitory effect on conditioned avoidance, but was highly effective in eliminating emotional defecation. While motor activity and emotional defection were blocked by chlorpromazine and prochlorperazine, perphenazine appeared selective for motor activity only (Taeschler and Cerletti, 1959).

The open-field behavior of rats, with "emotionality" measured as a function of the frequency of defecation, has been used as one index of emotionality on which the effects of chlorpromazine (2–10 mg/kg, s.c.) appear to be inhibitory (Brimblecombe, 1963; Janssen et al., 1960). The stress-induced reduction in appetitive behavior provided to rats by a novel environment was blocked by chlorpromazine (2 mg/kg) (Steinberg and Watson, 1959).

Aggressive behavior can be induced in rodents by isolation, and such behavior has been shown to be diminished by varying doses of chlorpromazine (Janssen et al., 1960). Doses, generally within approximately 10 mg/kg for several administrative routes, were shown effective in attenuating such isolation-induced aggression. It must be pointed out, however, that in addition to providing for enhanced aggressive behavior in rodents, isolation also significantly alters the threshold for a number of psychoactive compounds (Garattini and Sigg, 1969). In this respect, reduced ED threshold to the psychomotor effects of chlorpromazine in isolated rodents would be compatible with the results of such studies from which an aggression–reduction conclusion has been, perhaps prematurely, derived. Aggressive behavior induced by foot shock has also been attenuated by chlorpromazine (Brunaud and Siou, 1960; Chen et al., 1963). An alternative explanation may again be present in the analgesic properties of this agent, so that reduced aggressive behavior may be a simple concomitant of reduced pain.

In the cat, chlorpromazine was shown to increase sociability and decrease hostility (Norton et al., 1957), but there appears to be a differential effect on ''hostile'' behavior, depending on whether such animals are aggressive or docile initially. Aggressive behavior, for example, has been augmented by chlorpromazine in docile cats (Bradley and Hance, 1957). The augmentation of aggressivity by chlorpromazine in presumably docile cats (Plas and Naquet, 1961) is also accompanied by alterations in the dominance–submission hierarchy. In the monkey, chlorpromazine treatment (0.7–2.0 mg/kg, i.v.) usually results in marked attenuation of experimenter-directed hostility and aggression (Chen and Weston, 1960; Das et al., 1954).

There are several problems associated with the initiation as well as the evaluation of experimental studies with the phenothiazines in man. These problems reside with the availability of an otherwise behaviorally and pharmacologically uncontaminated subject population, the heterogeneity of motivational and emotional variables inherent in any such population, and the subjective and semantic problems posed by the introduction of drugs.

Psychomotor functions, as evaluated on several tasks, including digit copying, digit-symbol substitution, addition speed, pursuit rotor performance, visual discrimination, and tactual perception, were shown to be differently affected by chlorpromazine (200 mg). Generally there was a reduced score resulting in the drug-treated subjects (Kornetsky et al., 1959). However, such vigilance tasks as pursuit rotor performance, tapping speed, and continuously maintained performance were impaired by chlorpromazine to a greater degree than was a digit-symbol substitution test, which may generally be taken as an index of intellectual ability. The effect of chlorpromazine on these tasks was comparable to that produced by prolonged sleep deprivation. Those subjects that were minimally affected by chlorpromazine were greatly excited by dextroamphetamine following sleep deprivation (Kornetsky et al., 1959). Such individual variations in the depressant or stimulatory properties of psychoactive agents may well conform to the model of a dimensional framework in personality description within which the behavioral effects of drugs may be considered (Eysenck, 1960).

Subjects in whom a galvanic skin response was conditioned to a light flash did not show interference with the extinction of the unconditioned response as a result of chlorpromazine treatment, or any effect upon their response to an unconditioned stimulus, electric shock; there was, however, inhibition shown for the subsequent reestablishment of the response following extinction (Schneider and Costiloe, 1956).

In studies concerned with the comparative effects of four phenothiazines in 16 male students, a double-blind investigation using single oral doses of chlorpromazine, promethazine (25, 50, 100, 200 mg/day), perphenazine, and trifluoperazine (2, 4, 8, 16 mg), revealed similar, but variable, differences in behavior produced, as compared to the chlorpromazine effects. Psychomotor activity was inhibited, with concomitant confusion; changes in autonomic reactivity were accompanied by sedation; and mood anxiety was reduced (DiMascio et al., 1961). In a series of double-blind experiments (180) normal subjects, given a single dose of phenothiazines at four levels, and tested 2, 4 or 7 hours after the drug, showed: psychomotor retardation, impairment on intellectual tasks, and drowsiness resulting from chlorpromazine and promethazine; perphenazine and trifluoperazine led to an elevation of mood and apposite behavioral effects. It is of interest to note here that rather contrasting behavioral differences emerged, depending on whether the phenothiazines were aliphatic or piperazine (Klerman and DiMascio, 1961).

In humans where behavior was maintained by electric shock for an avoidance response which was further reinfoced by a point-loss system, chlorpromazine decreased avoidance responding without any effect upon escape behavior; this stands in contrast to pentobarbital, which decreased both avoidance and escape responding.

The effects of chlorpromazine on eyelid conditioning in normal subjects (25 mg, p.o.), given 5 hours or 1 hour prior to testing, was shown to lead to more conditioned eyelid responses than in a placebo-treated group. Chlorpromazine-treated subjects reported more of a subjective effect and performed at a higher level (Ludvigson, 1960).

Prolonged chlorpromazine administration (5 weeks) to nonpsychiatric patients (alcoholics) resulted in reduced critical flicker fusion values, initially, and then in normalizing with continued drug use (Hoehn-Saric et al., 1964). When visual afterimages were measured, using two strong light flashed at ¼-second duration, separated by hale-second intervals, the duration of the afterimage and its color were affected in children (average age 13.6 years). Chlorpromazine, in a single dose (1–2 mg/kg), reduced the duration of the afterimage and attenuated afterimage color; a reduction in the intensity of afterimage reds and oranges occurred, and the intensity of greys and whites was increased (Agathon, 1964). In a double-blind crossover study the threshold for auditory flutter fusion was significantly depressed in male subjects (21–30 years) given oral doses of chlorpromazine (25, 50 mg). Perphenazine (2, 4 mg, p.o.), in contrast, has no effect on threshold (Besser et al., 1966). Again, as previously indicated, a distinction in behavioral effects may be made between the aliphatic and piperazine phenothiazine derivatives. In a task requiring a Euclidean–Pythagorean summation of pitch and loudness, doses of chlorpromazine of 150 mg and higher, given daily to students and psychiatric patients, diminished summation. Tiredness and fatigue accompanied the initial daily drug administration (Bergström et al., 1964). In a binaural hearing synthesis test 60 patients with normal hearing (average age 29.5 years) were required to respond to questions with garbled speech, and repeat familiar words. Chlorpromazine (0.05 g, i.m.) reduced word synthesis, and this effect was attributed to its brain stem action (Preibisch-Effenberger and Knothe, 1965). Oral administration of chlorpromazine (100 mg) to 21 subjects affected pause time per work (an index of cognition during speech) and breathing rate at rest (Goldman-Eisler et al., 1966). In a double-blind crossover study students given chlorpromazine (50 mg), as compared with placebo (ascorbic acid, 50 mg), showed reduced verbal and numerical performance on the Morrisby differential test battery, accompanied by drowsiness and other side effects. Tests that involved judgments of conceptual relationships were also affected by this drug (Brimer et al., 1964).

# 7

# Barbiturates and Sedatives

The behavioral and biochemical effects of two additional classes of psychoactive compounds have been used as a further basis for relating metabolic changes in brain biogenic amines to changes in learning and memory. These classes of drug include the barbiturates and the benzodiazepines. The effects of representative agents upon the regional turnover of serotonin have been studied, and a generalized decrease was observed (Lidbrink et al., 1974). Sedative doses of a barbiturate produced a generalized reduction of serotonin turnover, whereas reduced serotonin turnover occurred only in the cerebral cortex with benzodiazepines. Brain serotonin content is also elevated during barbiturate sedation or anesthesia.

A rather interesting relationship of barbiturates to the regional disposition of biogenic amines in the brain may be developed on the basis of their effects upon monoamine oxidase activity. Pentobarbital produced an increase in monoamine oxidase activity in the telencephalon and brain stem and decreased activity in the diencephalon. Monoamine oxidase type A activity (for which serotonin is a substrate) was inhibited in the diencephalon, telencephalon, and brain stem by phenobarbital (Tagliente, 1979).

Pentobarbital has been rather generally applied to behavioral studies in animals and man with a variety of effects. Rats given pentobarbital (13 mg/kg) acquired conditioned avoidance responses without any drug effect, but avoidance behavior after acquisition was reduced if the drug administration was continued (Holmgren and Condi, 1964). It was also shown that conditioned motor reflexes could be developed in dogs under pentobarbital anesthesia (Teitelbaum et al., 1961). In the rhesus monkey lever-pressing responses learned to terminate painful stimulation were abolished by pentobarbital (Malis, 1962). The memory span in man was reduced by pentobarbital (100 mg/68 kg body weight, i.v.) (Quarton and Talland, 1962). The running memory span was narrowed by pentobarbital (100 mg/68 kg, i.v.) when compared with a placebo in a double-blind study (Talland and Quarton, 1965).

The effect upon memory consolidation of pentobarbital sodium was evaluated in rats which were given an injection of this agent, as compared with distilled water, following a daily trial for the acquisition of a maze response (Garg and Holland, 1968). The posttrial barbiturate-treated rats made significantly more errors in learning the maze response, suggesting that memory consolidation was impaired.

Increased response rates for learned responses have been reported as a result of phenobarbital treatment in rats (Kelleher et al., 1961) and pigeons (Bignami and Gatti, 1969). In contrast to this long-acting barbiturate, thiopental, an ultrashort-acting agent, produced an amnesic effect upon the recognition memory for pictures and the recall memory for word and letter associations.

Secobarbital, particularly when administered at bedtime, has been shown to exert anterograde amnesic effects, as assessed the following morning. After being given 100 mg of secobarbital, subjects were later wakened, asked to complete four tasks (e.g., sharpen a pencil, describe a familiar topic, write a check, describe an important event), and were then allowed to return to sleep. The next morning the subjects were awakened and asked to recall the tasks; a significant recall decrement occurred among those subjects that were given secobarbital at bedtime (Bixler et al., 1979).

In general, except for some studies in which barbiturate state dependency constitutes a basis for the effect of an agent upon learning or memory, barbiturates tend to impair acquisition and interfere with the retention of learned behavior. With barbiturates the performance of learned responses, which depend upon a motor component, appears to be facilitated, whereas a verbal or associative component of acquired behavior appears impaired. The extent of impairment in the latter case seems to relate to blood levels of the barbiturate at those times that performance is measured.

Highly representative of the benzodiazepines is chlordiazepoxide, which has been shown (10 mg/kg) to impair conditioned escape behavior acquisition by rats (Cicala and Hartley, 1965). Both chlordiazepoxide and diazepam (5 mg/kg) increased a pedal-pressing response for electrical stimulation to the posterior hypothalamus of rats (Olds, 1966), and in rabbits chlordiazedoxide impaired the acquisition of a two-way shuttle box avoidance response (Chisholm and Moore, 1970). In man the performance of a digit-symbol substitution task was impaired by chlordiazepoxide (20 mg), with the maximum effect (approximately 12% reduction in the mean number of correct responses as compared with placebo treatment) observed 60 minutes after drug treatment. Some impaired performance was still apparent in drug-treated subjects by 180 minutes after the drug (Besser and Steinberg, 1967).

There have been several reports regarding the amnesic effect of diazepam. This has been studied in rats (Soubrie et al., 1976) as well as in man. In the animal studies three benzodiazepines, namely, diazepam, chlordiazepoxide, and lorazepam, were individually given to rats (0.6–40 mg/kg) either 30 minutes prior to conditioned active avoidance trials or 30 minutes after. The benzodiazepines produced a dose-related reversal of behavioral inhibition for the avoidance task. Drugs given after the shock session did not affect shock-induced behavioral inhibition, thereby supporting the view that benzodiazepines interfere with the consolidation process (Soubrie et al., 1976). In man a possibly similar amnesic effect of diazepam has been reported (Mundow and Long, 1974). Verbal recall of visual, olfactory, or verbal stimuli presented to dental patients given 20 mg of diazepam was absent for the first stage of treatment. All 30 patients in this study were able to converse during the period for which subsequent amnesia became apparent (Foreman, 1974). There is some evidence that the peak effect of diazepam, in terms of its potential amnesic efficacy, has been noted in the interval of from 2 to 10 minutes following injection. In one series (Gregg et al., 1974) seven male and seven female patients were given an intravenous injection of diazepam (1 mg/7 lb. body weight, 1 mg/14 lb body weight, or 1 mg/21 lb body weight) or a placebo, and were then exposed to visual stimuli (line drawings of simple objects), auditory stimuli (common sounds), and painful stimuli (periosteal pressure applied to the clavicle, forehead, or ankle). Memory for the various stimuli, which were presented either immediately, 10, 20, or 30 minutes following drug injection, was tested 24 hours after each trial. All patients receiving the placebo indicated their recollection of the injection of the anesthetic (given 10 minutes after placebo injection), whereas those patients receiving diazepam (mean dose 7, 11, or 21 mg) showed only 57%, 50%, and 7% recall, respectively. A dose-related amnesia for all the sensory stimuli was apparent, with a peak effect when diazepam was given 10 minutes prior to the stimuli. For the highest dose of diazepam (1 mg/lb body weight) less than 30% of the stimuli were recalled, even when the internal between diazepam injection and stimulus presentation was 30 minutes. There was a statistically significant difference between the recall memory of male and female patients in this study, with the latter showing better recall than males after the intermediate and low doses of diazepam. This difference might best be attributed to sex-related differences in task motivation or attitude toward the experimenter (male). Inasmuch as the amnesic drug diazepam was presented prior to the stimuli for which subsequent amnesia was described, without any alteration of the consciousness level or vital functions, it would seem most appropriate to consider the effect as an anterograde amnesia.

In 144 patients given diazepam (10 mg, i.m.) as a premedicant before surgery, two patients showed hazy memory of the trip to the operating room, one had no recollection of the intravenous injection, and four had only a hazy memory of this event. 4% of the patients showed a partial amnesia (Pandit and Dundee, 1970). The diazepam premedication was given 60–90 minutes prior to anesthesia, and memory testing was carried out at 6 and/or 24 hours after anesthesia.

Intravenous diazepam was administered to patients prepared

for oral surgery. There was evidence of an anterograde amnesia, on the day of surgery, for oral injections (53.9%), drilling (23.3%), chiseling (28%), and use of an oral elevator (40.3%). When tested on a 1-week postsurgical follow-up visit, there was a 70.6% amnesia for the oral injection (Driscoll et al., 1972). Psychomotor performance, using a modified Bender Gestalt test, was also carried out in this study. A peak psychomotor deficit was observed after diazepam injection, with complete recovery by 1½ hours after injection. This finding partially separates the psychomotor components of the cognitive task from the consolidation process involved in the operative situation.

The amnesic effect of diazepam has also been studied in a nonoperative situation with 12 young intelligent male volunteers, ranging in age from 20 to 34 years. A decision-making task, a vigilance task, and a list of words to be remembered were presented. Intravenous infusion of either saline (1 ml/minute) or diazepam (0.24 mg/kg, 5 mg/minute) was then given for 3–4 minutes. There was only a slight reduction in the level of consciousness, and accurate short-term processing of input was preserved within 20 minutes of the diazepam injection (Clarke et al., 1970). The recall of three word lists was impaired, as was their recognition, suggesting a diazepam-induced anterograde amnesia with peak efficacy within the first 10 minutes within diazepam administration. Diazepam-related performance decrements have been related to presleep ingestion (Adams, 1974), and this drug has also been shown to impair driving skill (Linnoila, 1973), which may well represent a deleterious effect of the drug upon human motor learning (Linnoila et al., 1974). A positive effect of diazepam (5 mg) upon recall has been reported (Hartley, 1980), but this probably represents an improvement in sleep intervening between training and recall.

In other studies using tasks involving free and cued recall and mental imagery, there was a significant deficit in the learning of new material with a dose of diazepam as low as 0.3 mg/kg, although there was no appreciable impairment of recall for previously acquired tasks (Petersen and Ghoneim, 1980).

The effects of intravenous diazepam appear to show a consistently rapid-onset (2–3 minutes), brief (20–30 minutes), anterograde amnesia, with the duration of the amnesia being increased as a function of increases in dose (Gregg et al., 1974; Dundee & Pandit, 1972). This effect may be compared with that of lorazepam which, when given orally as well as intravenously, has a delayed onset of effect (30–40 minutes) and produces a prolonged amnesia, lasting up to 270 minutes. As compared with other preoperative benzodiazepines, lorazepam produced the greatest frequency of failure to recall the journey to the operating room (10% with 2 mg, 65% with 4 mg), to recall the intravenous injection (10 and 70%, respectively for 2 and 4 mg), and to recall an object shown after the injection (70 and 40%, respectively, for 2 and 4 mg). Whereas diazepam (10 or 20 mg, i.v.) exerts its greatest amnesic effect (85%) by 60 minutes after administration, as does flunitrazepam (0.5 or 1 mg), lorazepam (1, 2, or 4 mg) has its greatest effect (35–90%) by 90 minutes postinjection (McKay and Dundee, 1980).

Another benzodiazepine, flunitrazepam, principally used as a hypnotic, when given to normal subjects as bedtime (2 mg), impaired morning recall of several tasks presented when the subjects were awakened during the night (Bixler, 1979). It is apparent that the benzodiazepines, used as either preanesthetic agents or hypnotics, can exert potent anterograde memory effects.

# 8

# Mood Alterants

Up to this point almost all of the psychoactive agents considered to affect learning or memory have included barbiturates and sedatives; some attention may also be given to agents that have been employed clinically as mood stabilizers. Among these are the tricyclic compounds commonly utilized for the treatment of depression. It may be recalled, as mentioned earlier, that at least one biochemical effect of agents in this class is to impair the norepinephrine pump, whereby catecholamines are actively transported into the presynaptic nerve ending. Aside from its ability to interact with drugs which depend upon an intact norepinephrine pump for their action, such as guanethidine, tricyclics such as imipramine also interact to potentiate the effect of drugs which also act upon the norepinephrine pump, such as the amphetamines. The stimulant effect of amphetamine (1 mg/kg, i.p.) upon the performance of a nondiscriminative avoidance task by rats was potentiated by imipramine (10 mg/kg, i.p.) (Weissman, 1961). Several studies have indicated that the effects of imipramine in animals can be generally viewed as sedative (Battig, 1961; Hanson, 1961; Herr, et al., 1961; Maxwell and Palmer, 1961; Vernier, 1961; Sulser et al., 1962). In general the tricyclic compounds, which include imipramine, desipramine, etc. (iminodibenzyl derivatives) and amitriptyline, nortriptyline, protriptyline, etc. (dibenzocycloheptene derivatives), have been shown to be more effective when used clinically as antidepressant medication than monoamine oxidase inhibitors (Wechsler et al., 1965). Among the tricyclic compounds themselves, amitriptyline, which is intermediate in action between imipramine and chlorpromazine, was shown to be slightly more effective in depressive disorders characterized by agitation, anxiety, and schizophreniclike symptoms.

Imipramine, which is structurally similar to chlorpromazine, has been shown to induce or enhance the resting rhythm of the electroencephalogram (EEG): at low doses, in experimental animals, there is synchronization of the cortical EEG and a decrement in fast and low amplitude activity; at intermediate doses, desynchronization of EEG activity occurs, with a slowing in frequency; and at high doses, imipramine produces hypersynchronization of EEG activity, with the possibiligy of EEG seizures.

Several studies have attributed the effect of imipramine to its action on brain monoamines, although this relationship remains to be explored considerably further before any descriptive statement can be made regarding a central mechanism of action for this compound or corollary of its behavioral effects.

An absence of any significant effect of imipramine on monoamine oxidase activity has been shown in several studies (Exer and Pulver, 1960; Kivalo et al., 1961; Pletscher and Gey, 1959, 1962), and a lack of effect on brain monoamines has also been indicated in rats (Sulser et al., 1962; Vernier, 1961). In contrast to these findings, however, there have been reports of elevated levels of brain serotonin resulting from imipramine treatment (Costa et al., 1960; Kivalo et al., 1961). In mice treated with imipramine hydrochloride (20 mg/kg) there was an elevation in whole brain serotonin, a slight elevation in its chief metabolite in brain, 5-HIAA and an increase in brain serotonin turnover time, with no alteration in brain monoamine oxidase activity (Essman, 1970b). These findings have tentatively suggested that one central effect of this compound in mice may be to increase the synthesis and degradation of serotonin in brain. The brain level of imipramine, following injection (40 mg/kg, i.p.), reached a peak at 45 minutes after such treatment, with a brain level of 14 $\mu$g/g (Gilette et al., 1961). A 30% inhibition of brain cholinesterase activity has been reported with injection of 10 mg/kg of imipramine (Pulver et al., 1960), and an inhibition of respiratory activity in rat brain cortex slices and a reduction in oxidative phosphorylation in rat brain mitochondria have also been reported (Abadon et al., 1961).

The effect of imipramine on the central nervous system has been interpreted as nonspecific and stimulatory for neurons, whereas for glia a proposed specific effect on RNA synthesis has been proposed (Hydén, 1963). These conclusions were based on experiments in which the RNA content of single cells was altered by imipramine treatment, such that there was an 18% increase in neuronal RNA and a 45% decrease in glial RNA. This finding bears some relationship to the suggestion that compounds that elevate neuronal RNA and deplete glial RNA may be effective in antagonism of the amnesic effect of ECS (Essman, 1966; Essman and Golod, 1968; Essman and Essman, 1969). Some support for this relationship may be found in that imipramine-treated mice given ECS immediately following acquisition training for a single-trial passive avoidance response showed a significantly reduced incidence of ECS-induced retrograde amnesia than did control-treated mice (Essman, 1970a).

The behavioral effects of imipramine, in animals, may be broadly viewed as sedative, with only a very minimal effect on spontaneous locomotor activity. In behavioral studies rats trained to acquire a maze response showed an increase in response latency in the acquisition of such behavior independent of the nature of the motivated stimulus. In doses of 5–20 mg/kg, i.p., error performance in a water maze was decreased; however, response time was increased (Latz, 1964). Conditioned avoidance responses have been reduced at high doses of imipramine (100 mg/kg, p.o.) in rats (Theobald, 1959); however, at lower doses conditioned avoidance responses were not negatively affected, and performance thereof appeared to be enhanced (Maxwell and Palmer, 1961; Maxwell, 1964). It appears as though discrete conditioned avoidance responses are negatively affected by imipramine in animals, at high doses, within a range in which induced synchronization of the electrocorticogram is a corrollary. At doses of 5–20 mg/kg, i.p., the response rate and incidence of shock avoidance were decreased by imipramine treatment (Theobald et al., 1964; Carlton and Didamo, 1961), although other studies have not consistently demonstrated a response decrement in animals treated with higher doses of imipramine (Scheckel and Boff, 1964; Heise and Boff, 1962). There has been some indication (Shchelkunov, 1963) that the effect of imipramine on performance becomes more apparent when the reinforcing stimulus employed was food rather than shock. The reduction of food reinforcement, produced by imipramine, did not affect the percentage of shocks taken by the animal (Goldberg and Johnson, 1974).

A variety of studies would appear to indicate that at low doses imipramine acts as a mild analeptic, whereas at high doses it serves as a depressant. Discriminatory behavior is improved or facilitated, particularly in the case of classical secretory or motor responses when low doses of imipramine are given, and under such dose conditions, maze errors and nondiscriminated avoidance behavior has been observed to be facilitated.

Certain similarities between central effects of imipramine and those of lithium salts have been pointed out (Essman, 1970b), which perhaps lends some support to the view (Schou, 1963) that these compounds fall within the common category designated as *normothymoleptics*, or mood stabilizers. The alterations of the EEG in the direction of a recruiting response, resulting in high-amplitude slow waves in cats and rabbits, and the reduction or suppression of arousal, produced by electrical stimulation of the reticular formation, or by auditory or painful stimulation, have been shown for imipramine (Sigg, 1959). The increase in the arousal threshold to reticular stimulation by imipramine has also been demonstrated in cats (Bradley and Key, 1959), and in doses of 0.1–2.0 mg/kg imipramine was effective in blocking the activation of electrocortical responses induced by sensory stimulation. A critical parameter in the evaluation of the central effects of imipramine appears to reside in the dose at which this compound is administered; for example, low doses led to decreased arousal thresholds for sensory stimuli and direct electrical stimulation of the reticular formation, whereas higher doses (8–20 mg/kg) depressed the excitability of the arousal system (Rubio-Chevannier et al., 1961). Alterations in threshold for the rage response also appear to be dose dependent in that low doses (2–5 mg/kg) resulted in decreased threshold for rage responsiveness, whereas higher doses (8–10 mg/kg) decreased autonomic responsivity, caused rage to disappear, and increased threshold. These findings may possibly point toward the direct or indirect enhancement of hypothalamic excitability, which could possibly serve to account for the clinically antidepressant nature of imipramine action. Amitriptyline (0.1–1.0 mg/kg) and imipramine (0.05–3.00 mg/kg) did not alter the elaboration of conditioned defensive motor responses in cats to sequential auditory and visual stimuli that were reinforced by ECS. Differentiation of the conditional stimuli was not affected at higher drug doses (2.0, 0.1 mg/kg), although there was an increased rate of interstimulus interval responding. Conditioned and unconditioned responses were decreased at higher doses (3.0–10.0 mg/kg) of the drugs (Vinogradov, 1969).

Imipramine effects have also been studied for their possible role in memory consolidation, based upon the premise that amnesic effects associated with the elevation of brain serotonin might be blocked by tricyclics. The turnover of brain serotonin is reduced after the administration of imipramine or chlorimipramine (Tissari and Suurhasko, 1972). A parallel observation has been made in the cerebrospinal fluid of depressed patients, where inhibition of 5-HIAA efflux out of the CSF led to a reduced metabolite accumulation rate after treatment with amitriptyline and imipramine (Post and Goodwin, 1974). These findings suggest a decreased serotonin turnover in the central nervous system during treatment with tricyclics. A related observation which may, in part, account for the reduction in serotonin turnover by tricyclics is that *in vitro* studies with rabbit brain have shown that imipramine and desipramine inhibit monoamine oxidase (Roth and Gillis, 1974).

The retrograde amnesic effects of ECS upon a passive avoidance response by mice was reduced by 14% when imipramine (20 mg/kg) was given 1 hour prior to the amnesic stimulus (Essman, 1970b). Amitriptyline (10 mg/kg) reduced the acquisition of an active avoidance response in mice by 30%. The elevation of brain serotonin that followed the amnesic ECS stimulus was blocked in animals that had been treated by one of these tricyclics, thereby again favoring the view that interruption of memory consolidation by a rise of brain serotonin could be blocked by drugs which prevent the brain serotonin rise after the amnesic stimulus is initiated.

There have been a variety of compounds which can be broadly classed within an area considered as indirect stimulants. However, the nature of such compounds and their interrelationship with one another is of such a diverse nature, and their behavioral effects have sometimes been rather far removed from their intended clinical use.

Recent clinical interest in the use of lithium salts in the treatment of the manic phase of manic-depressive illness, and the variety of metabolic effects and behavioral alterations induced by compounds within the lithium family, suggest that lithium salts, as possible indirect stimulants of central nervous system activity, may be useful to consider both experimentally as well as clinically within this general area.

The initial studies from which the clinical application of lithium salts to the treatment of the manic phase of manic-depressive illness emerged, were conducted in guinea pigs (Cade, 1949). It was noted that the result of the administration of lithium salts to these animals was lethargy and protection from urea-induced convulsions. There has been little experimental work dealing with the effect of lithium salts on behavior since most of these considerations have been explored in human subjects within the context of therapeutic application. The effect of lithium on the electrical activity of the nervous system has been considered (Mayfield and Brown, 1966), and the results of EEG studies indicate a widening of the frequency spectrum and diffuse slowing. Background rhythm in these recordings has been both potentiated as well as disorganized by lithium treatment, with sensitivity to hyperventilation also occurring. There is some indication that cerebral adenosine diphosphate (ADP) and respiration are stimulated by lithium, as indicated from studies of its effects on isolated rat brain mitochondria (Kral et al., 1967).

It was noted that in man there was a higher retention and tolerance to lithium during manic attack, as compared with healthy persons, and that this increase in retention is reduced following the attenuation of the manic attack (Trautner et al., 1955). Following the ingestion of lithium salts it was noted that whereas animal subjects excreted 50–70% manic patients excreted less than 20%. It should, however, be pointed out that different doses of lithium salts were given to the control and manic groups (Gershon and Yuwiler, 1960).

Another hypothesis concerned with the effect of lithium has suggested central nervous system catecholamines, which increased during mania and decreased during depression. Norepinephrine, available to central adrenergic receptors, has been shown in animal studies to be decreased by lithium chloride (Schanberg et al., 1967). A decrease in the brain level of normetanephrine and an increase in the level of deanimated catecholes resulted from lighium chloride treatment (Schanberg et al., 1967), suggesting that it may decrease the availability of norepinephrine to adrenergic receptor sites in mania. There has been some suggestion that the relative rates of release and re-uptake of norepinephrine at central adrenergic nerve endings may be related to alterations in mood states; (Sulser et al., 1964). These data have indicated that the therapeutic efficacy of lithium treatment in manic states may partially result from an increased re-uptake of norepinephrine, with a resulting decrease in norepinephrine available for interaction with receptor sites.

There has been some degree of experimental work relating the effects of lithium to other electrolytes. Following lithium chloride treatment in rats there was an elevation of calcium and magnesium excretion after 12 days, whereas phosphate excretion rose after 20 days (Gotfredsen et al., 1969). Lithium chloride injection in rats led to an elevation of the brain glycogen level, and in its specific activity in brain blood, glucose levels were also affected during the first 2 hours of lithium chloride treatment, following which there was a decrease in level (Plenge et al., 1969). In rats given oral doses of lithium salts there was no recorded effect on brain amine levels; however, there was a reduced depletion of 5-hydroxytryptamine in the nerve terminals of lithium-treated animals that were given a tryptophan hydroxylase inhibitor (Corrodi et al., 1969). These authors have concluded that prolonged administration of low doses of lithium salts leads to a reduction in the activity of 5-hydroxytryptamine neurons or, possibly, the inhibition of 5-hydroxytryptamine release at nerve terminals following impulse stimulation. An earlier conclusion regarding the central effect of lithium on amines was that it did not alter brain amine levels (Schou, 1967). This same investigator suggested earlier (Schou,

1963) that there were parallels between the therapeutic effects of lithium salts and imipramine, which were classed as normothymoleptics, in that both of these compounds did not affect "normal behavior," led to no apathy or impairment of consciousness or intellectual functions, and had no euphoriant or mood-depressive properties. These suggested parallels have been studied in mice (Essman, 1970c), and several behavioral and biochemical correlates of acute lithium salt treatment have emerged.

The administration of doses of lithium carbonate, ranging from 1.18 to 4.70 mEq/kg, in mice resulted in detectable amounts of brain lithium by 15 minutes following intraperitoneal injection and persisting for at least 45 minutes following injection. Brain magnesium concentration was significantly elevated for at least 60 minutes following treatment. Brain serotonin concentration was elevated at 15 minutes following lithium injection, and at this time, for the lowest dose, there was a significant reduction in the brain serotonin turnover rate, and an elevation in turnover time, suggesting that brain serotonin synthesis and degradation at one specific time following lithium treatment was reduced. It was also found that a conditioned avoidance response, for which posttraining ECS resulted in a retrograde amnesia in animals tested 24 hours following the training ECS sequence, was reinstated in approximately 30% of the animals by 48 or 72 hours later where such animals had been pretreated with 2.35 mEq/kg of lithium carbonate 30 minutes prior to training.

In a clinical study, patients suffering from affective psychoses, when treated with lithium carbonate, showed that during the course of therapy, clinical recovery was accompanied by a rise in total body water and a significant increase in intracellular water, suggesting that altered electrolyte levels in the central nervous system may be related to such pathology or the mechanism whereby lithium treatment effects clinical recovery (Mangioni et al., 1969).

# 9

# General Anesthetics

The potentially amnesic effect of general anesthetics has been considered in a number of studies in both animals and man. A detailed basis upon which the effects of anesthesia relate to brain organization and function as well as depending upon cellular properties and evoking responses has been provided (Clark and Waugh, 1979). One agent that has been considered is diethyl ether, which was shown to produce a retrograde amnesia for a conditioned response in mice (Essman and Jarvik, 1960). A similar effect of ether anesthesia upon the retention of an avoidance response in rats was also shown (Pearlman et al., 1961). A study of the time course over which diethyl ether, administered in an anesthetic dose to mice after acquisition of a one-trial avoidance response, was effective in producing a retrograde amnesia (Abt et al., 1961) indicated that virtually complete amnesia was produced by anesthesia given within 8 minutes after a single training trial. Between 16 and 20 minutes after training, ether produced amnesia in 50–60% of the animals.

By 24 minutes after training, ether anesthesia produced amnesia in only 20% of the mice. It was also shown (Essman and Jarvik, 1961) that ether anesthesia immediately after learning produced a complete retrograde amnesia for a passive avoidance response, when tested 24 hours after training. Anesthesia with ether, 1 hour after training, had no effect upon the retention of the avoidance behavior. The finding that anesthesia with diethyl ether is capable of producing a time-dependent retrograde amnesia in rodents supports the view that changes associated with the effects of the anesthetic or of the anesthesia state are capable of interfering with the memory consolidation process. The result also stands as a contradiction of the view (Burns, 1958) that rapidly induced anesthesia does not produce retrograde amnesia.

In a clinical investigation (Artusio, 1955) with 135 patients, ether anesthesia effects upon memory were assessed during plane 1 of anesthesia. In plane 1 (the onset of anesthesia until some analgesia was achieved) of stage 1 anesthesia there was no change in memory for recent or past events, and simple problems could be solved. In plane 2 of anesthesia there was some analgesia, although pain responses could still be elicited, and simple instructions were followed. In postoperative memory testing there was total amnesia for all experiences during this plane of anesthesia, although memory for recent and past events was intact. In plane 3 there was complete anesthesia, although during this period the patients were still verbally responsive, and special senses were intact. During plane 3 of ether anesthesia there was diminution of memory for recent events; memory for past events, although ultimately reduced, was intact for a longer period than the former.

These studies in man and the concurrent animal investigation indicate that anterograde as well as retrograde amnesia may occur with diethyl ether anesthesia. It is also suggested that the duration of anesthesia or the actual loss of consciousness are not necessarily requisites for amnesia. Clinical studies in particular indicate that, like the amnesic effects of benzodiazepines, ether-induced amnesia is associated with analgesia. It is quite likely that those molecular changes that account for the disruption of memory consolidation or interfere with memory retrieval can be activated by ether analgesia. This contradicts the long-time view that loss of consciousness is a requirement for retrograde amnesia. The electrophysiological correlates of search necessary for short-term memory have been shown to be altered by the anesthetic agent enflurane (Adam and Collins, 1979). This may bear upon a prior observation (Adam and Collins, 1978) that the late component of the visual evoked potential, or the averaged scalp potential, reflects the search process for short-term memory. Enflurane exposure, by virtue of repeated contact with this anesthetic agent in operative procedures, may also exert effects upon cognitive processes. Trace concentrations of inhaled enflurane have been shown to produce significant increases in reaction time and decrease digit recall in volunteer subjects (Bruce and Bach, 1975). Similar findings have been reported for the inhalation of trace quantities of halothane (Bruce et al., 1974; Bruce and Bach, 1976). At subanesthetic doses of halothane (to 200 ppm) there was no impairment of a complex reaction time task or of immediate recall, as measured by digit span (Cook et al., 1978).

The issue of anesthesia-induced amnesia has not always been consistently supported. For example, for 26 healthy subjects to whom either halothane, Forane, thiopental, or nitrous oxide followed by halothane, was administered rapidly 30 seconds after a 10-second presentation of a visual stimulus, no retrograde amnesia was apparent when recall was tested 24 hours later (Bahlman et al., 1972). Such objects as a clock, camera, automobile, or beer can were described in great detail.

Nitrous oxide, given at subanesthetic doses, has also been cited as a potentially amnesic agent. However, its potential in this respect appears to be dose related. Short-term memory or the input necessary to its fixation has been impaired by subanesthetic doses in man (Steinberg and Summerfield, 1957). The agent was given to volunteer subjects instructed to acquire a rote learning task, at a partial pressure of 0.33 Pa — a third of the partial pressure required for anesthesia. A concentration dependence for retrograde amnesia from nitrous oxide has been suggested (Parbrook, 1967), although at partial pressures between 0.2 and 0.5 Pa no impairment of input or short-term recall (30 seconds after input) was found (Robson et al., 1960). An elevation of the partial pressure impaired later recall (2–5 minutes). The relationship between the concentration of nitrous oxide and its amnesic effect in man has not always been consistent between studies or within the same study. At a low partial pressure (0.2 Pa) nitrous oxide did not affect recall, but both short-term recall and long-term recall were reduced when 0.3 Pa was used (Parkhouse et al., 1960). Long-term recall was abolished at 0.4 Pa, and short-term recall was reduced. A significant impairment of reaction time and digit recall has been reported at doses of inhaled nitrous oxide as low as 50 ppm (Bruce and Bach, 1976). A decision task was reduced by breathing 20 or 30% nitrous oxide, and at 30% there was a decrement in short-term memory performance (Garfield et al., 1975). Other investigators have failed to demonstrate effects of trace amounts of nitrous oxide upon human performance (Smith and Shirley, 1977). This lack of significant cognitive or performance effects of nitrous oxide has been noted for trace doses (0.4%), but subanesthetic doses (20–30%) impaired immediate recall (Cook et al., 1978).

The use of a premedication with a general anesthetic also may contribute to the effect upon memory. The use of a narcotic as a preoperative medication in obstetric patients within 6 hours of general anesthesia (Wilson and Turner, 1969) reduced the frequency of unpleasant stimuli recalled during a cesarean section by 18%. Diazepam used as a premedication apparently increased by 17.4% the incidence of unpleasant stimulus recall associated with a cesarean section (Turner and Wilson, 1969). This finding contrasts with the studies cited earlier in support of diazepam as an anterograde amnesic—even when used by itself in subanesthetic doses. When given intravenously (0.24 mg/kg) to healthy volunteers, recall was impaired for at least 30 minutes (Clarke et al., 1970). This effect has been sufficiently well documented so that clinical use, for example, several minutes prior to local anesthetic injection, reduced recall of the latter to 16% with 10 mg and 0% with 30 mg (Keilty and Blackwood, 1969).

It is apparent that the potentiation as well as the antagonism of the memory effects of general anesthetics by other nonanesthetics depends upon the interaction of these agents centrally. General anesthetics elevate sensory thresholds and depress the reticular activating system of the brain. There is also some indication that the neurotransmitter status is altered by general anesthetic agents, and such changes may reflect the central effect of the agent rather than the consequence of the anesthesia. In our own studies we have observed an elevation of brain serotonin and a reduction of its turnover in the brains of animals exposed to diethyl ether or nitrous oxide. Partial inhibition of the active elimination of the acidic metabolite of serotonin from the brain also occurred. It is tempting to speculate that potentiation or antagonism of the amnesic effect of general anesthetics depends upon the molecular effect of the interactive agent. Studies are still required to delineate this possible mode of action.

# 10

# Ethanol

In considering the relationship between ethanol and the process of learning and memory, a distinction between the acute and chronic effects of this agent becomes useful. It is well known that impairment of performance can occur with both acute and chronic ethanol administration (Weiss and Laties, 1962) and that chronic ethanolism can impair the acquisition of responses and the recall of recent experiences. There is some question, however, as to the degree to which such effects reside in: (1) the central physiological effect of ethanol, (2) a drug-induced cellular change approximating a neurological basis for a chronic brain syndrome, or (3) a metabolic lesion based upon a deficiency state where vitamin and/or electrolyte content losses could independently contribute to altered sensory, motor, cognitive, intellectual, or performance functions. It should be apparent that if disturbances of memory are to be ascribed to ethanol, then there are probably several forms of ethanol amnesia. Two forms have been described (Ryback, 1970) consisting of a state-dependent form and a "blackout" form. The former condition has been applied to a number of central nervous system depressants and cholinergic agents (Overton, 1966) in animals (Crow, 1966; Ryback, 1969a,b) and in man (Storm and Caird, 1967; Goodwin et al., 1969), indicating that stimuli learned during a state following ethanol ingestion are best recalled in a similar later ethanol state. There is some controversy as to the genuine nature of universality of the state-dependent concept, particularly in view of the obvious falacy that the ethanol state, where performance is maximally compromised, should confer a unique synaptic circumstance where memory is better recalled. To consider state dependency as a consolidation process which has occurred during the ethanol state, almost precludes the possibility of dependency. For example, we have shown that ethanol given to mice potentiates the amnesic effect of ECS given after avoidance conditioning. Such a potentiating effect is observed as an increase in time after conditioning, where ECS will produce a retrograde amnesia. Retention or amnesia was tested 24 hours after training where there was no longer an ethanol state. It would seem reasonable, therefore, on basic as well as clinical grounds, to question the validity of a state-dependent amnesic effect of ethanol. The experiment cited above may be taken as yet another example of an ethanol amnesia—a potentiated amnesia. One suggested basis for this effect is that both ethanol and ECS lead to an increase in brain serotonin content, and an elevation of brain serotonin can produce amnesia (Essman, 1970a). A cumulative or additive effect of the two agents could increase the course of time over which memory consolidation occurs. A separation of the amnesic and facilitative effects of acute ethanol administration has been investigated. At doses of 0.75–4.5 g/kg, given posttraining, ethanol facilitated the acquisition of a passive avoidance task. At a dose of 3 g/kg, posttrial, ethanol facilitated retention, but the same dose given 10 minutes pretraining produced a retention deficit (Alkana and Parker, 1979). These findings suggest an interaction between the temporal gradient for memory consolidation and the time course over which ethanol exerts those central effects that are cognidisruptive. The early phase of acute ethanol facilitation of consolidation could represent the sedative effect of ethanol or the reduction of extraneous sensory stimulation. Another explanation may relate to the observation that ethanol, when given acutely, elevates brain levels of methionine enkephalin and $\beta$-endorphin, whereas with chronic treatment these peptides are reduced by 70% in the anterior pituitary, requiring approximately 2 weeks after withdrawal to become reinstated to baseline levels (Schulz et al., 1980). The analgesic effect of these peptides could account for changes in behavior based upon shock-based performance and retention.

The blackout amnesia induced by ethanol refers to a profound short-term memory deficit associated with an acute elevation in the blood ethanol level (Ryback, 1969a,b). Under these circumstances cues to the recent memory loss, ingestion of ethanol, or prompted recognition fail to provide for recall. There remains some question of the possible accompaniments of a rapid, acute rise in blood ethanol level that could account for an apparently nonreversible and irretrievable memory loss. Hypoglycemia, hypomagnesemia, dehydration, pH change, and so on all represent possible factors which may result from the elevated blood ethanol and which may account, either individually or collectively, for the observed amnesia.

The combination of ethanol abuse and nutritional deficiency serve as a basis for Wernicke's disease and Korsakoff's syndrome characterized, among several neurological findings, by a disorder of memory. There are impairment of recent memory, a disorder in new learning, and intervals of retrograde amnesia. When recovery from these disorders has occurred, there is still a residual amnesia for the acute phase of the illness. Among those areas of the brain involving neuronal and myelin degeneration and gliosis, are the mammillary bodies, fornices, thalamic nuclei, and hypothalamus. It is apparent, therefore, that memory disturbances resulting from the chronic effects of ethanol involve structural changes which are not apparent for those amnesias to which acute ethanol treatment may contribute.

# 11

# Stimulants

The action of central nervous system stimulants, such as the amphetamines, can be enhanced if the level of brain serotonin has been reduced. For example, interruption of the ascending serotoninergic pathways in the rat with lesions of the medial forebrain bundle, leading to a 60–84% decrease in telencephalic serotonin, produced a threefold enhancement of amphetamine effect (Green and Harvey, 1974). An increased rate of operant conditioning response was observed. The effect of amphetamines upon learning or memory appears only indirectly related to their effect upon brain serotonin metabolism or dependency upon the level of brain serotonin. What appears more directly to be behaviorally relevant for the effect of amphetamines are the tasks upon which its potential effects on learning or memory are assessed. It may be noted, however, that amphetamines in doses exceeding 5 mg/kg release the extragranular stores of serotonin into the extraneuronal space, but the depletion of serotonin does not occur (Fuxe and Ungerstedt, 1968).

The effects of amphetamines upon performance have been critically assessed (Weiss and Laties, 1969), and it has been suggested that performance levels lowered by fatigue, and work-performance decrements may be enhanced by these drugs. Such performance factors are often difficult to separate from the performance measurers in learning and memory tasks. Similarly, motivational components of learning or memory tasks may influence the effects of amphetamines upon such behaviors. Diamphetamine has been shown to increase the rate of conditioning in man (Franks and Trouton, 1958), and several tests of abstract reasoning, sentence completion, writing speed, and free association were enhanced by *d*-amphetamine (Nash, 1962). The solution of arithmetic problems, reduced error incidence, and decreased performance decrement due to fatigue were also noted in subjects given a single oral dose of 10 mg of diamphetamine.

For tasks more directly related to memory processes, amphetamines have also been shown to exert a facilitative effect. Metamphetamine (15 mg/68 kg, i.v.) provided for an increased recall of strings of digits from 8 to 20 times when these were presented in different time sequences (Talland and Quarton, 1965). Acquisition of paired-associate verbal stimuli of low associative value was enhanced by *d*-amphetamine, but no effect upon the recall of these associated stimuli was found (Hurst et al., 1969).

The effects of metamphetamine upon short-term memory was investigated in subjects instructed to reproduce lists of digits after various delay times following their presentation (Crow and Bursill, 1970). Error rates for the drug-treated subjects exceeded those of the controls at all delay intervals, although not significantly. There were also no differences between the error rate changes before and after treatment for the drug- and control-treated subjects.

The effects of amphetamines have been observed to facilitate learning in hyperactive children (Conners and Eisenberg, 1963), and Porteus maze performance was improved by *d*-amphetamine in normal as well as in hyperactive children (Conners et al., 1964). A similar result was obtained when the quantitative score on the Porteus maze test was studied in children with an intercurrent lesion of the central nervous system (hyperkinetic) and in normal controls (Lasagna and Epstein, 1968). Nonorganic subjects showed a 4.8%

increase in maze test quotients after $d$-amphetamine, and the hyperkinetic (organic) groups showed a 23.8% increase for the same task after $d$-amphetamine.

Another group of central nervous system stimulants which has taken on possible significance for their effects upon learning and memory processes is the analeptics, which include strychnine, picrotoxin, and pentylenetetrazol. Strychnine tonics for the geriatric population as a remedy for, among other things, "memory loss," "forgetfulness," "memory lapses," and "improved concentration" were common applications called to one's attention on the labels of such products common to the pharmacists' shelves 75 years ago, and to some extent are available today. There have been various rationales upon which the presumed learning and memory facilitation by strychnine have been based. These include a drug-induced increase in brain excitability coincident with the learning experience (Lashley, 1917), — a premise by which improved maze acquisition by rats was explained. They also lead to a presumed inhibition of cholinesterase activity (only demonstrated *in vitro* — Nachmansohn, 1938), used to account for a reduced incidence of maze acquisition errors by rats (McGaugh, 1961), and to the observation that six daily strychnine injections facilitated behavior in rats and led to an increase (27%) in the whole brain content of RNA (Carlini and Carlini, 1965).

There is rather consistent agreement regarding the central stimulant effect of strychnine, but some controversy regarding its efficacy in facilitating either learning or memory. The acceleration of visual acuity (Walsh, 1947), its effect upon appetitive behavior, its effect upon shock threshold, and seizure threshold — all introduce methodological problems that limit conclusions regarding strychnine as a facilitative drug. These limitations may all or individually apply to such studies in which the maze performance of rats was increased by strychnine given before or after training (McGaugh and Petrinovich, 1965; McGaugh, 1966, 1968). Another possibly important factor contributing to presumed behavioral facilitation by strychnine is the distribution of experience in learning trials. Rats given strychnine prior to massed trials required fewer trials and made fewer errors in acquiring a maze response, but no effect of the drug was apparent when the trials were spaced over longer intervals (Livecchi and Dusewicz, 1969). This finding again supports the notion of an antifatigue administration upon maze acquisition with either massed or spaced trials (Dusweicz and Livecchi, 1969). The absence of a posttrial effect of strychnine argues against its presumed proconsolidation effect. Strychnine sulfate, in eight doses ranging from 0.005 to 0.60 mg/kg, failed to have any facilitative effect upon avoidance learning (Oglesby and Winter, 1973), again casting doubt upon the memory effect of strychnine as contrasted with its performance effects. The posttrial administration of strychnine sulfate to rats did not modify avoidance discrimination or task acquisition (Oglesby and Winter, 1974).

Another factor which may be important for the behavioral effects of strychnine concerns its neonatal administration and the variable of handling. Rat pups were given either strychnine or saline injections and either handled or nonmanipulated between 2 and 5 days of age. Although strychnine was without effect upon active avoidance learning by the rats at 45 days of age, the handled animals showed significantly more avoidance behavior than the nonmanipulated controls (Schaefer et al., 1974).

The view that behavioral facilitation by analeptics represents (1) an interaction with motivated behavior, (2) an antifatigue effect, or (3) an increased level of activation may, in addition to applying to strychnine, also apply to picrotoxin and pentylenetetrazol. The posttrial treatment of rats with picrotoxin has been reported to facilitate maze learning (Breen and McGaugh, 1961). The poorer learners among the rats showed facilitation (fewer errors) at a dose of picrotoxin (1.0 mg/kg) that did not alter the error incidence among the good learners. Semichronic picrotoxin treatment of rats, posttrial (1.0 mg/kg) improved the maze-acquisition behavior (Garg and Holland, 1968), although this agent has also been shown to be without effect upon maze learning in other studies (Prien et al., 1963).

On the basis of its selective reduction in short inhibitory postsynaptic currents, while it has no effect upon long inhibitory postsynaptic currents or excitatory postsynaptic currents, it has been suggested that pentylenetetrazol selectively blocks a cholinergic postsynaptic potential and acts postsynaptically (Wilson and Escueta, 1974). There have, in fact, been clinical applications of pentylenetetrazol for the treatment of memory disorders in geriatric patients with arteriosclerosis or associated chronic brain syndrome

(Wolff, 1962), as well as for the treatment of senile attentional and social disorders (Goodhart and Helenore, 1963). The use of pentylenetetrazol in animal studies has yielded results which, on one hand, support its role as a facilitatory agent in subconvulsive doses (Irwin and Benuazizi, 1966; Hunt and Krivanek, 1966; McGaugh, 1966; Krivanek and McGaugh, 1968; Hunt and Bauer, 1969), and, on the other hand, have failed to find a facilitatory effect (Bunch and Mueller, 1941; Heron and Carlson, 1941; Kahan, 1966; Bovet et al., 1966). It has been shown that rats given saline injections from 15 to 35 days of age and/or maturity prior to being tested for acquisition of a maze response, made more response errors than rats that were not injected; pentylenetetrazol (15 mg/kg) during development or at maturity counteracted the disruptive effect of saline (Stein, 1974).

In convulsive doses, pentylenetetrazol has been shown to produce a retrograde amnesic effect. This may be accounted for by the convulsion as well as by the central effect of the drug, independent of the convulsion. A retrograde amnesic effect of pentylenetetrazol was produced when a convulsion occurred after an avoidance conditioning trial in rats (Pearlman et al., 1961). The retrograde amnesic effect occurred even when the interval between training and drug treatment was as long as 8 hours. This profound effect may very likely be accounted for by repetitive seizure episodes, which may spontaneously occur after an initial drug-induced convulsion, or may be precipitated by sensory stimuli, particularly auditory, which occur during the postconvulsive period. In mice pretreated with lidocaine to block pentylenetetrazol-induced convulsions, the drug still produced a retrograde amnesia for a passive avoidance response (Essman, 1968). Experiments in this investigation did not support an RNA-related mechanism to account for the amnesic effect. A brain RNA decrement occurred when convulsions were precipitated, but when the convulsions were blocked, brain RNA concentration was not affected. Pentylenetetrazol convulsions also provide for a temporal gradient of retrograde amnesia if convulsive, but not excessively high doses are given. The disruption of a conditioned taste aversion in rats has been shown for this agent (Millner and Palfai, 1974); the drug given within 5 seconds after conditioned taste aversion training disrupted the retention of the aversive behavior, whereas, when given 10 minutes before or after taste aversion training, it has no effect upon the retention of the conditioned aversion.

In primates the effect of pentylenetetrazol has been evaluated on the acquisition of discrimination learning problems. Immediate posttrial injections improved the acquisition of difficult discriminations but had no effect upon easy problems (Bowman et al., 1979); 10 mg/kg provided for optimal facilitation when given 1 minute after training. Although discrimination learning by the rhesus monkey was facilitated by the immediate posttraining injection of pentylenetetrazol, learning set was unaffected (Bowman et al., 1980).

It may be of further interest to note that a current standard compilation of prescribable approved drugs in the United States (*Physician's Desk Reference*, 1982) lists at least six preparations containing 100 mg of pentylenetetrazol, the indications for which have been variously given as "cerebral stimulant," "to enhance mental and physical activity," and "indicated in the treatment of memory defects."

Another, and perhaps more commonly encountered stimulant, having a place in the pharmacology of learning and memory, is caffeine. The action of this methyl xanthine upon learning and memory has, like other central stimulants, been dual in nature. Some investigators (Lashley, 1917) have noted a dose-related retardation of maze learning in rats, or (Veronin and Napalkov, 1963) inhibition of chains of alimentary reflexes. It was suggested (Pavlov, 1927) that negative conditioned reflexes are impaired by the drug, whereas positive conditioned reflexes are enhanced, depending upon the caffeine-induced reduction in internal inhibition. The increased locomotor activity of caffeine, observed in some studies (Dews, 1953), which could contribute to its effects upon learning, have been shown in other studies (Greenblatt and Osterberg, 1961) to depend upon predrug baseline activity levels. If initially high, the drug exerts little locomotor stimulant effect. Caffeine given to mice during the nadir of their activity cycle (4 pm) significantly increased subsequent locomotor activity, but the same dose (25 mg/kg) given during the activity peak (4–8 am) depressed locomotor activity levels (Essman, 1971). Thus several variables become immediately apparent, which, in animal studies, appear to govern the direction in which the effects of caffeine alter behavior.

These include: (1) the complexity of a choice task, (2) the active or passive nature of avoidance behavior, (3) the degree of locomotor activity effect, and (4) baseline or periodic variations upon which the drug effect is imposed.

In man, caffeine (1.5 g), given 2½–3 hours prior to presenting a list of nonsense syllables to be learned, provided for better learning of those stimuli for which there were pleasant associations and also an increase in the number of consonants learned (Tolman, 1917). There appear to be considerable interindividual differences in the effects of the caffeine in coffee upon simple learning functions in man. Coffee given 20, 100, or 140 minutes prior to adding or memory span tasks increased the accuracy with which performance occurred (Gililand and Nelson, 1939), but there was considerable variability in the magnitude of the effect. It would be difficult to generalize from such studies and speculate about the potentially facilitative effect of coffee consumption upon tasks requiring learning or depending upon the efficiency with which memory consolidation takes place. Just as there are wide variations in the caffeine content in different coffees, there are individual differences in the absorption, duration of effect, and magnitude of central action. Just as noted from animal studies, the central effects of caffeine and coffee appear to depend upon the activation and behavioral baselines upon which the drug is superimposed.

Performance of four measures on an automobile driving simulator was significantly enhanced by initial and supplemental doses of caffeine (Regina et al., 1974), suggesting that sustained task performance requiring motor learning can be facilitated by the drug. The reduction of drowsiness and increase in alertness produced by caffeine served as a basis for administering 300 mg of the drug to 60 volunteer college students then given the paced sequential memory task (Mitchel et al., 1974). A significant interaction was observed between the effects of caffeine and the presence of the pill. It would appear that the placebo effect of the pill—providing for enhanced memory task performance—was facilitated by caffeine. The use of stimulant drugs in hyperactive children has been given some prior attention, but also related to caffeine (Cole, 1975), particularly with a view toward its use by children. In doses equivalent to approximately two cups of coffee over a 4–5-hour period, caffeine did not benefit any of 25 hyperkinetic children (Gross, 1975). Most of the children were, in fact, worsened by caffeine, as compared with other stimulants such as methylphenidate and amphetamine. Such findings could again be in agreement with the view that baseline activation determines the extent to which behavioral efficacy of caffeine may be provided, and, unlike other stimulants, caffeine does not produce a paradoxical effect upon a hyperexcited state.

As an example of how caffeine may exert dual effects in a learning–memory paradigm, mice were given the drug after one maze training trial preceding another by 24 hours (Stripling and Alpern, 1974). A dose-dependent disruption of performance occurred on the 24-hour trial. When caffeine was given prior to a training trial, performance was facilitated. It was suggested that caffeine disrupted the long-term stores of memory for the initial training and also provided for proactive facilitation of maze learning. In the first circumstance it would appear that caffeine interferes with the memory consolidation process, whereas in the second condition consolidation may be rendered more efficient through increased performance at learning.

A chemical relative of caffeine, uric acid, has also been implicated both behaviorally and biochemically in learning and memory processes. The endogenous level of uric acid has been suggested as mediating such functions as intellectual and cognitive behavior (Orowan, 1955), primarily on the basis of its potential as a central nervous system stimulant. One can certainly derive anecdotal evidence in support of a positive effect of uric acid from the clinical history of eminent persons who were hyperuricemic; a potent counterargument, however, is the question of whether the intellectual or cognitive ability of such persons was any different from that of normouricemic individuals who also achieved eminence. A low, but statistically significant, correlation was found between the uric acid level of army recruits and their performance scores on a well-standardized intelligence test. A number of factors, other than a purely facilitative property of endogenous uric acid, may contribute to such a relationship; these include increased activation level, greater antifatigue potential, and sustained alertness. These same factors may, in part, also account for the observations that academic achievement, defined by rank, publications, and prominence in one's discipline, is also associated with a higher level of uric acid (Brooks and Mueller, 1966).

The behavioral role of uric acid has been extensively reviewed (Essman, 1970c) and in animal studies has been shown to increase response times and decrease the incidence of errors made during the learning of a simple maze task by mice. Uricase, in a dose sufficient to reduce endogenous uric acid to allantoin (1.65 mg/kg), led to an increase in both maze response times and errors. Treatment with uric acid prior to conditioning an avoidance response in a single trial, reduced the incidence of retrograde amnesia for that response produced by posttraining ECS. With ECS there was only a 20% incidence of response retention; however, in uric-acid-treated mice, depending upon dose (0.5–20.0 mg/kg), there was from 47 to 73% retention of the conditioned avoidance response. These data suggested that uric acid, without affecting unconditioned behavior, seizure susceptibility, or threshold of response to the unconditioned stimulus (foot shock), apparently facilitated memory consolidation either by (1) decreasing the consolidation time, thereby reducing the effective interval within which stimuli were capable of disrupting the consolidation process, or (2) reducing the central electrical and/or biochemical effect that accounts either for consolidation disruption or amnesia, or (3) shifting the locus of the central effect to a site where its memory disruptive effects are reduced, or (4) acting in competition with other molecules formed, released, or activated by the amnesic stimulus to reduce their effect.

There are two observations made in conjunction with the possible proconsolidation effect of uric acid which provide support for an effect on the molecular level. One such finding is that uric acid, administered parenterally, is capable of elevating brain RNA and able to block the RNA-reducing effect of at least one amnesic stimulus, ECS. Another finding is that the elevation of brain serotonin by ECS, another corollary of its amnesic effect, is attenuated if animals have been pretreated with uric acid. We have observed that the intracranial injection of serotonin in mice produces a retrograde amnesia (Essman, 1973c) and that the site of maximal effect is the medial hippocampus. One of the effects that intrahippocampal serotonin injection shares in common with ECS, in addition to their effect of amnesic events, is their ability to produce a time-related, regional, cellular, and organelle-specific inhibition of protein synthesis (Essman, 1972). Uric acid has been shown (1) to attenuate the amnesic effect of (a) ECS, (b) intrahippocampal serotonin injection, and (c) parenteral butyric acid injection, and (2) to block the inhibition of protein synthesis normally produced by such treatments (Essman and Essman, 1977). The common denominator in these studies where uric acid facilitates memory consolidation by reducing the interfering effects of several treatments is that the elevation of brain serotonin (common to those amnesic stimuli considered) and the related inhibition of protein synthesis (the consequence of serotonin elevation) are attenuated or blocked by uric acid treatment. Whether this relationship also applies to endogenous uric acid remains in question, and whether drugs which, in the clinical situation, provide for increased uric acid levels, such as thiazides, also relate to its proconsolidation effect offer interesting questions which can possibly be partially answered in the clinical situation. Certainly, in this regard, antiuricogenic and uricosuric agents, such as colchicine and allopurinol, also deserve examination for effects that may be mediated upon learning and memory processes.

There are two observations, which have been made in conjunction with the possible proconsolidation effect of uric acid, which provide support for an effect on the molecular level. One such finding is that uric acid, administered parenterally, is capable of elevating brain RNA and able to block the RNA-reducing effect of at least one amnesic stimulus, ECS. Another finding is that the elevation of brain serotonin by ECS, another corollary of its amnesic effect, is attenuated if animals have been pretreated with uric acid. We have observed that the intracranial injection of serotonin in mice produces a retrograde amnesia (Essman, 1973c) and that the site of maximal effect is the medial hippocampus. One of the effects that intrahippocampal serotonin injection shares in common with ECS, in addition to their effect of amnesic events, is their ability to produce a time-related, regional, cellular, and organelle-specific inhibition of protein synthesis (Essman, 1972). Uric acid has been shown (1) to attenuate the amnesic effect of (a) ECS, (b) intrahippocampal serotonin injection, and (c) parenteral butyric acid injection, and (2) to block the inhibition of protein synthesis normally produced by such treatments (Essman and Essman, 1977). The common denominator in these studies where uric acid facilitates memory consolidation by reducing the interfering effects of several treatments is that the elevation of brain serotonin (common to those amnesic stimuli considered) and the related inhibition of protein synthesis (the consequence of serotonin elevation) are attenuated or blocked by uric acid treatment. Whether this relationship also applies to endogenous uric acid remains in question, and whether drugs which, in the clinical situation, provide for increased uric acid levels, such as thiazides, also relate to its proconsolidation effect offer interesting questions which can possibly be partially answered in the clinical situation. Certainly, in this regard, antiuricogenic and uricosuric agents, such as colchicine and allopurinol, also deserve examination for effects that may be mediated upon learning and memory processes.

A related methyl xanthine, which, like uric acid, acts to facilitate maze acquisition and reduces the amnesic effect of ECS in mice, is trimethyl uric acid (Essman, 1971). There is evidence that this agent stimulates brain RNA synthersis and reduces brain serotonin content — these effects being rather dose specific (10 mg/kg) in mice; uric acid appears to be more specific for its selective neurochamical effects. However, its potential clinical utility remains at present undefined. Certainly its clinical applicability would appear warranted if only its neurochemical effects were considered adequate to justify its use as a facilitative agent in learning and memory.

A stimulant which has been utilized clinically, at least partially on the basis of its reputed biochemical effects (stimulation of RNA polymerase activity in the rat brain), is magnesium pemoline (Glasky and Simon, 1966), although other groups have failed to replicate the biochemical observation. Behavioral facilitation in a series of animal studies was suggested for this drug (Plotnikoff, 1966 a,b,c), where response acquisition was facilitated, more rapid task relearning after ECS was observed, and recovery of pre-ECS avoidance behavior occurred. The amnesic effect of ECS was reduced by magnesium pemoline in rats (Stein and Brink, 1969) and a similar effect was found in man. Patients given magnesium pemoline showed some facilitation of learning and memory tasks given after ECS therapy (Small and Small, 1967; Small et al., 1968).

With magnesium pemoline, as with other central nervous system stimulants, there is the possiblitiy that sustained performance or attention are less compromised. Increased errors were noted, for example, under control conditions for a non-motivated continuous attention task. Magnesium pemoline, as well as caffeine and methylphenidate, prevented the error increase in these human subjects (Orzack et al., 1968). This agent, like other central stimulants, has been used in the treatment of childhood hyperkinesis (Page et al., 1974). Its efficacy in bringing about improved cognitive and perceptual functioning, as measured on test performance, without appreciable side effects and with a single daily dosage supports its clinical usefulness as an alternative to the amphetamines and methylphenidate for the management of hyperkinesis and associated learning problems.

Memory test performance among a geriatric population with documented memory defects was significantly improved by magnesium pemoline (Cameron, 1966). A 10% increase in memory score on the Wechsler memory quotient was achieved in subjects given the drug (25–125 mg/day) after 1 month. The acute administration of magnesium pemoline (25 or 37.5 mg, p.o.) to normal healthy males 3 hours before verbal and motor learning tasks had no effect upon learning, memory, or performance (Smith, 1967). Similarly, acute treatment of college students with magnesium pemoline (6.25–25.0 mg, p.o.) 2½ hours prior to a learning task that depended upon the ability to discriminate light cues, failed to alter the rate at which the correct response was learned (Burns et al, 1967).

There has been the suggestion that magnesium pemoline increases the excitatory properties of a strong stimulus in a learning situation, without necessarily affecting performance (DiGiusto and King, 1972) in the absence of a discrete conditioned stimulus. This observation raises the interesting issue of sensory facilitation with stimulants such as magnesium pemoline and might possibly explain why for some subjects (senile geriatric, hyperactive children, intellectually defective, etc.) the effects, if due to a sensory enhancement, are more apparent than in a normal population where its antifatigue effects appear to be the most apparent. Random geriatric populations in whom there are no signs of organic brain pathology, intellectual deterioration, or perceptual dysfunction do not necessarily show any benefit on memory tasks from magnesium pemoline. In one such study (Gilbert et al., 1973) subjects given the drug did not differ from placebo-treated controls in their performance on the Wechsler adult intelligence scale vocabulary subtest or the Guild memory test. From data obtained on a mood scale administered at the beginning and end of the study there was some indication that the drug increased depression and worrisomeness.

# 12

# Nicotine

The effects of nicotine upon performance in the behavioral realm and upon brain amines in the biochemical sector of its action constitute major issues with which the clinical pharmacology of its learning and memory effects is concerned. In animal studies increased locomotor activity levels followed the acute intravenous injection over a dose range of 0.18–0.43 mg/kg (Bonta et al., 1960), whereas with chronic injection (0.5–0.1 mg/kg, s.c. or i.p.) a significant decrease in the running time of rats was observed (Eisenberg, 1948, 1954). In man the effects of nicotine appear to reduce performance, but this effect may be related to a number of factors other than the central action of the drug *per se*. The nicotine content of a single inhaled cigarette (estimated at approximately 1–2 $\mu$g/kg equivalents in the blood), given ten times over a 6-hour period, increased the onset of fatigue and did not affect vigilance or tracking behavior (Heimstra, 1962). Tracking performance was decreased by the inhalation of four cigarettes over a brief time period (Wenzel and Davis, 1961). Aside from the absence of information regarding blood levels of nicotine at the time of performance evaluation, which was lacking in these studies, there are other issues that render the results extremely difficult to interpret. There is no clear separation between the physiological and behavioral effects of the gas phase of cigarette smoke quite apart from those of nicotine. There is also the question of what relationship metabolites of nicotine, formed by hepatic metabolism, bear to the observed effects. Dosage, absorption, and elimination are subject to wide intra- as well as interindividual variations, and the cumulative dosage and cumulative effect over time remain unknowns, still to be defined.

Animal studies of learning and memory provide some insights into both the effects of nicotine upon these processes as well as the neurochemical substrates of these processes affected by nicotine. The effects of nicotine upon learning in rodents has been shown to be related to the baseline behavior upon which the drug effect is imposed. Nicotine (0.1 mg/kg) given prior to maze learning trials facilitated the acquisition of younger rats (55, 61 days), which were better learners. Older rats (131, 158 days), which were poorer maze learners, did not show any alterations in their learning behavior with nicotine (Linuchev and Michelson, 1965). In mice, nicotine (0.5 mg/kg) facilitated the learning of an avoidance response in strains that were poor learners, but in strains that were good avoidance learners, avoidance conditioning was impaired (Bovet et al., 1966). Other conditions where nicotine acts to facilitate learning include younger versus older rats (Robustelli, 1966), task difficulty (Bovet-Nitti, 1966), younger versus older mice (Oliverio, 1967), morning versus evening (Bovet et al., 1967), and reactive versus nonreactive rats (Garg and Holland, 1968).

A cholinergic mechanism relating nicotine action upon learning to the central effect of the drug has been suggested by some results. It was found that the facilitation of memory consolidation could be achieved by the posttraining administration of atropine (Evangelista and Izquierdo, 1971), and when given prior to a shuttle avoidance task, its stimulant effect upon performance added to the stimulant effect of nicotine (Evangelista and Izquierdo, 1972). In the same study the stimulant action of nicotine was antagonized by prolonged pretreatment with atropine. The authors maintain that the drug effect, specific to the hippocampus, represents a probably electrical effect at that site. The interaction of nicotine and atropine in the hippocampus may be viewed as a cholingeric response to an amnesic stimulus and could constitute another basis upon which the neurochemical effect of this drug could be related to memory consolidation. Nicotine sulfate (1.0 mg/kg) given to mice 15 minutes prior to avoidance conditioning increased the amnesic effect of a posttraining ECS (Essman, 1969). When given 60 minutes prior to training, nicotine in the same dose reduced the amnesic effect of a posttraining ECS (Essman et al., 1968). ECS given to mice reduced the bound acetylcholine pool of the cerebral cortex by 88% and the ACh content of the synaptic vesicles in this region by 30% within 10 minutes after convulsion. For mice that were treated with nicotine sulfate 45 minutes earlier, ECS did not significantly reduce the vesicular ACh content (Essman, 1971b). These findings support the role of cholinergic mechanisms operative in memory consolidation insofar as nicotine action in reversing the cholinergic changes attendant upon retrograde amnesia are concerned.

An adrenergic mechanism for the action of nicotine upon learning has been proposed (Fulginiti and Orsingher, 1973) and supported by some experimental data. Rats showed facilitation by nicotine of a conditioned response. This facilitative effects was significantly reduced if the animals were pretreated with $\alpha$-methyl-$p$-tyrosine, a tyrosine hydroxylase inhibitor which leads to reduced brain levels of catecholamines. The blockade of nicotine facilitation of learning by $\alpha$-methyl-$p$-tyrosine was abolished by nialamide, a monoamine oxidase inhibitor providing for sustained increases in brain catecholamines. The facilitative action of nicotine was thus shown to depend upon brain levels and/or metabolism of catecholamines.

A role for brain serotonin in the action of nicotine upon learning and memory has also been indicated. As previously noted, nicotine exerts a biphasic effect upon the amnesic effect of ECS and this effect appears time dependent. Coincident with the nicotine-induced antagonism of the ECS-induced amnesia there was: (1) increased availability of centrally active peripheral metabolites of nicotine, (-) cotinine, and 3-pyridylacetic acid, (2) blockade of the serotonin-elevating effect of ECS, and (3) an increase in brain serotonin turnover rate.

In addition to those factors mentioned there are others which have implications for the clinical pharmacology of nicotine in learning and memory. One of these is the development of tolerance, which may easily develop and can persist for prolonged periods after withdrawal. This may be one condition that, in particular, may account for differences in the acute and chronic effects of nicotine upon learning and memory in man, and more generally address the issue of cigarette smoke and how it affects such processes. A possible model applicable to man, which relates to this problem, is the observation (Stolerman et al., 1973) that chronic tolerance produced in rats by nicotine injected, orally ingested with drinking water, or subcutaneously implanted could persist for as long as 90 days after drug treatment. If facilitation of learning or memory were associated with either acute or chronic tolerance to nicotine, then maintenance of the tolerance state could constitute an important condition for such effects to be continued. In another respect, failure to maintain the tolerance state could itself be a basis for a secondary but real disruptive effect from nicotine.

In a clinical context of its broader psychoactive effects, nicotine is a mood alterant. As such, its subjective effect upon mood and affect, like that of any other psychoactive agent, can independently constitute a basis for its effect upon learning or memory in man. For example, smoking while involved in a learning or memory task may provide a subjective basis upon which cognitive performance is altered. For example, consideration of such factors as the nicotine content of cigarettes, diurnal variations, and differences in puffing rate contributed to the subjective report of mood change in habitual smokers before and after smoking (Ague, 1973). Dose-dependent effects of nicotine on pleasantness, aggression, anxiety, and tension were observed. Such factors may well, depending upon the learning or memory conditions, serve as motivational states upon which response changes can be based.

The multiple ways in which several of the brain biogenic amines are involved in the clinical pharmacology of learning and memory offer interesting future prospects for agents that may provide further insight into the biochemical substrates of learning or memory or for the molecular relationships of specific drugs for these processes.

# 13

# Procaine

The use of procaine hydrochloride or stabilized forms of this local anesthetic in geriatric populations as an agent to interrupt aging processes, reverse depression, and promote learning and memory has warranted some brief consideration of its place in the clinical pharmacology of learning and memory. Learning and memory was assessed in rats chronically treated with procaine, using a 13-choice maze (Aslan et al., 1965). Among control rats, 24-month-old animals made more errors per trial, had longer maze running times, and showed longer running times per trial than 10-month-old rats. Procaine-treated, 24-month-old rats showed fewer maze errors than control rats, had shorter maze running times, and shorter running times per trial than non-drug-treated control rats of the same age. These measures of learning and memory for the procaine-treated 24-month-old rat were comparable with those obtained from control rats of 10 months of age. The use of stabilized procaine hydrochloride (Gerovital H-2) in geriatric populations has been viewed as a possible route toward the use of this compound as an antidepressant or vehicle through which cognitive changes accompanying senility and arteriosclerotic brain disease might be modified (Smigel et al., 1960; Kral et al., 1967). Changes were observed in somatization and anxiety/depression by the third week of treatment with this agent in a group of depressed geriatric patients (Sakalis et al., 1974); no changes in memory were observed, however. One point upon which the presumed mechanism of procaine action has been based for basic investigation and clinical use is particularly notable, namely, that monoamine oxidase, which regulates the catabolism of catecholamines and indole amines, has been observed to increase in activity with aging (Robinson et al., 1972). This increase was noted in human platelets and plasma and was correlated with an age-related increase in the hindbrain. Norepinephrine levels decreased with age, whereas the serotonin content remained fairly uniform with age in the human hindbrain, but the serotonin metabolite 5-HIAA increased sharply after the age of 65. This latter observation could indicate a change in serotonin turnover in the hindbrain with aging. Procaine has been shown to be a monoamine oxidase inhibitor (MacFarland and Besbris, 1974; MacFarlane, 1975). The drug was shown to be a reversible, competitive inhibitor of monoamine oxidase, suggesting that it may interfere with aging-related enzyme increments and favor the restoration of amine substrate and/or turnover rates characteristic of the pre-aging nervous system. This action of procaine as a monoamine oxidase inhibitor contrasts with the mode of inhibitor action of other more traditional agents, such as pargyline and phenylzine, which are irreversible inhibitors, and tranylcypromine, which is a partially reversible inhibitor. It is subject to question whether the efficacy of a monoamine oxidase inhibitor as an antidepressant in clinical use or its effect upon learning and memory processes depends upon the reversibility of enzyme inhibition. In particular, these findings to raise the question of the extent to which clinically utilized monoamine oxidase inhibitors serve to modify either learning or memory.

A difference in the effects of iproniazid and tranylcypromine upon a dark-avoidance conditioned response was demonstrated in mice (Bucci and Bovet, 1974). Iproniazid (25.5 and 100 mg/kg) decreased the percentage of conditioned responses, whereas tranylcypromine (2.5 and 5.0 mg/kg) caused a marked increase in the percentage of conditioned responses 5 hours after administration. The point in time at which maximal facilitation of conditioned response performance after tranylcypromine treatment occurred, was coincident with a maximal increase in brain norepinephrine after monoamine oxidase inhibition. It may be of interest to consider that iproniazid-induced conditioned response impairment relates well in time to maximal elevation in brain serotonin. The difference in the time course in the change in these brain amines by different monoamine oxidase inhibitors in different concentrations could constitute a determinant of the outcome upon learned behavior. This view is further supported in studies demonstrating a biphasic effect of tranylcypromine on learned behavior in rats (Bucci, 1974). An initial depressant effect of the drug upon spontaneous motor activity and a learned conditioned response was observed, but by 5 hours after drug treatment, conditioned avoidance behavior and locomotor activity were stimulated. The initial substrate of monoamine oxidase that increases after enzyme inhibition is serotonin, and by 5 hours brain norepinephrine has maximally increased. The biphasic effect of tranylcypromine may be viewed in terms of which brain amines are elevated at those times where learned behavior is measured.

In man the effects of tranylcypromine upon conditioning and learning have been studied in an attempt to relate possible effects of this monoamine oxidase inhibitor to its arousal effect (Weckowicz et al., 1974). No significant difference in eyelid conditioning between drug- and placebo-treated subjects was observed, except for a relationship, in the placebo group only, between eyelid conditionability and anxiety score. Paired-associate learning among placebo-treated subjects was facilitated by a higher anxiety score. The apparently facilitative effects of the anxiety level upon eyelid conditioning and paired-associate learning appeared to be eliminated by tranylcypromine which, regardless of differences in noted depression or anxiety, did not facilitate conditioning and learning. An issue of some importance in this study is the time course over which the action of tranylcypromine may be expected to act. This could well be a considerable disparity in time between the antidepressant effects of this agent and its effects upon either learned behavior—which is most probably an effect upon performance—or the acquisition or retention of behavior.

Like the time course and central effects of clinically utilized monoamine oxidase inhibitors, some further definition of these parameters for procaine is indicated. As a weak inhibitor of monoamine oxidase, which is reversible and competitive, procaine probably avoids some of the toxic and untoward effects encountered with other monoamine oxidase inhibitors. It is not immediately apparent, however, if the possibly unique mode of monoamine oxidase inhibition and the associated stimulantlike effect of procaine are adequate to account for possibly facilitative effects upon learning or memory.

Another consideration that applies to procaine is the degree to which its action may depend upon smooth muscle effects or cerebral vascular resistance. In this regard some comparison with agents such as vasodilators and mediators of altered ganglion cell metabolism might be in order.

# 14

# Papaverine and Hydergine

Increased cerebral blood flow and decreased cerebral-vascular resistance result from the administration of the nonspecific smooth muscle relaxant papaverine. This agent has been employed with varied success in the treatment of a variety of symptoms in the geriatric patient, including mental confusion (LeBrecque, 1966), chronic brain syndrome secondary to cerebral arteriosclerosis (Stern, 1970; Ritter et al., 1971; McQuillan et al., 1974), and psychological and psychophysical test performance (Smith et al., 1968). Some studies (Bazo, 1973) have indicated that papaverine has little effect upon intellectual function or cognition when given for 12 weeks to a population with cerebral arteriosclerosis with cerebrovascular insufficiency. However, other studies (Bambasova et al., 1974) have indicated that the drug did improve intellectual functions and verbal communication and reduced anxiety and depression in patients with arteriosclerotic dementia.

Similar disorders of cognition, relevant to learning and memory, have been treated in patients with senile dementia or compromised cerebral circulatory functions using the dihydrogenated ergot alkaloid hydergine. This agent has been reported to have varied success, but appears to favorably compare with and even provide for more effective therapeutic promise than papaverine (Gerin, 1969; Banen, 1971; Rao and Norris, 1972). In a double-blind study in which hydergine and papaverine were compared the former drug provided significantly enhanced cognitive and intellectual function (Bazo, 1973). A combination of hydergine with thioridazine proved to be beneficial in the treatment of several pathological states characteristic of senescence and cerebral atherosclerosis (Predescu et al., 1974) and indicates that hydergine therapy may provide a favorable baseline upon which to superimpose the potentially beneficial effects of other central stimulants in the elderly. Hydergine was found to be markedly more beneficial than papaverine in the treatment of a number of selected symptoms associated with aging (Rosen, 1975). On rated symptomatology there was twice the improvement noted with hydergine than with papaverine, in particular, mental alertness, which appears to be a significant factor underlying the motivational as well as persistence aspects of performance on tasks that require new learning or the retrieval of recent memory. Partially underlying the rationale for the clinical use of papaverine and ergot alkaloids, particularly for decreased learning ability and compromised memory functions in aging, is the possibility that cerebral vasodilatation and altered cerebral blood flow will permit the access of endogenous as well as exogenous substances to the central nervous system, where they may exert a positive effect. Aside from one suggestive study (Predescu et al., 1974), where the presumed transport and central action of a stimulant have been enhanced by combination with an ergot preparation, little use has been made clinically of this approach to the pharmacotherapy of geriatric cognitive dysfunction. It would appear that considerable merit lies in the use of such an approach. A possibly related issue and one for which some preliminary comment may be offered concerns the effects of proteins, peptides, and amino acids upon learning and memory. An increased blood flow could make these selectively or, as an aggregate, more readily available for central transport and provide for effects, either directly or secondary to their availability, which account for improved cognitive functions.

# 15

# Peptides

Analogs of adrenocorticotropic hormone (ACTH) or melanocyte stimulating hormone (MSH) have been used to investigate changes in learned behavior and the retrieval of acquired responses. Several studies in animals have indicated facilitation of shuttle box avoidance in rats (Beatty et al., 1970) with ACTH using a high-intensity conditioning foot shock. Other studies (Stratton and Kastin, 1974) found that at a low level of foot shock in a shuttle box avoidance rats given MSH showed improved acquisition. Positively reinforced learned behavior has also been facilitated by the administratin of ACTH (Guth, et al., 1971) or MSH (Stratton and Kastin, 1975).

Some limited data for the effects of one analogue of ACTH, consisting of the amino acids 4–10, are available from studies in man. In subjects treated with $ACTH_{4-10}$ greater attention was rendered to stimuli presented in a visual discrimination paradigm (Sandman et al., 1975). The attention requirements of subjects for a continuous reaction time task were improved for subjects given ACTH$_{4-10}$ (Gaillard and Sanders, 1975). A failure to observe any effect of ACTH$_{4-10}$ upon the serial learning of paired-associate stimuli or short-term memory for numbers has been noted. These tasks may be less dependent upon attentional factors, which in other studies with this peptide appear to be maximally affected. The effects of ACTH$_{4-10}$ (30 mg, s.c.) upon the performance of 20 depressed patients on a test battery designed to evaluate memory consolidation was assessed 90 minutes before and 150 minutes after injection, given 30 minutes after a unilateral electroconvulsive shock. No positive effect upon memory consolidation was observed (d'Elia and Frederiksen, 1980a). In a similar study (d'Elia and Frederiksen, 1980b) there was no evidence that a single dose of ACTH$_{4-10}$ could improve retrieval of memory after a single unilateral ECT.

The central effects of synthetic ACTH analogues have been considered and relate in a most interesting way to some of the points considered in earlier discussions. After chronic peptide administration to the rat it was found that midbrain gamma-aminobutyric acid and serotonin concentrations were reduced, norepinephrine turnover was increased, and serotonin turnover was decreased (Leonard, 1974). There are many questions about peptide-induced facilitation of learning and memory processes, particularly in man, which remain to be answered.

Notable among these are issues of disposition, absorption, transport, and stability of parenterally administered compounds, the amino acid composition and/or sequence of which appears to make them quite specific as activators of cognitive functions. Again, as previously discussed for other agents, effects upon fatigue, vigilance, attention, and motivation are all issues that limit the specificity of peptides for the enhancement of learning and/or memory. The chronicity of treatment, the dose regimen, and the indirect contributions of peptides to the hormonal status of the adrenal, particularly after chronic administration, all represent factors which can affect the outcome of behavior studies, especially those in which task performance requires complex responses to stimuli of low associative value or situations of little failure risk.

Other peptides have also been considered as possible proconsolidation agents, or perhaps more generally as effectors against memory loss in a more clinical context (Kent, 1981). As previously mentioned in the context of the dysmnesias, vasopressin is one such peptide. One advantage offered with this agent is that it can be effectively administered via a nasal spray, thereby obviating parenteral injection. A profound traumatic amnesia reported in two patients was effectively treated with vasopressin (Oliveros and Jandali, 1978) to the extent that both mood and memory had almost improved to pretrauma levels. Improved test performance for attention, concentration, and motor tasks was noted in subjects given vasopressin by nasal spray, 3 times per day for 3 days (Legros et al., 1978). Improved memory functions after vasopressin treatment have also been reported in at least one patient with Korsakoff's syndrome (LeBorce et al., 1978). These preliminary clinical studies support earlier animal investigations showing that vasopressin was capable of sustaining avoidance behavior, facilitating acquisition, that it antagonizes the retrograde amnesic effects of several agents and reverses the memory dysfunction seen in vasopressin deficiency (de Wied, 1965, 1971; Van Wimersma Greidanus et al., 1971; Lande et al., 1972; Rigter et al., 1974; de Wied, et al., 1975a).

Another posterior pituitary peptide, which in contrast to vasopressin has been suggested to act as a proamnesic agent is oxytocin (Bohus et al., 1978). A transient impairment of recall, without notable effect upon learning, was produced in human volunteers given large doses of intranasal (15 i.u./day) or intravenous (200mU/minute for 6 or 8 hours) oxytocin (Ferrier et al., 1980).

The major difference between the requirements for the administration in man of peptides and other agents used to affect learning or memory is that the former must be injected or inhaled rather than ingested. This not only introduces a more potent placebo effect, greater intersubject variability, and a difference in the time course of presumed maximal action, but it also limits the subject population where this route of administration becomes acceptable or is tolerated. A motivational variable clearly emerges for the subject willing to tolerate a series of injections with a goal of improved cognitive performance, as compared with those subjects that are either not risktakers or view the goal as not worth the treatment. These considerations place limitations upon the extent to which the clinical use of peptides for the enhancement of learning and memory may be indicated and further evaluation appears warranted.

# Some Concluding Observations

There have been numerous other pharmacological agents which have been considered to possess a role in the mediation of learning and memory processes and as such could have clinical applicability in man. These include such compounds such as niacin, glutamic acid, thyroxine, pyridoxine, trace metals, and so on. A major consideration in the application of these agents as well as others to learning or memory processes is the behavioral baseline upon which effects are superimposed and against which effects are evaluated. Differences in the drug effect between a control population and one with arteriosclerotic changes, mental deficiency, learning disabilities, perceptual disorders, and so on, may not always represent the best basis for clinical evaluation. The separation of performance effects (motor acceleration, antifatigue, etc.) from sensory effects (lowered sensory threshold, increased vigilance, etc.), from behavioral effects (increased motivation, interest, attention, etc.) essentially constitutes the most fundamental requirement for defining a clinical pharmacology of learning and memory. The need for such a pharmacology exists on several levels of function and dysfunction, but it appears more apparent that drug effects upon learning and memory processes depend upon the central biochemical action of the drug and the central mechanism to which the cognitive functions are tied. Several of these interdependencies of drug action and underlying mechanism have been either proposed or experimentally supported, but others still await such definition. It is through such definition that a clinical pharmacology of learning and memory will evolve and its pharmacopoeia will increase.

# References

Abadon, P. N., Ahmed, K., and Scholefield, P. G. Biochemical studies on Tofranil. *Can. J. Biochem.* 39: 551–558, 1961.

Abood, L. G. Effect of chlorpromazine on phosphorylation of brain mitochondria. *Proc. Soc. Exp. Biol. Med.* 88: 688–690, 1955.

Abt, J. P., Essman, W. B., and Jarvik, M. E. Ether-induced retrograde amnesia for one-trial conditioning in mice. *Science* 133: 1477–1478, 1961.

Adam, N., and Collins, G. I. Late components of the visual evoked potential to search in short-term memory. *Electroencephalogr. Clin. Neurophysiol.* 14: 147–156, 1978.

Adam, N., and Collins, G. I. Alteration by enflurane of electrophysiologic correlates of search in short-term memory. *Anesthesiology* 50: 93–97, 1979.

Adams, R. G. Pre-sleep ingestion of 2 hypnotic drugs and subsequent performance. *Psychopharmacologia* 40: 185–190, 1974.

Adolfsson, R., Gottfries, C. G., Oreland, L., Roos, B. E., and Winblad, B. Reduced levels of catecholamines in the brain and increased activity of monoamine oxidase in platelets in Alzheimer's disease. Therapeutic implications. In: Katzman, R., Terry R. D., and Bick, K. L. (Eds.) *Alzheimer's Disease and Related Dementias.* New York: Raven Press, 1978, pp. 441–451.

**159**

Agathon, M. Intéret de la méthode des images consécutives dans l'étude de l'action des drogues psychotropes. *Rev. Neuropsych. Infant. Hyg. Ment. Enfan.* 12: 209–216, 1964.

Aggeler, P. M., O'Reilly, R. A., and Leong, L. Potentiation of anticoagulant effects of warfarin by phenylbutazone. *N. Engl. J. Med.* 276: 496–501, 1967.

Ague, C. Nicotine and smoking: Effect upon subjective changes in mood. *Psychopharmacologia (Berlin)* 30: 323–328, 1973.

Albert, M. S., Butters, N., and Levin, J. Temporal gradients in the retrograde amnesia of patients with alcoholic Korsakoff's disease. *Arch. Neurol.* 36: 211–216, 1979.

Alkana, R. L., and Parker, E. S. Memory facilitation by post-training injection of ethanol. *Psychopharmacology* 66: 117–119, 1979.

Alpern, H. P., and Jackson, S. J. Short term memory: A neuropharmacologically distinct process. *Behav. Biol.* 22: 133–146, 1978.

Alpern, H. P., and Marriott, J. G. Short term memory: Facilitation and disruption with cholinergic agents. *Physiol. Behav.* 11: 571–575, 1973.

Anderson, P. Organization of hippocampal neurons and their interconnections. In: Issacson, R., and Pribam, K. (Eds.) *The Hippocampus.* London: Plenum Press, 1975.

Anisman, H., and Kokkindis, C. Effect of scopolamine, *d*-amphetamine and other drugs affecting catecholine on spontaneous alternation and locomotive activity in mice. *Psychopharmacologia* 45: 55–63, 1975.

Anisman, H., Kokkindis, C., Glazier, S., and Remington, G. Differentiation of response biases elicited by scopolamine and *d*-amphetamine: Effects on habituation. *Behav. Biol.* 18: 401–417, 1976.

Anzelark, G., Crow, T., and Greenberg, T. Impaired learning and decreased cortical norepinephrine after bilateral locus coeruleus lesions. *Science* 181: 682–684, 1973.

Aprison, M. H. On a proposed theory for the mechanism of action of serotonin in the brain. *Rec. Adv. Biol. Psychiat.* 4: 133–146, 1962.

Artusio, J. F., Jr. Ether analgesia during major surgery. *JAMA* 157: 33–36, 1955.

Aslan, A., Vrabiescu, A., Domilescu, C., Campeanu, L., Costiniu, M., and Stanescu, S. Long-term treatment with procaine (Gerovital H$_3$) in albino rats. *J. Gerontol.* 20: 1–8, 1965.

Avioli, L. V., Birge, S., Lee, S. W., and Slatopolsky, E. The metabolic fate of vitamin D$_3$-$^3$H in chronic renal failure. *J. Clin. Invest.* 47: 2239–2252, 1968.

Avis, H. H., and Pert, A. A comparison of the effects of muscarine and nicotinic anticholinergic drugs on habituation and fear conditioning. *Psychopharmacologia* 34: 209–222, 1974.

Bahlman, S. H. Eger, E. I., II, and Cromwell, T. H. Anesthetics and amnesia. *Anesthesiology* 36: 191, 1972.

Baldessarini, R. J., and Fischer, J. E. Serotonin metabolism in rat brain after surgical diversion of the portal venus circulation. *Nature (London) New Biol.* 245: 25–27, 1973.

Bambasova, E., Bilkova, J., and Budinska, K. Papaverin in the treatment of psychiatric patients. *Activ. Nerv. Sup. (Praha)* 16: 192–193, 1974.

Banen, D. An ergot preparation (Hydergine) for relief of symptoms of cerebrovascular insufficiency. *J. Am. Geriatr. Soc.* 20: 22–29, 1971.

Baratti, C. M., Huygen, P., Mino, J., Merlo, A., and Gardella, J. Memory facilitation with post trial injections of oxotremerine and physostigmine in mice. *Psychopharmacology* 64: 85–88, 1979.

Barkov, N. K. The analgesic properties of certain phenothiazine derivatives. *Bull. Exp. Biol. Med.* 50: 950–952, 1961a.

Barkov, N. K. The influence of phenothiazine derivatives on the action of analgesics. *Bull. Exp. Biol. Med.* 51: 185–188, 1961b.

Barrter, F. C., Pronove, P., and Gill, J. R., Jr. Hyperplasia of the juxtaglomerular complex with hyperaldosteronism and hypokalemic alkalosis: A new syndrome. *Am. J. Med.* 33: 811–828, 1962.

Bartlet, A. L. The 5-hydroxytryptamine content of mouse brain and whole mice after treatment with some drugs affecting the central nervous system. *Brit. J. Pharmacol.* 15: 140–146, 1960.

Battig, K. Die Wirkung pharmakologischer Stoffe auf verschiedene Funktionen des Verhaltens der Ratte. *Pflüger's Arch. Ges. Physiol.* 274: 59, 1961.

Bazo, A. An ergot alkaloid preparation (Hydergine) versus papaverine in treating common complaints of the ages: Double-blind study. *J. Am. Geriatr. Soc.* 21: 63–71, 1973.

Beatty, D. A., Beatty, W. A., Bowman, R. E., and Gilchrist, J. C. The effects of ACTH adrenalectomy and dexamethasone on the acquisition of an avoidance response in rats. *Physiol. Behav.* 5: 939–944, 1970.

Bergström, L., Häkkinen, V., Jauhiainen, T., and Kahri, A. The effects of chlorpromazine on the percentual manifold of the sense of hearing. *Ann. Acad. Sci. Fenn., Ser. A: V. Medica* 106: 1–12, 1964.

Berry, S., and Thompson, R. Prediction of learning rate from hippocampal electroencephalogram. *Science* 200: 1298–1300, 1978.

Besser, G. M., Duncan, C., and Quilliam, J. P. Modification of the auditory flutter fusion threshold by centrally acting drugs in man. *Nature* 211: 751, 1966.

Besser, G. M., and Steinberg, H. L'interaction du chlordiazepoxide et du dextroamphetamine chez l'homme. *Thérapie* 22: 977–990, 1976.

Bignami, G., and Gatti, G. L. Analysis of drug effects on multiple fixed ratio 33-fixed interval 5 min. in pigeons. *Psychopharmacologia* 15: 310–332, 1969.

Bixler, E. O., Scharf, M. B., Soldatos, C. R., Mitsky, D. J., and Kales, A. Effects of hypnotic drugs on memory. *Life Sci.* 25: 1379–1388, 1979.

Blass, J. P., and Gibson, G. E. Abnormality of a thiamin-requiring enzyme in patients with Wernicke–Korsakoff syndrome. *N. Engl. J. Med.* 297: 1367–1370, 1977.

Blogovski, M. Exploration of an elevated maze used as a neuropharmacological test (in French). *Compt. Rend.* 249: 2868–2870, 1959.

Bloomer, H. A., Barton, L. J., and Meddock, R. K., Jr. Penicillin-induced encephalopathy in uremic patients. *JAMA* 200: 121–123, 1967.

Blozouski D., Cudennec, A., and Garrigou, D. Deficits in passive-avoidance following atropine in the developing rat. *Psychopharmacology* 54: 139–143, 1977.

Bohus, B., Urban, I., Van Wimersma Greidanus, T. B., and de Wied, D. Opposite effects of oxytocin and vasopressin on avoidance behaviour and hippocampal theta rhythm in the rat. *Neuropharmacology* 17: 239–247, 1978.

Boissier, J. F., Dumont, C., Ratouis, R., and Pagny, J. Tentative de pharmacologie prévisionnelle dans le domaine des neuroleptiques: actions sédative centrale et adrénolytique de la *N*(diméthoxy-s, 4-phénéthyl)*N*' (chloro-2-phényl) pipérazine. *Arch. Int. Pharmacodyn. Therap.* 133: 29–49, 1961.

Boissier, J. R., and Simon, P. Dissociation of two components in the investigation of behavior of the mouse. *Arch. Int. Pharmacodyn. Therap.* 147: 372-387, 1964.

Boissier, J. R., Simon, P., and Lwoff, J. M. Use of a specific reaction of mice (method of the perforated board) for the study of psychotropic drugs (in French). *Thérapie* 19: 571–589, 1964.

Bonta, I. L., Delver, A., Simons, L., and deVos, C. J. A newly developed motility apparatus and its applicability into pharmacological designs. *Arch. Int. Pharmacodyn. Therap.* 129: 381–394, 1960.

Bovet, D., Bovet-Nitti, F., and Oliverio, A. Action of nicotine on spontaneous and acquired behavior of rats and mice. *Ann. N.Y. Acad. Sci.* 142: 261–267, 1967.

Bovet, D., McGaugh, J. L., and Oliverio, A. Effects of posttrial administration of drugs on avoidance learning of mice. *Life Sci.* 5: 1309–1315, 1966.

Bovet-Nitti, F. Facilitation of simultaneous visual discrimination by nicotine in the rat. *Psychopharmacologia* 10: 59–66, 1966.

Bowen, D. M., and Davison, A. N. Extrapyramidal diseases and dementia. *Lancet* 1: 1199–1200, 1975.

Bowen, D. M., Flack, R. H., Smith, G. B., White, P., and Davison, A. N. Brain decarboxylase activities as indices of pathological changes in senile dementia. *Lancet* 1: 1247–1249, 1974.

Bowen, D. M., Smith, C. B., and Davison, A. N. Molecular changes in senile dementia. *Brain* 96: 849–856, 1973.

Bowen, D. M., Smith, C. B., White, P., and Davison, A. N. Neurotransmitter-related enzymes and indices of hypoxia in senile dementia and other abiotrophies. *Brain* 99: 459–496, 1976.

Bowen, D. M., White, P., Spillane, J. A., Goodhart, M. J., Curzon, G., Iwangoff, P., Meier-Ruge, W., and Davison, A. An. Accelerated aging or selective neuronal loss as an important cause of dementia? *Lancet* 1: 11–14, 1979.

Bowman, R. E., Heironimus, M. P., Forbes, J., Leary, R. W., and Harlow, H. F. Facilitation of discrimination learning but not of learning set by post-training injections of pentylenetetrazol in rhesus monkeys. *Behav. Neurol. Biol.* 28: 89–98, 1980.

Bowman, R. E. Heironimus, M. P., and Harlow, H. F. Pentylenetetrazol: Post-training injection facilitates discrimination learning in rhesus monkeys. *Physiol. Psychol.* 7: 265–268, 1979.

Boyd, W., Graham-White, I., and Blackwood, G. Clinical effects of choline in Alzheimer senile dementia. *Lancet* 2: 711, 1977.

Bradley, P. B., and Hance, A. J. The effect of chlorpromazine and methopromazine on the electrical activity of the brain in the cat. *Electroencephal. Clin. Neurophysiol.* 9: 2, 1957.

Bradley, P. B., and Key, B. J. A comparative study of the effects of drugs on the arousal system of the brain. *Br. J. Pharmacol.* 14: 340, 1959.

Breen, R. A., and McGaugh, J. L. Facilitation of maze learning with posttrial injections of picrotoxin. *J. Comp. Physiol. Psychol.* 54: 498–501, 1961.

Brierly, J. The neuropathology of amnestic states. In: Whitty, C., and Zangwill, O. (Eds.) *Amnesia,* 2nd ed. London: Butterworths, 1977.

Brimblecomb, R. W. Effects of psychotropic drugs on open-field behavior in rats. *Psychopharmacologia* 4: 139–147, 1963.

Brimer, A., Schnieden, H., and Simon, A. The effect of chlorpromazine and chlordiazepoxide on cognitive functioning. *Br. J. Psychiat.* 110: 723–725, 1964.

Brin, M., Tal, M., Ostashever, A. A., and Kalinsky, H. Effect of thiamine deficiency on activity of erythrocyte hemolysate transketolase. *J. Nutr.* 71: 273–280, 1960.

Bronstein, P. M., Neiman, H., Wolkoff, F. D., and Levine, M. J. The development of habituation in the rat. *Animal Learn. Behav.* 2: 92–96, 1974a.

Bronstein, P. M., Neiman, H., Wolkoff, F. D., and Levine, M. J. Age related differences in rats' spontaneous alternation. *Animal Behav.* 2: 288, 1974b.

Brooks, G. W., and Mueller, E. Serum urate concentrations among university professors; relation to drive, achievement, and leadership. *JAMA* 195: 415–418, 1966.

Brooks, S. M., Werk, E. E., Ackerman, S. J., Sullivan, I., and Thrasher, K. Adverse effects of phenobarbital on corticosteroid metabolism in patients with bronchial asthma. *N Engl. J. Med.* 286: 1125–1126, 1972.

Brown, B. B. CNS drug actions and interactions in mice. *Arch. Int. Pharmacodyn. Therap.* 128: 391–414, 1960.

Brown, K., and Warburton, D. Attention of stimulus sensitivity by scopolamine. *Psychonomic Soc.* 22: 297–298, 1971.

Bruce, D. L., and Bach, M. J. Psychologic studies of human performance as affected by traces of enflurane and nitrous oxide. *Anesthesiology* 42: 194–196, 1975.

Bruce, D. L., and Bach, M. J. Effects of trace anesthetic gases on behavioral performance of volunteers. *Br. J. Anaesth.* 48: 871–875, 1976.

Bruce, D. L., Bach, M. J., and Arbit, J. Trace anesthetic effects on perceptual, cognitive and motor skills. *Anesthesiology* 40: 453–458, 1974.

Brunaud, M., and Siou, G. Action des substances psychotropes chez le rat, sur un état d'agressivité provoqué. In: Bradley, P. B., Deniker, P., and

Radouco-Thomas, C. (Eds.) *Neuropsychopharmacology,* vol. I. Amsterdam: Elsevier, 1960, pp. 282–286.

Brush, F. R., Davenport, J. W., and Polidora, V. J. TCAP: Negative results in avoidance and water maze learning and retention. *Psychon. Sci.* 4: 183–184, 1966.

Bucci, L. The biphasic effect of small doses of tranylcypromine on the spontaneous motor activity and learned conditioned behavior in rats. *Pharmacology (Basel)* 12: 354–361, 1974.

Bucci, L., and Bovet, D. The effect of iproniazid and tranylcypromine studied with a dark-avoidance conditioned schedule. *Psychopharmacologia (Berlin)* 35: 179–188, 1974.

Buchel, L., Levy, J., and Tanguy, O. The importance of antagonism and synergism in the pharmacological study of neuroleptics (in French). *J. Physiol. (Paris)* 54: 771–786, 1962.

Buckholtz, N. S., and Bowman, R. E. Retrograde amnesia and brain RNA content after TCAP. *Physiol. Behav.* 5: 911–914, 1970.

Buczko, W., and Tarasiewicz, S. The influence of albumin degradation products (ADP) on the central action of caffeine. *Acta Med. Pol.* 17: 111–117, 1976.

Bunch, M. E., and Mueller, C. G. The influence of metrazol upon maze learning ability. *J. Comp. Psychol.* 32: 569–574, 1941.

Burns, B. D. *The Mammalian Cerebral Cortex.* London: Edward Arnold, 1958, p. 90.

Burns, J. T., House, R. F., Fensch, F. C., and Miller, J. G. Effects of magnesium pemoline and dextroamphetamine on human learning. *Science* 155: 849–851, 1967.

Buxton, D. A., Brimdlecombe, R. W., French, M. C., and Redfern, P. H. Brain acetylcholine concentration and acetylcholinesterase activity in selectively-bred strains of rats. *Psychopharmacology* 47: 97–99, 1976.

Cade, J. F. J. Lithium salts in the treatment of psychotic excitement. *Med. J. Australia* 36: 349, 1949.

Carlsson, A., and Winblad, B. Influence of age and time interval between death and autopsy on dopamine and 3-methoxytyramine levels in human basal ganglia. *J. Neurol. Trans.* 38: 271–276, 1976.

Cameron, D. E. Presidential address. Society of Biological Psychiatry Meeting. Washington, D.C., 1966.

Carlini, G. R. S., and Carlini, E. A. Effects of strychnine and *Cannabis Sativa* (marihuana) on the nucleic acid content in brain of the rat. *Med. Pharmacol. Exp.* 12: 21–26, 1965.

Carlton, P. Some effects of scopolamine, atropine and amphetamine in three behavioral situations. *Pharmacologist* 3: 60, 1961.

Carlton, P. Cholinergic mechanism in the control of behavior by the brain. *Psychol. Rev.* 70: 19–39, 1963.

Carlton, P. Scopolamine, atropine and light-reinforced responding. *Psychonomic Sci.* 5: 347–348, 1966.

Carlton, P., and Adokat, C. Attenuated habituation due to parachlorophenylalanine. *Pharmacol. Biochem. Behav.* 1: 657–663, 1973.

Carlton, P. L., and Didamo, P. Augmentation of the behavioral effects of amphetamine by atropine. *J. Pharmacol. Exp. Therap.* 132: 91–96, 1961.

Carlton, P., and Markiewicz, B. Behavioral effects of atropine and scopolamine. In: Furchgott, E. (Ed.) *Pharmacological and Biophysical Agents and Behavior.* New York: Academic Press, 1971.

Carpenter, M. *Human Neuroanatomy.* Baltimore: Williams and Wilkens, 1976.

Casey, J. F., Lasky, J. J., Klett, C. J., and Hollister, L. E. Treatment of schizophrenic reactions with phenothiazine derivatives. A comparative study of chlorpromazine, triflupromazine, mepazine, prochlorperazine, perphenazine and phenobarbital. *Am. J. Psychiat.* 117: 97–105, 1960.

Cerletty, J. M., and Engbring, N. Y. Azotemia and glucose intolerance. *Ann. Intern. Med.* 66: 1097–1108, 1967.

Chamberlain, T. J., Rothschild, G. H., and Gerard, R. W. Drugs affecting RNA and learning. *Proc. Nat. Acad. Sci.* 52: 918–924, 1963.

Chen, G., Bohner, B., and Bratton, A. C., Jr. The influence of certain central depressants on fighting behavior in mice. *Arch. Int. Pharmacodyn.* 142: 30–34, 1963.

Chen, G. M., and Weston, J. K. The analgesic and anesthetic effect of 1-(1-phenylcyclohexyl) piperdine HC on the monkey. *Anesth. Analg.* 39: 132–137, 1960.

Cherkin, A., and Harroun, P. Anesthesia and memory processes. *Anesthesiology* 34: 469–474, 1971.

Chisholm, D. C., and Moore, J. W. Effects of chlordiazepoxide on the acquisition of shuttle avoidance in the rabbit. *Psychon. Sci.* 19: 21–22, 1970.

Cicala, G. A., and Hartley, D. L. The effects of chlordiazepoxide on the acquisition and performance on a conditioned escape response in rats. *Psychol. Rec.* 15: 435–440, 1965.

Clark, D. L., and Waugh, N. Anesthesia and learning. *Anesthesiology* 50: 84–87, 1979.

Clarke, P. R., Eccersley, P. S., Frisby, J. P., and Thornton, J. A. The amnesic effect of diazepam (Valium). *Br. J. Anaesth.* 42: 690–697, 1970.

Cohen, E. L., and Wurtman, R. J. Brain acetylcholine: control by dietary choline. *Science* 191: 561–562, 1976.

Cole, S. O. Hyperkinetic children: The use of stimulant drugs evaluated. *Am. J. Orthopsychiat.* 45: 28–37, 1975.

Conners, C. K., and Eisenberg, L. The effects of methylphenidate on symptomatology and learning in disturbed children. *Am. J. Psychiat.* 120: 458–464, 1963.

Conners, C. K., Eisenberg, L., and Sharpe, L. Effects of methylphenidate (Ritalin) on paired-associate learning and Porteus maze performance in emotionally disturbed children. *J. Consult. Psychol.* 28: 14–22, 1964.

Cook, L., and Weidley, E. Behavioral effects of some psychopharmacological agents. *Ann. N.Y. Acad. Sci.* 66: 740–752, 1957.

Cook, L., Weidley, E., Morris, R. W., and Mattis, P. A. Neuropharmacological effects of chlorpromazine (thorazine hydrochloride). *J. Pharmacol.* 113: 11–12, 1953.

Cook, T. L., Smith, M., Starkweather, J. A., Winter, P. M., and Eger, E. I. II. Behavioral effects of trace and subanesthetic halothane and nitrous oxide in man. *Anesthesiology* 49: 419–424, 1978.

Corrodi, H., Fuxe, K., and Schou, M. Effect of prolonged lithium administration on cerebral monoamines in the rat. *Proc. 2nd International Meeting of the International Society for Neurochemistry,* 1969, p. 136.

Costa, E., Garattini, S., and Valzelli, L. Interactions between reserpine, chlorpromazine, and imipramine. *Experientia* 16: 461, 1960.

Cote, L. J., and Kremzner, L. T. Changes in neurotransmitter systems with increasing age in human brain. *Trans. Am. Soc. Neurochem.* 5: 83, 1974.

Courvoisier, S., Ducrot, R., and Julou, L. Nouveaux aspect espérimentaux de l'activité centrale des dérivés de la phénothiazine. In: Garattini, S., and Ghetti, V. (Eds.) *Psychotropic Drugs.* Amsterdam: Elsevier, 1958, p. 373.

Courvoisier, S., Fournel, J., Ducrot, R., Kolsky, M., and Koetschet, P. Propriétés pharmaco-dynamics du chlorhydrate de chloro-3-(diméthyl-amino-3'-propyl)-10-phénothiazine (4560R.P.): Etude expérimentale d'un nouveau corps utilisé dans l'anesthésie potentialisée et dans l'hibernation artificielle. *Arch. Int. Pharmacodynam.* 92: 305–361, 1953.

Cox, T. The effects of physostigmine during the acquisition of avoidance behavior as a function of intersession interval. *Quart. J. Exp. Psych.* 26: 387–394, 1974.

Crabbe, J. C., and Alpern, H. P. Facilitation and disruption of long-term storage of memory with neural excitants. *Pharmacol. Biochem. Behav.* 1: 197–202, 1975.

Crow, L. T. Effects of alcohol on conditioned avoidance responding. *Physiol. Behav.* 1: 89–91, 1966.

Crow, T. J., and Bursill, A. E. An investigation into the effects of metamphetamine on short-term memory in man. In: Costa, E., and Garattini, S. (Eds.) *Amphetamines and Related Compounds.* New York: Raven Press, 1970, pp. 889–895.

Daniels, D. The effect of TCAP on acquisition of discrimination learning in the rat. *Psychonom. Sci.* 7: 5–6, 1967.

Das, N. N., Dasgupta, S. R., and Werner, G. Changes in behavior and EEG in rhesus monkeys caused by chlorpromazine. *Arch. Int. Pharmacodyn.* 99: 451–457, 1954.

David, K. L., and Yamamura, H. I. Cholinergic under-activity in human memory disorders. *Life Sci.* 23: 1729–1734, 1978.

Davies, P. Neurotransmitter-related enzymes in senile dementia of the Alzheimer type. *Brain Res.* 171: 319–327, 1979.

Davies, P., and Maloney, A. J. F. Selective loss of central cholinergic neurons in Alzheimer's disease. *Lancet* 2: 1403, 1976.

Davies, P., and Verth, A. H. Regional distribution of muscarinic acetylcholine receptor in normal and Alzheimer's-type dementia brains. *Brain Res.* 138: 385–392, 1978.

Davis, K. L., Mohs. R. C., Trinklenberg, J. R., Pfefferbaum, A., Hollister, L. E., and Kopell, B. S. Physostigmine: Improvement of long term memory processes in normal humans. *Science* 201: 272–274, 1978a.

Davis, K. L., Mohs, R. C., Tinklenberg, J. R., Hollister, L. E., Pfefferbaum, A., and Kopell, B. S. Physostigmine: Enhancement of long-term memory functions on normal subject. *Science* 201: 274–276, 1978b.

Davis, K. L., Mohs, R. C., Tinklenberg, J. R., Hollister, L. E., Pfefferbaum, A., and Kopell B. S. Cholinomimetics and memory. The effect of choline chloride. *Arch. Neurol.* 37: 49–52, 1980.

Davis, R. E. Environmental control of memory fixation in goldfish. *J. Comp. Physiol. Psychol.* 65: 72–78, 1968.

Deadwyler, S. A., Montgomery, D., and Wyers, E. J. Passive avoidance and carbachol excitation of the caudate nucleus. *Physiol. Behav.* 8: 631–635, 1972.

Delay, J., and Deniker, P. Trente-huit cas de psychoses traitées par la cure prolongée et continue de 4560RP. In:*Compt. rend. Congrès des Al. Neurol.* Paris: Masson et Cie., 1952.

Delay, J., Deniker, P., and Harl, J. M. Utilisation en thérapeutique d'une phénothiazine d'action centrale élective (4560RP). *Ann. Méd. Psychol.* 110: 112–117, 1952.

d'Elia, G., and Frederiksen, S. O. $ACTH_{4-10}$ and memory in ECT-treated and untreated patients. I. Effect on consolidations. *Acta Psychiat. Scand.* 62: 418–428, 1980a.

d'Elia, G., and Frederiksen, S. O. $ACTH_{4-10}$ and memory in ECT-treated patients and untreated controls. II. Effect on retrieval. *Acta Psychiat. Scand.* 62: 429–435, 1980b.

Destrade, C. Soumireu-Mourat, B., and Cardo, B. Effect of post trial hippocampal stimulation of acquisition of operant behavior in the mouse. *Behav. Biol.* 8: 713–724, 1973.

Deutsch, A. J., and Weiner, N. J. Analysis of extinction through amnesia. *J. Comp. Physiol. Psych.* 69: 179–184, 1969.

Deutsch, J. The cholinergic synapse and the site of memory. *Science* 174: 788–794, 1971.

Deutsch, J., Hamburg, M., and Dahl, H. Anticholinesterase-induced amnesia and its temporal aspects. *Science* 151: 221–223, 1966.

Deutsch, J., and Leibowitz, S. Amnesia or reversal of forgetting by anticholinesterase, depending on time of injection. *Science* 153: 1017–1018, 1966.

de Wied, D. The influence of the posterior and intermediate lobe of the pituitary and pituitary peptides on the maintenance of a conditioned avoidance response in rats. *Int. J. Neuropharmacol.* 4: 157–167, 1965.

de Wied, D. Long term effect of vasopressin on the maintenance of a conditioned avoidance response in rats. *Nature* 232: 58–60, 1971.

de Wied, D., Bohus, B., and van Wimersma Greidanus, T. j. B. Memory deficit in rats with hereditary diabetes insipidus. *Brain Res.* 85: 152–156, 1975a.

de Wied, D., Witter, A., and Greven, H. M. Behaviourally active ACTH analogues. *Biochem. Pharmacol.* 24: 1463–1468, 1975b.

Dews, P. B. The measurement of the influence of drugs on voluntary activity in mice. *Br. J. Pharmacol. Chemother.* 8: 46–48, 1953.

Dews, P. B. Comparison of effects of phenobarbital and chlorpromazine on discriminatory performance in pigeons. *J. Pharmacol.* 116: 16, 1956.

DiGiusto, E. L., and King, M. G. Magnesium pemoline: Enhancement of performance. *Psychol. Rep.* 30: 863–866, 1972.

DiMascio, A., Havens, L. L., and Snell, J. E. A comparison of four phenothiazine derivatives: A preliminary report on the assessment of chlorpromazine, promethiazine, perphenazine, and trifluoperazine. In: Wortis, J. (Ed.) *Recent Advances in Biological Psychiatry, vol. 3.* New York: Grune & Stratton, 1961, pp. 68–76.

Doherty, J. E., and Perkins, W. H. Digoxin metabolism in hypo- and hyperthyroidism. *Ann. Intern. Med.* 64: 489–507, 1966.

Domer, F. R., and Schueler, F. W. Investigations of the amnesic properties of scopolamine and related compounds. *Arch. Int. Pharmacodyn. Therap.* 127: 449–458, 1960.

Domino, K., and Domino, E. Effects of scopolamine and metascopolamine and methscopolamine on acquisition and retention of rat on one-way shuttlebox behavior and total brain acetylcholine. *Arch. Int. Pharmacodynam.* 224: 248–257, 1976.

Drachman, D. A. Memory and cognitive function in man: Does the cholinergic system have a specific role? *Neurology* 27: 283–290, 1977.

Drachman, D. A. Memory, dementia, and the cholinergic system. In: Katzman, R., Terry, R. D., and Bick, K. L. (Eds.) *Alzheimer's Disease: Senile Dementia and Related Disorders,* vol. 7. Aging. New York: Raven Press, 1978, pp. 141–148.

Drachman, D. A., and Arbit, J. Memory and the hippocampal complex. *Arch. Neurol.* 5: 15–61, 1966.

Drachman, D. A., and Leavitt, J. Human memory and the cholinergic system. A relationship to aging. *Arch. Neurol.* 30: 113–121, 1974.

Drew, W. G., Loren, R. C. Miller, C. C., and Bauch, E. C. Effects of THC, LSD-25 and scopolamine on continuous, spontaneous alternation in the Y-maze. *Psychopharmacologia* 32: 171–182, 1973.

Dreyfus, P. N. Clinical application of blood transketolase determinations. *N. Engl. J. Med.* 267: 596–598, 1962.

Driscoll, P., and Battig, K. Cigarette smoke and behavior: some recent developments. *Rev. Environ. Health* 1: 118–133, 1973.

Driscoll, E. J., Smilack, Z. H., Lightbody, P. M., and Fiorucci, R. D. Sedation with intravenous diazepam. *J. Oral Surg.* 30: 332–343, 1972.

Dundee, J. W., and Pandit, S. K. Anterograde amnesic effects of pethidine, hyoscine, and diazepam in adults. *Br. J. Pharmacol.* 44: 140–144, 1972.

Dundee, J. W., and Richard, R. K. Effect of azotemiz upon the action of intravenous barbiturate anesthesia. *Anesthesiology* 15: 333–346, 1954.

Dusewicz, R. A., and Livecchi, S. G. The effects of posttrial administration of strychnine upon maze learning. *Psychol. Rec.* 19: 461–463, 1969.

Ebel, A., Hermetet, C., and Mandel, P. Comparison of acetylcholinesterase and choline acetyltransferase in the temporal cortex of DBA and C57 mice.

*Nature (London) New Biol.* 242: 56–58, 1973.

Eggar, S., Linesay, P. S., and Dawson, R. K. Ontogenetic aspects of central cholinergic involvement in spontaneous alternation behavior. *Develop. Psychobiol.* 6: 289–299, 1973.

Egyhazi, E., and Hyden, H. Experimentally induced changes in the base composition of the ribonucleic acid of isolated nerve cells and their obligodendroglial cells. *J. Biophys. Biochem. Cytol.* 10: 403–410, 1961.

Ehringer, H., Hornykiewicz, O., and Lechner, K. The effect of chlorpromazine on catecholamine and 5-hydroxytryptamine metabolism in the rat brain (in German). *Arch Exp. Pathol. Pharmakol.* 239: 507–519, 1960.

Eisenberg, J. M. The effect of nicotine on maze learning ability of albino rats. *Fed. Proc.* 7: 31–32, 1948.

Eisenberg, J. M. The effect of nicotine on maze behavior of albino rats. *J. Psychol.* 37: 291–295, 1954.

Ellen, P., Aitken, W., Sims, T., and Stahl, J. Cholinergic blockade septal lesions and DRC performance in the rat. *J. Comp. Physiol. Psych.* 89: 409–420, 1975.

Englert, E., Brown, H., Willardson, D. G., Wallach, S., and Simons, E. L. Metabolism of free and conjugated 17-hydroxycorticosteroids in subjects with uremia. *J. Clin. Endocr.* 18: 36–48, 1958.

Ernsting, M. J. E., Kafoe, W. F., Nauta, W. T., Oosterhuis, H. K., and DeWarrt, C. Biochemical studies on psychotropic drugs. I. The effects of psychotropic drugs on γ-aminobutyric acid and glutamic acid in brain tissue. *J. Neurochem.* 5: 121–127, 1960.

Essman, W. B. Facilitation of memory consolidation by chemically induced acceleration of RNA synthesis. *Proc. XXIII International Congress on Physiological Sciences,* 1965, p. 470.

Essman, W. B. Effect of tricyanoaminopropene on the amnesic effect of electroconvulsive shock. *Psychopharmacologie* 9: 426, 1966.

Essman, W. B. Electroshock-induced retrograde amnesia in seizure-protected mice. *Psychol. Rep.* 22: 929–935, 1968.

Essman, W. B. Mediation of memory consolidation: Behavioral and biochemical effects of nicotine and nicotine metabolites. *Proc. 4th Congress on Pharmacology,* Basel, 1969, p. 289.

Essman, W. B. The role of biogenic amines in memory consolidation. In: Adam, G. (Ed.) *The Biology of Memory.* Budapest: Hungarian Academy of Sciences, 1970a.

Essman, W. B. Central nervous system metabolism, drug effects, and higher functions. In: Smith, W. L. (Ed.) *Drugs and Cerebral Function. Springfield: Chas. Thomas, 1970b, pp. 151–175.*

Essman, W. B. Some neurochemical correlates of altered memory consolidation. *Trans. N.Y. Acad. Sci.* 32: 948–973, 1970c.

Essman, W. B. Drug effects and learning and memory processes. *Adv. Pharmacol. Chemother.* 9: 241–330, 1971a.

Essman, W. B. Some neurochemical correlates of altered memory consolidation. *Trans. N.Y. Acad. Sci.,* 1971b.

Essman, W. B. Retrograde amnesia and cerebral protein synthesis: Initiation and inhibition of 5-hydroxytryptamine. *Totus Homo.* 4: 61–67, 1972.

Essman, W. B. Neuromolecular modulation of experimentally induced retrograde amnesia. *Confinia Neurol.* 35: 1–22, 1973a.

Essman, W. B. Nicotine-related neurochemical changes: some implications for motivational mechanisms and differences. In: Dunn, W. J., Jr. (Ed.) *Smoking Behavior.* Washington, D.C.: Winston, 1973b, pp. 51–65.

Essman, W. B. Effetti dell'elettroshock sulla neurochimica del sistema nervoso centrale, II, *Rass. Clin. Scient.* 49: 5–23, 1973c.

Essman, W. B. Brain 5-hydroxytryptamine and memory consolidation. In: Costa, E., Gessa, G. L., and Sandler, M. (Eds) *Advances in Biochemical Psychopharmacology, vol. II. Serotonin: New Vistas. Biochemical Behavioral Clinical Studies.* New York: Raven Press, 1974, pp. 265–274.

Essman, W. B. Diurnal differences in altered brain 5-hydroxytryptamine-related regional protein synthesis. *Pharmacologie* 6: 313–322, 1975.

Essman, W. B. Serotonin in learning and memory. In: Essman, W. B. (Ed.) *Serotonin in Health and Disease, vol. III.* New York: Spectrum, 1978a, pp. 69–143.

Essman, W. B. Morphine action in myocardial metabolopathies. In: Adler, M. L., Manara, L., and Samanin, R. (Eds.) *Factors Affecting the Action of Narcotics.* New York: Raven Press, 1978b, pp. 125–131.

Essman, W. B., and Alpern, H. Single trial learning: Methodology and results with mice. *Psych. Rep.* 15: 731–740, 1964.

Essman, W. B., and Essman, S. G. Enhanced memory consolidation with drug-induced changes in brain RNA and serotonin metabolism. *Pharmako-Psychiat. Neuropsychopharm.* 12: 28–34, 1969.

Essman, W. B., and Essman, S. G. Amine regulation of protein synthesis in retrograde amnesia. In: Delgado, J. M. R., and DeFeudis, F. (Eds.) *Behavioral Neurochemistry.* New York: Spectrum, 1977, pp. 25–61.

Essman, W. B., and Golod, M. I. Reduction of retrograde amnesia by TCAP: Drug dosage and electroshock intensity. *Comm. Behav. Biol.* 1: 183–187, 1968.

Essman, W. B., and Jarvik, M. E. The retrograde effect of ether anesthesia on a conditioned avoidance response in mice. *Am. Psychol.* 15: 498, 1960.

Essman, W. B., and Jarvik, M. E. Impairment of retention for a conditioned response by ether anesthesia in mice. *Psychopharmacologia* 2: 172–176, 1961.

Essman, W. B., Steinberg, M. I., and Golod, M. I. Alterations in the behavioral and biochemical effects of electroconvulsive shock with nicotine. *Psychonom. Sci.* 12: 107–108, 1968.

Essman, W. B., and Sudak, F. N. Effect of body temperature reduction on response acquisition in mice. *J. Appl. Physiol.* 17: 113–116, 1962.

Etienne, P., Gauthier, S., and Dastoor, D. Lecithin in Alzheimer's disease. *Lancet* 2: 1206, 1978.

Evangelista, A. M., and Izquierdo, I. The effect of pre- and post-trial amphetamine injections on avoidance responses of rats. *Psychopharmacologia (Berlin)* 20: 42–47, 1971.

Evangelista, A., and Izquierdo I. Effects of avoidance or avoidance condition: interaction with nicotine and comparison with *N*-methylatropine. *Psychopharmacologia* 27: 241–248, 1972.

Exer, B., and Pulver, R. Some metabolic effects of Tofranil and metabolites. *Chimia* 14: 30, 1960.

Eysenck, H. J. *Experiments in Personality.* London: Routledge and Kegan, 1960.

Feigley, D. A. Effects of scopolamine on activity and passive avoidance learning in rats of different ages. *J. Comp. Physiol. Psych.* 87: 26–36, 1974.

Feigley, D. A. Parsons, P., Hamilton, L. W., and Spear, N. E. Development of habituation to novel environments in the rat. *J. Comp. Physiol. Psych.* 79: 443–452, 1972.

Feigley, D. A., and Spear, N. E. Effect of age and punishment condition on long term retention of the rat of active and passive avoidance learning. *J. Comp. Physiol. Psych.* 73: 515–526, 1970.

Ferrier, B. M., Kennett, D. J., and Devlin, M. C. Influence of oxytocin on human memory processes. *Life Sci.* 27: 2311–2317, 1980.

Fibiger, H., Lytle, L., and Campbell, B. Cholinergic modulation of adrenergic arousal in the developing rat. *J. Comp. Physiol. Psych.* 72: 384–389, 1970.

Finch, C. E. Cellular pacemakers of aging in mammals. In: Harris, R., and Viza, D. (Eds.) *Proc. 1st European Conference on Cell Differentiation.* Munkesgaard, Copenhagen, 1972, pp. 123–126.

Finch, C. E. Neurochemical and neuroendocrine changes during aging in rodent models. In: Katzman, R., Terry, D., and Bick, K. L. (Eds.) *Alzheimer's Disease: Senile Dementia and Related Disorders.* New York: Raven Press, 1978, pp. 461–468.

Fishman, M. W., and Schuster, C. R. The effect of chlorpromazine and pentobarbital on behavior maintained by electric shock on point loss avoidance in humans. *Psychopharmacology* 66: 3–11, 1979.

Flexner, L. B., and Flexner, J. A. Intracerebral saline: Effect on memory of trained mice treated with puromycin. *Science* 159: 330–331, 1968.

Foreman, P. A. Control of the anxiety/pain complex in dentistry. *Oral Surg. Med. Pathol.* 37: 337–349, 1974.

Franks, C. M., and Trouton, D. Effects of amobarbital sodium and dexamphetamine sulfate on the conditioning of the eyeblink response. *J. Comp. Physiol. Psychol.* 51: 220–222, 1958.

Fry, W., Krumins, R., Fry, F., Thomas, G., Borbely, S., and Ades, H. Origins and distribution of some efferent pathways from the mammillary nuclei of the cat. *J. Comp. Neurol.* 120: 195–258, 1963.

Fulginiti, S., and Orsingher, O. A. Further evidence in support of a common adrenergic mechanism for the facilitation action on learning of amphetamine and nicotine in rats. *J. Pharmacol.* 25: 580–581, 1973.

Fuxe, K., and Ungerstedt, U. Histochemical studies on the effect of (+) amphetamine, drugs of the imipramine group and tryptamine on the central catecholamine and 5-hydroxytryptamine. *Eur. J. Pharmacol.* 4: 135–144, 1968.

Gadusek, F. J., and Kalat, J. W. Effects of scopolamine on retention of taste aversion learning in rats. *Physiol. Psych.* 3: 130–132, 1975.

Gaillard, A. W. K., and Sanders, A. F. Some effects of ACTH 4–10 on performance during a serial learning task. *Psychopharmacologia (Berlin)* 42: 201–208, 1975.

Garattini, S., and Sigg, E. B. *Aggressive Behavior.* Amsterdam: *Excerpta Medica,* 1969.

Garfield, M. J., Garfield, F. B., and Sampson, J. Effects of nitrous oxide on decision-strategy and sustained attention. *Psychopharmacologia* 42: 5–10, 1975.

Garg, M., and Holland, H. C. Consolidation of maze learning: The effects of posttrial injections of a stimulant drug (Picrotoxin). *Psychopharmacologia* 12: 96–103, 1968.

Garg, M., and Holland, H. C. Consolidation and maze learning: A further study of posttrial injections of a stimulant drug (nicotine). *Int. J. Neuropharmacol.* 7: 55–59, 1968.

Geller, I., and Hartmann, R. Attenuation of "conflict" behavior with cinanserin (2'-[3-dimethylaminopropylthio] cinnamanilide hydrochloride), a serotonin antagonist: Reversal of the effects with 5-hydroxytryptophan (5-HTP) and alpha-methyltryptamine. *Fed. Proc.* 32: 817, 1973.

George, G., and Mellanby, J. A further study on the effect of physostigmine on memory in rats. *Brain Res.* 81: 133–144, 1974.

George, G., Mellanby, J., and Mellanby, H. When does inhibition of AChE cause amnesia in rats? *Brain Res.* 122: 568–574, 1977.

Gerin, J. Symptomatic treatment of cerebrovascular insufficiency with Hydergine. *Curr. Therap. Res.* 11: 539–546, 1969.

Gershon, S., and Yuwiller, A. Lithium ion: A specific psychopharmacological approach to the treatment of mania. *J. Neuropsychiat.* 1: 229–241, 1960.

Gey, K. I., and Pletscher, A. Einfluss von Chlorpromazin und Chlorprothixen auf den Monoaminstoffwechsel des Rattenhirns. *Helv. Physiol. Pharmacol. Acta* 19: C22–C24, 1961.

Ghoneim, M. M., and Mewaldt, S. P. Studies on human memory. The interactions of diazepam, scopolamine, and physostigmine. *Psychopharmacology* 52: 1–6, 1977.

Giarman, N., and Pepeu, G. Drug induced changes in brain acetylcholine. *Br. J. Pharmacol.* 19: 226–234, 1962.

Gilbert, J. G., Donnelly, K. J., Zimmer, L. E., and Kubis, J. F. Effect of magnesium penoline and methylphenidate on memory improvement and mood in normal aging subjects. *Int. J. Aging Hum. Dev.* 4: 35–51, 1973.

Gilette, J. R., Dingell, J. V., Sulser, V., Kuntzmen, R., and Brodie, B. B. Isolation from rat brain of a metabolic product, desmethylimipramine, that mediates the antidepressant activity of imipramine (Tofranil). *Experientia* 17: 417, 1961.

Gililand, A. R., and Nelson, D. The effects of coffee on certain mental and physiological functions. *J. Gen. Psychol.* 21: 339–348, 1939.

Glasky, A. J., and Simon, L. N. Magnesium pemoline: Enhancement of brain RNA polymerases. *Science* 151: 702–703, 1966.

Glick, S. D., Crane, L., Barker, L., and Mittag, T. Effects of N-hydroxyethyl-pyrolidinium methiodide, a choline analogue, on passive avoidance behavior in mice. *Neuropharmacol.* 14: 561–564, 1975.

Glick, S. D., and Greenstein, S. Differential effects of scopolamine and mecamylamine on passive avoidance behavior. *Life Sci.* 11: 169–179, 1972.

Glick, S. D., Mittag, T., and Green, J. Central cholinergic correlates of impaired learning. *Neuropharmacol.* 12: 291–296, 1973.

Goldberg, M. E., and Johnson, H. E. Potentiation of chlorpromazine-induced behavioural changes by anticholinesterase agents. *J. Pharm. Pharmacol.* 61: 60–61, 1964.

Goldman-Eisler, F., Skarbek, A., and Henderson, A. Breath rate and the selective action of chlorpromazine on speech behavior. *Psychopharmacologia* 8: 415–427, 1966.

Gonatas, N. K., Anderson, W., and Evangelista, I. The contribution of altered synapses in the senile plaque: An electron microscopic study in Alzheimer's dementia. *J. Neuropathol. Exp. Neurol.* 26: 25–39, 1967.

Gonzalex, L. P., and Altshuler, H. L. Scopolamine effects of suppression of operant responding. *Physiolog. Psych.* 7: 156–162, 1979.

Goodwin, D. W., Powell, B., and Brenner, D. Alcohol and recall: State-dependent effects in man. *Science* 163: 1358–1360, 1969.

Gotfredsen, C. F., Mellerup, E. T., and Rafaelsen, O. J. Lithium and some other psychopharmaca. Effect on electrolyte distribution and excretion in rat. *Proc. 2nd International Meeting of the International Society for Neurochemistry,* 1969, p. 196.

Gottfries, C. G., Gottfries, I., and Roos, B. E. The investigation of homovanillic acid in the human brain and its correlation to senile dementia. *Br. J. Psychiat.* 115: 563–574, 1969.

Gottfries, C. G., Gottfries, I., and Roos, B. E. Homovanillic acid and 5-hydroxyindole acetic acid in cerebrospinal fluid related to mental and motor impairment in senile and presenile dementia. *Acta Psychiatr. Neurol. Scand.* 46: 99–103, 1970.

Gottfries, C. G., Kjallquist, A., Ponten, U., Roos, B. E., and Sundbarg, G. Cerebrospinal fluid pH and monoamine and glucolytic metabolites in Alzheimer's disease. *Brit. J. Psychiat.* 124: 280–287, 1974.

Gottfries, C. G., Oreland, L., Wiberg, A., and Winblad, B. Lowered monoamine oxidase activity in brains from alcoholic suicides. *J. Neurochem.* 25: 667–673, 1975.

Goodhart, R. S., and Helenore, J. C. (Eds.) *Modern Drug Encyclopedia and Therapeutic Index,* 9th ed. New York: Rueben H. Donnelley, 1963.

Graf, C. L. Effects of scopolamine on inhibitory mechanisms. *Physiol. Psych.* 2: 164–170, 1974.

Green, S. E., and Summerfield, A. Central and peripheral cholinergic involvement in the habituation of investigatory head poking in rats, *J. Comp. Physiol. Psych.* 9: 1398–1407, 1977.

Green, T. K., and Harvey, J. A. Enhancement of amphetamine action after interruption of ascending serotonergic pathways. *J. Pharmacol. Exp. Therap.* 190: 109–117, 1974.

Greenblatt, E. N., and Osterberg, A. C. Effect of drugs on the maintenance of exploratory behavior in mice. *Fed. Proc.* 20: 397, 1961.

Gregg, J. M., Ryan, D. E., and Levin, K. H. The amnesic actions of diazepam. *Oral Surg.* 32: 651–664, 1974.

Grieco, N. H., Pierson, R. N., Jr., and Pi-Sunyer, F. X. Comparison of the circulatory and metabolic effects of isoproterenol, epinephrine, methoxamine in normal and asthmatic subjects. *Am. J. Med.* 44: 863–872, 1968.

Groh, G., and Lemieux, M. The effects of three psychotropic drugs on spider web formation. In: Lehmann, H. E., and Ban, T. A. (Eds.) *The Butyrophenones in Psychiatry.* Quebec: Quebec Psychopharmacological Assoc., 1964, p. 53.

Gross, M. D. Caffeine in the treatment of children with minimal brain dysfunction or hyperkinetic syndrome. *Psychosomatics* 16: 26–27, 1975.

Grote, S. S., Moses, S. G., Robins, E., Hudgens, R. W., And Croninger, A. B. A study of selected catecholamine metabolizing enzymes: A comparison of depressive suicides and alcoholic suicides with controls. *J. Neurochem.* 23: 791–802, 1974.

Gurowitz, E. M., Lubar, J. R., Ain, B. R., and Gross, D. A. Disruption of passive avoidance learning by magnesium pemoline. *Psychon. Sci.* 8: 19–20, 1967.

Guth, S., Levine, S., and Seward, J. P. Appetitive acquisition and extinction with exogenous ACTH. *Physiol. Behav.* 7: 195–200, 1971.

Hamburg, M., Retrograde amnesia produced by intraperitoneal injection of physostigmine. *Science* 156: 973–974, 1967.

Hamilton, L. W. Behavioral effects of unilateral and bilateral septal lesions in rats. *Physiol. Behav.* 5: 855–859, 1970.

Handley, G. W., and Calhoun, W. H. Serial discrimination reversal learning: Effects of scopolamine. *Bull. Psychon. Sci.* 10: 422–424, 1977.

Hanson, H. M. The effects of amitriptyline, imipramine, chlorpromazine and nialamide on avoidance behavior. *Fed. Proc.* 20: 396, 1961.

Harris, W. S., and Goodman, R. M. Hyperreactivity to atropine in Down's syndrome. *N. Engl. J. Med.* 279: 407–410, 1968.

Hartelius, H. Further experiences of the use of malononitrile in the treatment of mental illness. *Am. J. Psychiat.* 107: 95–101, 1950.

Hartley, L. Diazepam: Human learning of different materials. *Prog. Neuro-Psychopharmacol.* 4: 193–197, 1980.

Haycock, J. W., Deadwyler, S. A., Sideroff, S. J., and McGaugh, J. C. Retrograde amnesia and cholinergic systems in caudate-putamen complex and dorsal hippocampus of rats. *Exp. Neurol.* 41: 201–213, 1973.

Hearst, E. Effects of scopolamine on discriminated responding in the rat. *Int. J. Pharmacol. Exp. Theor.* 126: 349–358, 1959.

Heimstra, N. W. Social influence on the response to drugs. II. Chlorpromazine and iproniazid. *Psychopharmacologia* 3: 72–78, 1962.

Heise, G. A., and Boff, E. Continuous avoidance as a baseline for measuring behavioral effects of drugs. *Psychopharmacologia* 3: 264–282, 1962.

Heise, G. A., Krarbich, B., Lilie, N. L., and Martin, R. A. Scopolamine effects of development of alternation in the rat. *Pharmacol. Biochem. Behav.* 3: 993–1002, 1975.

Heise, G. A., Laughlin, N., and Keller, C. A behavioral and pharmacological analysis of reinforcement withdrawal. *Psychopharmacologia* 16: 345–368, 1970.

Heron, W. T., and Carlson, W. S. The effects of metrazol shock on retention of the maze habit. *J. Comp. Physiol. Psychol.* 32: 307–309, 1941.

Herr, F., Stewart, J., and Charest, M. P. Tranquilizers and antidepressants: A pharmacological comparison. *Arch. Int. Pharmacodyn. Therap.* 134: 328–342, 1961.

Hier, D. B., and Caplan, L. R. Drugs for senile dementia. *Drugs* 20: 74–80, 1980.

Hindmarch, I., Parrot, A. C., and Lanza, M. The effect of an ergot alkaloid derivative (Hydergine) on aspects of psychomotor performance, arousal, and cognitive processing ability. *J. Clin. Pharmacol.* 19: 726–732, 1979.

Hirsch, M. J., and Wurtman, R. J. Lecithin consumption elevates acetylcholine concentrations in rat brain and adrenal gland. *Science* 202: 223–225, 1978.

Ho, B. T., McIsaac, W. M., Tansey, L. W., and Walker, K. E. Inhibitors of monoamine oxidase. III. 9-substituted-$\beta$-carbolines. *Proc. R. Soc. London. Ser. B.* 127: 219–221, 1969.

Hoehn-Saric, R., Bacon, E. F., and Gross, M. Effects of chlorpromazine on flicker fusion. *J. Nerv. Ment. Dis.* 138: 287–292, 1964.

Holmes, J. H., Nakamoto, S., and Sawyer, K. C. Changes in blood composition before and after dialysis with the Kolff turn coil kidney. *Trans. Am. Soc. Artif. Int. Organs* 4: 16–23, 1958.

Holmgren, B., and Condi, C. Conditioned avoidance reflex under pentobarbital. *Bol. Inst. Estudios Medicos Biologicos* 22: 21–38, 1964.

Hughes, R. N., and Trowland, R. Physostigmine effects on activity and reactions to novelty. *Life Sci.* 19: 793–796, 1976.

Hunt, E. B., and Bauer, R. H. Facilitation of learning by delayed injections of pentylenetetrazol. *Psychopharmacologia* 16: 139–146, 1969.

Hunt, E. B., and Krivanek, J. The effects of pentylenetetrazol and methylphenoxypropane on discrimination learning. *Psychopharmacologia* 9: 1–16, 1966.

Hunt, H. F. Some effects of drugs on classical (type S) conditioning. *Ann. N.Y. Acad. Sci.* 65: 258–267, 1956.

Hurst, P. M., Radlov, R., Chubb, N., and Bagley, S. K. Effects of $d$-amphetamine on acquisition, persistence, and recall. *Am. J. Psychol.* 82: 307–319, 1969.

Hydén, H. In: *Proc. IVth International Congress on Biochemistry,* Vienna, 1958. London: Pergamon Press, 1959, vol. 3.

Hydén, H. A molecular basis of neuron-glia interaction. In: Schmitt, F. O. (Ed.) *Macromolecular Specificity and Biological Memory.* Cambridge, Mass.: The M.I.T. Press, 1962, pp. 55–69.

Hydén, H. Biochemical and functional interplay between neuron and glia. *Rec. Adv. Biol. Psychiat.* 6: 31, 1963.

Hydén, H., and Egyhazi, E. Nuclear RNA changes of nerve cells during a learning experiment in rats. *Proc. Nat. Acad. Sci. (U.S.A.)* 48: 1366–1373, 1962.

Hydén, H., and Egyhazi, E. Glial RNA changes during a learning experiment in rats. *Proc. Nat. Acad. Sci. (U.S.)* 49: 618–624, 1963.

Hydén, H., and Egyhazi, E. Changes in RNA content and base composition in cortical neurons of rats in learning experiment involving transfer of handedness. *Proc. Nat. Acad. Sci. (U.S.)* 52: 1030–1035, 1964.

Hydén, H., and Hartelius, H. Stimulation of the nucleoprotein production in the nerve cells by malononitrile and its effect on psychic functions in mental disorders. *Acta. Psychiat. (Suppl.)* 48, 1948, 117 pp.

Hydén, H., and Lange, P. W. Brain-cell protein synthesis specifically related to learning. *Proc. Nat. Acad. Sci. (U.S.)* 65: 898–904, 1970.

Hydén, H., and Lange, P. W. Protein synthesis in hippocampal nerve cells during reversal of handedness in rats. *Brain Res.* 45: 314–317, 1972.

Hydén, H., Lange, P. W. Mihailovic, L. J., and Petrovic-Minic, B. Changes of RNA base composition in nerve cells of monkeys subjected to visual discrimination and delayed alternation performance. *Brain Res.* 65: 215–230, 1974.

Hydén, H., Lange, P. W., and Seyfried, C. Biochemical brain protein changes produced by selective breeding for learning in rats. *Brain Res.* 61: 446–451, 1973.

Iqbal, K., Wisniewski, H. M., Grundke-Iqbal, I., Korthals, J. K., and Terry, R. D. Chemical pathology of neurofibrils: Neurofibrillary tangles of Alzheimer's presenile-senile dementia. *J. Histochem. Cytochem.* 23: 563–569, 1975.

Irwin, S. Correlation in rats between the locomotor and avoidance suppressant potencies of eight phenothiazine tranquilizers. *Arch. Int. Pharmacodyn.* 132: 279–286, 1961.

Irwin, S., and Benuazizi, A. Pentylenetetrazol enhances memory functions. *Science* 152: 100–102, 1966.

Izquierdo, J. A., Baratti, L. M., Torrelio, M., and Arévalo, L. Effects of food deprivation, discrimination, experience and physostigmine on choline acetylase and acetylcholine esterase in the.dorsal hippocampus and frontal cortex of rats. *Psychopharmacologia* 33: 103–110, 1973.

Jacobs, B. L. Evidence for the functional interaction of two central neurotransmitters. *Psychopharmacologia* 39: 81–86, 1974.

Jaffard, R., Destrade, C., Durkin, T., and Ebel, A. Memory formation as related to genotypic or experimental variations of hippocampal cholinergic activity in mice. *Physiol. Behav.* 22: 1093–1096, 1979.

Jaffard, R., Ebel, A., Destrade, L., Ayad, G., Mandel, P., and Cardo, B. The role of hippocampal cholinergic mechanisms in the acquisition of a barpress response. *Pharmacol., Biochem. Behav.* 5: 371–374, 1976.

Jaffard, R. Ebel, A., Destrade, L., Durkin, T., Mandel, P., and Cardo, B. Effects of hippocampal electrical stimulation on LTM and on cholinergic mechanisms in three inbred strains of mice. *Brain Res.* 133: 277—289, 1977.

Janssen, P. A., Van De Westeringh, C., Jageneau, A. H., Demoen, P. J., Hermans, B. K., Van Daele, G. H., Schellekens, K. H., Vander Eycken, C. A., and Niemegeers, C. J. Chemistry and pharmacology of CNS depressants related to 4-(4-hydroxyphenylpiperidino) butyrophenone. I. Synthesis and screening data in mice. *J. Med. Pharm. Chem.* 1: 281–297, 1960.

Jarvik, M. E., and Essman, W. B. A simple one-trial learning technique for mice. *Psychol. Rep.* 6: 290, 1960.

Jenden, D. J. The neurochemical basis of acetylcholine precursor loading as a therapeutic strategy. In: Davies, K. L., and Berger, P. A. (Eds.) *Brain Acetylcholine and Neuropsychiatric Disease.* New York: Plenum Press, 1979, pp. 483–514.

Kahan, S. A. The effects of metrazol on operant response rats. *Physiol. Behav.* 1: 117–123, 1966.

Karczmar, A. Overview: Cholinergic drugs and behaviour—what effects may be expected from a "cholinergic diet?" In: Growdon, J., Wurtman, R. J., and Barbeau, A. (Eds.) *Uses of Choline and Lecithin in Neurological and Psychiatric Disorders.* New York: Raven Press, 1979.

Karczmar, A., and Dun, N. Cholinergic synapses: Physiological, pharmacological and behavioral correlates. In: Lipton, M., DiMascio, A., and Killam, D. (Eds.) *Psychopharmacology: A Generation of Progress.* New York: Raven Press, 1978, pp. 293–305.

Katz, J. J., and Halstead, W. C. Protein organization and mental function. *Comp. Psychol. Monogr.* 20: 1–38, 1960.

Keilty, S. R., and Blackwood, S. Sedation for conservative dentistry. *Br. J. Chin. Pract.* 23: 365–367, 1969.

Kelleher, R. T., Fry, W., Deegan, J., and Cook, L. Effect of meprobamate on operant behavior in rats. *J. Pharmacol. Exp. Therap.* 133: 271–280, 1961.

Kent, S. Can drugs halt memory loss? *Geriatrics* 36: 34–42, 1981.

Kety, S. S. The central physiological and pharmacological effects of the biogenic amines and their correlations with behavior. In: Quinton, G. C., Melneckich, T., and Schmidt, F. (Eds.) *The Neurosciences.* New York: Rockefeller University Press, 1967, pp. 444–452.

Kidd, M. Paired helical filaments in electron microscopy of Alzheimer's disease. *Nature (London)* 197: 192–193, 1963.

Kivalo, E., Rinne, U. K., and Karinkanta, H. The effect of imipramine on the 5-hydroxy-tryptamine content and monoamine oxidase activity of the rat brain and on the excretion of 5-hydroxyindoleacetic acid. *J. Neurochem.* 8: 105, 1961.

Klerman, G. L., and DiMascio, A. Psychological effects of piperazone phenothiazine. *Fed. Proc.* 20: 393, 1961.

Kneip, P. Climbing impulse and climbing test (in German). *Arch. Int. Pharmacodyn. Therap.* 126: 238–245, 1960.

Kornetsky, C. Alterations in psychomotor functions and individual differences in responses produced by psychoactive drugs. In: Uhr, L., and Muller, J. G. (Eds.) *Drugs and Behavior.* New York: John Wiley, 1960, pp. 297–312.

Kornetsky, C., Vates, T. S., and Kessler, E. K. A comparison of hypnotic and residual psychological effects of single dose of chlorpromazine and secobarbital in man. *J. Pharmacol. Exp. Therap.* 127: 51–54, 1959.

Kral, V. A., Solyom, L., and Enesco, H. E. Effect of short-term oral RNA therapy on the serum uric acid level and memory function in senile versus senescent subjects. *J. Am. Geriat. Soc.* 15: 364–372, 1967.

Krivanek, J., and McGaugh, J. L. Effects of pentylenetetrazol on memory storage in mice. *Psychopharmacologia* 12: 303–321, 1968.

Ksir, L. Scopolamine effects on two trial delayed response performance in the rat. *Psychopharmacologia* 34: 127–134, 1974.

Ksir, L. Scopolamine and amphetamine effects on discrimination: Interaction with stimulus control. *Psychopharmacologia* 43: 37–41, 1975.

Lande, S., Flexner, J. B., and Flexner, L. B. Effect of corticotrophin and desglycinamide⁹-lysine⁹vasopressin on suppression of memory by puromycin. *Proc. Nat. Acad. Sci. (U.S.)* 69: 558–560, 1972.

Lasagna, L., and Epstein, L. C. The use of amphetamine in the treatment of hyperkinetic children. *J. Nerv. Ment. Dis.* 146: 136–146, 1968.

Lashley, K. S. The effect of strychnine and caffeine upon rate of learning. *Psychobiology* 1: 141:–170, 1917.

Latz, A. Alterations in the performance of mice on a learned task after the administration of anti-depressant drugs. *Fed. Proc.* 23: 103, 1964.

Leaton, R. N., and Rech, R. Locomotor activity increases produced by intrahippocampal and intraseptal atropine in rats. *Physiol. Behav.* 8: 539–541, 1972.

LeBlanc, J. Effect of chlorpromazine on swimming time of rats at different temperatures. *Proc. Soc. Exp. Biol. Med.* 98: 648–650, 1958.

LeBoeuf, A., Lodge, J., and Eames, P. G. Vasopressin and memory in Korsakoff syndrome. *Lancet* 2: 1370, 1978.

LeBorce, A., Lodge, J., and Eames, Pl G. Basopressin and memory in Korsakoff syndrome. *Lancet* 2: 1370, 1978.

LeBrecque, D. C. Papaverine hydrochloride as therapy for mentally confused geriatric patients. *Curr. Therap. Res.* 8: 106–111, 1966.

Legros, J. J., Gilot, P., Seron, X., Claessens, J., Adam, A., Moeglen, J. M., Audibert, A., and Berchier, P. Influence of vasopressin on learning and memory. *Lancet* 1: 41–42, 1978.

Lehmann, H. E., and Hanrahan, G. E. Chlorpromazine, a new inhibiting agent for psychomotor excitement and manic states. *Am. Med. Assoc. Arch. Neurol. Psychiat.* 71: 227–237, 1954.

Leith, N. J., and Barrett, R. J. Effects of hippocampal microinjection of *d*-amphetamine and scopolamine on activity behavior in rats. *J. Comp. Physiol. Psych.* 88: 285–299, 1974.

Leonard, B. E. The effect of two synthetic ACTH analogues on the metabolism of biogenic amines in the rat brain. *Arch. Int. Pharmacodyn.* 20: 242–253, 1974.

Lewis, M. F., and Mertens, H. W. Behavioral changes from chronic exposure to pesticides used in aerial application. *Aerospace Med.* 44: 290–293, 1973.

Lewis, P., and Shute, L. The cholinergic limbic system: Projections to hippocampal formation, medial cortex, nuclei of the ascending cholinergic, reticular system and the subfornical organ and supraoptic crest. *Brain* 90: 521–539, 1967.

Lewis, S. Maze acquisition and nucleic acid metabolism: Effects of two malononitrile derivatives. Paper presented at Meeting of Eastern Psychological Association, Boston, Apr. 1967.

Lewis, S., and Essman, W. B. Maze acquisition and RNA material: Effects of two malononitrile derivatives. Unpublished material, 1967.

Lidbraink, P., Corrodi, H., and Fuxe, K. Benzodiazepines and barbiturates: Turnover changes in central 5-hydroxytryptamine pathways. *Eur. J. Pharmacol. (Amsterdam)* 26: 35–40, 1974.

Liljequist, R., and Mattila, M. J. Effect of physostigmine and scopolamine on the memory functions of chess players. *Med. Biol. 57: 402–405,* 1979.

Lindan, O., Quastel, J. H., and Sved, S. Biomedical studies on chlorpromazine. I. The effect of chlorpromazine on respiratory activity of isolated rat brain cortex. *Can. J. Biochem. Physiol.* 35: 1135–1144, 1957.

Linnoila, M. Effects of diazepam, chlordiozepoxide, thioridazine, haloperidole, flupenthixole and alcohol on psychomotor skills related to driving. *Anuales Medicinae Experimentalis et Biologiae Fenniae* 51: 125–132, 1973.

Linnoila, M., Saario, I., and Maki, M. Effect of treatment with diazepam or lithium and alcohol on psychomotor skills related to driving. *Eur. J. Clin. Pharmacol.* 7: 337–342, 1974.

Linuchev, M. N., and Michelson, M. J. Action of nicotine on the rats of elaboration of food motor conditioned reflexes in rats of different ages. *Activ. Nerv. Sup.* 7: 25–30, 1965.

Lishman, W. *Organic psychiatry: The Psychological Consequences of Cerebral Disorder.* Oxford: Blackwell, 1978.

Livecchi, S. G., and Dusewicz, R. A. Effects of pre-trial strychnine on maze learning. *Psychol. Rep.* 24: 735–736, 1969.

Lowenthal, D. T., and Reidenberg, M. M. The heart rate response to atropine in uremic patients, obese subjects before and during fasting, and patients with other chronic illnesses. *Proc. Soc. Exp. Biol. Med.* 139: 390–393, 1972.

Luckens, M. M., and Malone, M. H. Cardiovascular effects of reserpine, yohimbine, and reserpine–yohimbine mixtures on intact anesthetized dog. *J. Pharm. Sci.* 62: 1268–1290, 1973.

Ludvigson, H. W., The effects of chlorpromazine and 4-amphetamine on eyelid conditioning. Ph.D. Thesis, State University of Iowa, 1960.

MacFarlane, M. D. Procaine HC1 (Gerovital H3): A weak, reversible, fully competitive inhibitor for monoamine oxidase. *Fed. Proc.* 34: 108–110, 1975.

MacFarlane, M. D., and Besbris, H. Procaine (Gerovital H3) therapy: Mechanism of inhibition of monoamine oxidase. *J. Am. Geriatr. Soc.* 22: 365–371, 1974.

Malis, J. L. Effects of drugs on the regulation of an aversive stimulus in the monkey. *Fed. Proc.* 2: 327, 1962.

Mandel, P., Ayad, J. C., Hermetet, L., and Ebel, A. Correlation between choline acetyltransferase activity and learning ability in different mice strains and their offspring. *Brain Res.* 72: 65–70, 1974.

Mangioni, A., Andreoli, V., Cabibbe, F., and Mandelli, V., Body fluids distribution in manic and depressed patients treated with lithium carbonate. *Proc. 2nd International Meeting of the International Society for Neurochemistry*, 1969, pp. 279–280.

Marriott, J. G., and Alpern, H. P. An analysis of the time dependent aspects of short term memory in mice. *Behav. Biol.* 9: 85–91, 1973.

Maxwell, D. R. The relative potencies of various antidepressant drugs in some laboratory tests. In: Bradley, P. B., Flügel, F., and Hoch, P. (Eds.) *Neuropsychopharmacology, vol. 3.* Amsterdam: Elsevier, 1964, pp. 501–506.

Maxwell, D. R., and Palmer, H. T. Demonstration of anti-depressant or stimulant properties of imipramine in experimental animals. *Nature* 191: 84–85, 1961.

Maxwell, D. R., Palmer, H. T., and Ryall, R. W. A comparison of the analgesic and some other central properties of methotrimeprazine and morphine. *Arch. Int. Pharmacodyn. Therap.* 132: 60–73, 1961.

Mayfield, D., and Brown, R. G. The clinical laboratory. Electroencephalographic effects of lithium. *J. Psychiat. Res.* 4: 207–219, 1966.

McCoy, D. Some effects of scopolamine on acquisition and extinction performance in rats. *Psycholg. Rep.* 30: 867–873, 1972.

McEntee, W. J., and Mair, R. G. Memory impairment in Korsakoff's psychosis: A correlation with brain noradrenergic activity. *Science* 202: 905–907, 1978.

McEntee, W., J., and Mair, R. G. Memory enhancement in Korsakoff's psychosis by clonidine: Further evidence for a noracrenergic deficit. *Ann. Neurol.* 7: 466–470, 1980.

McGaugh, J. L. Facilitative and disruptive effects of strychnine sulphate on maze learning. *Psychol. Rep.* 8: 99–104, 1961.

McGaugh, J. L. Time-dependent processes in memory storage. *Science* 153: 1351–1358, 1966.

McGaugh, J. L. Drug facilitation of memory and learning. In: Efron, D. H. (Ed.) *Psychopharmacology: A Review of Progress, 1957–1967.* Washington, D.C.: U.S. Gov't. Printing Office, 1968.

McGaugh, J. L., and Petrinovich, L. Effects of drugs on learning and memory. *Int. Rev. Neurobiol.* 8: 139–196, 1965.

McGeer, E. G., and McGeer, P. L. Neurotransmitter metabolism in the aging brain. In: Terry, R. D., and Gershon, S. (Eds.) *Aging, vol. 3.* New York: Raven Press, 1976, pp. 389–403.

McKay, A. C., and Dundee, J. W., Effect of oral benzodiazepines on memory. *Brit. J. Anaesth.* 52: 1247–1257, 1980.

McKim, W. A. The effects of scopolamine and physostigmine on fixed interval behavior in the rat. *Psychopharmacologia* 39: 237–244, 1974.

McNutt, L. 1,1,3-Tricyano - 2 amino - 1-propene; a pharmacological attempt to enhance learning ability. *Proc. 75th Annual Convention of the American Psychological Association, vol. 2,* 1967, pp. 77–78.

McQuillan, L. M., Lapec, C. A., and Vibal, S. R. Evaluation of EEG and clinical changes associated with Pavabid therapy in chronic brain syndrome. *Curr. Therap. Res.* 16: 49–58, 1974.

Meek, J. L., Bertilsson, L., Cheney, D. L., Zsilla, G., and Costa, E. Aging-induced changes in acetylcholine and serotonin content of discrete brain nuclei. *J. Gerontol.* 32: 129–131, 1977.

Meyer, M. E., Severson, G. A., and Thompson, R. W. Scopolamine methscopolamine and response conditioned inhibition in rats. *Physiol. Psych.* 4: 43–44, 1976.

Miczek, K. A., and Grossman, S. P. Punished and unpunished operant behavior after atropine administered to VMH of squirrel monkeys. *J. Comp. Physiol. Psych.* 81: 318–330, 1972.

Millner, J. R., and Palfai, T. Metrazol disrupts conditioned aversion produced by $L_1Cl$: A time dependent effect. *Res. Rpts. NIMH*, no. MH23235, 1974.

Milner, B. Amnesia following operation on the temporal lobes. In: Whitty, C., and Zangwill, O. (Eds.) *Amnesia*, (1st ed.) London: Butterworths, 1966.

Mitchel, V. E., Ross, S., and Hurst, P. M. Drugs and placebos: Effects of caffeine on cognitive performance. *Psychol. Rep.* 35: 875–883, 1974.

Mitchell, J. C., and King, F. A. The effects of chlorpromazine on water maze learning, retention, and stereotyped behavior in the rat. *Psychopharmacologia* 1: 463–468, 1960.

Mitchell, J. R., Cavanaugh, J. H., Arias, L., and Oates, J. A. Guanethidine and related agents. III. Antagonism by drugs which inhibit the norepinephrine pump in man. *J. Clin. Invest.* 49: 1596–1604, 1970.

Mohs, R. C., Davis, K. L., and Hollister, L. E. Choline chloride effects on memory in the elderly. *Neurobil. Aging* 1: 21–25, 1980.

Mohs, R. C., Davis, K. L., Tinklenberg, J. R., Hollister, L. E., Yesavage, J. A., and Kopell, B. S. Choline chloride treatment of memory deficits in the elderly. *Am. J. Psychiat..* 136: 1275–1277, 1979.

Molimard, R., Marillaud, A., Paille, A., Le Devehat, C., Lemoine, A., and Dougny, M. Impairment of memorization by high doses of pyridoxine in man. *Biomedicine* 32: 88–92, 1980.

Mollenauer, S., Plotnick, R., and Bean, J. Effects of scopolamine on smell discrimination in the rat. *Physiol. Psych.* 4: 357–360, 1976.

Morley, B. J., and Russin, R. The effects of scopolamine on extinction and spontaneous recovery. *Psychopharmacology* 56: 301–304, 1978.

Morrison, C. F., and Armitage, A. K. Effects of nicotine upon free operant behavior of rats and spontaneous motor activity of mice. *Ann. N.Y. Acad. Sci.* 142: 268–276, 1967.

Moss, D. E., and Rogers, J. B. Effects of cobra neutoxin on retention of a brightness discrimination in rats. *Pharmacol. Biochem. Behav.* 3: 1147–1178, 1975.

Müller, G. E., and Pilzecker, A. Experimentelle Beiträge zur Lehre vom Gedächtnis. *Z. Psychol.* 1: 1–288, 1900.

Mundow, L. S., and Long, S. V. The amnestic value of diazepam at forceps delivery. *Irish J. Med. Sci.* 143: 101–104, 1974.

Nachmansohn, D. Sur l'action de la strychnine. *Seance Soc. Biol.* 129: 941–943, 1938.

Nagy, M. Z., Murphy, J. M., and Ray, D. Development of behavioral arousal and inhibition on the Swiss webster mouse. *Bull. Psychon. Soc.* 6: 146–148, 1975.

Nash, H. Psychologic effects of amphetamines and barbiturates. *J. Nerv. Ment. Dis.* 134: 203–217, 1962.

Nauta, J. Hippocampal projections and related neural pathways in the midbrain of the cat. *Brain* 81: 319–340, 1958.

Neill, D. B. Frontal-striatal control of behavioral inhibition in the rat. *Brain Res.* 105: 89–103, 1976.

Norton, S., DeBeer, E. J., and Tamburro, J. Comparison of the effects of chlorpromazine and pentobarbital on cat behaviour. *J. Pharmacol.* 119: 173, 1957.

O'Brien, J. P., and Sharp, A. R. The influence of renal disease on the insulin (I$^{131}$) disappearance curve in man. *Metabolism* 16: 76–83, 1967.

Ogg, C. S., Toseland, P. A., and Cameron, J. S. Pulmonary tuberculosis in patient on hemodialysis. *Br. Med. J.* 2: 283–284, 1968.

Oglesby, M. W., and Winter, J. C. Post-trial strychnine: Lack of effect on conditioned avoidance learning. *Fed. Proc.* 32: 818, 1973.

Oglesby, M. W., and Winter, J. C. Strychnine sulfate and piracetam: lack of effect on learning in the rat. *Psychopharmacologia (Berlin)* 36: 163–173, 1974.

Olds, M. E. Facilitatory action of diazepaim and chlordiazepoxide on hypothalamic reward behavior. *J. Comp. Physiol. Psychol.* 62: 136–140, 1966.

Oliverio A. Analysis of the "anti-fatigue" activity of amphetamine. *Role of Central Adrenergic Mechanisms II Farmaco* (Milan) 6: 441–449, 1967.

Oliveros, J. C., Jandali, M. K., Timsit, J. R., Berthier, M., Remy, R., Behghezal, A., Auditbert, A., and Moeglen, J. M. Vasopressin in amnesia. *Lancet* 1: 42, 1978.

Orowan, E. The origin of man. *Nature* 175: 683–684, 1955.

Orzack, M. H., Taylor, C. L., and Kornetsky, C. A research report on the antifatigue effects of magnesium pemoline. *Psychopharmacologia* 13: 413–417, 1968.

Otis, L. S. Dissociation and recovery of a response learned under the influence of chlorpromazine of saline. *Science* 143: 1347–1348, 1964.

Overstreet, D. H. Reduced behavioral effects of pilocarpine during chronic treatment with DFP. *Behav. Biol.* 11: 49–58, 1974.

Overstreet, D. H. Pharmacological approaches to habituation of the acoustic startle response in rats. *Physiol. Psych.* 5: 230–238, 1975.

Overstreet, D. H., Russell, R. W., Vasquez, B. J., and Dalglish, F. W. Involvement of muscarinic and nicotinic receptors in behavioral tolerance to DFP. *Pharmacol. Biochem. Behav.* 2: 45–54, 1974.

Overton, D. A. State-dependent learning produced by depressant and atropine-like drugs. *Psychopharmacologia* 10: 6–31, 1966.

Page, J. G., Janicki, R. S., Bernstein, J. E., Curran, C. F., and Mitchell, F. A. Pemoline (Cylirt) in the treatment of childhood hyperkinesis. *J. Learning Disabil.* 7: 498–503, 1974.

Pandit, S. K., and Dundee, J. W. Pre-operative amnesia. *Anaesthesia* 24: 493–499, 1970.

Parbrook, G. D. The levels of nitrous oxide analgesia. *Brit. J. Anaesth.* 39: 974–982, 1967.

Parker, J. P., Beirne, G. J., and Desai, J. N. Androgen-induced increase in red cell 2,3-diphosphoglycerate. *N. Engl. J. Med.* 287: 381–383, 1972.

Parkhouse, J., Henrie, J. R., and Duncan, G. M. Nitrous oxide analgesia in relation to mental performance. *J. Pharmacol. Exp. Therap.* 128: 44–54, 1960.

Pavlov, I. P. *Conditioned Reflexes.* London: Oxford Univ. Press, 1927.

Pazzagli, A., and Pepeu, G. Amnesic properties of scopolamine and brain acetylcholine in the rat. *Int. J. Neuropharm.* 4: 291–296, 1964.

Pearlman, C. A., Jr., Sharpless, S. K., and Jarvik, M. E. Retrograde amnesia produced by anesthetic and convulsant agents. *J. Comp. Physiol. Psychol.* 54: 109–112, 1961.

Peele, T. *The Neuroanatomical Basis for Clinical Neurology.* New York: McGraw-Hill, 1977.

Perl, D. P., and Brody, A. R. Alzheimer's Disease: X-ray spectrometric evidence of aluminum accumulation in neurofibrillary tangle-bearing neurons. *Science* 208: 297–299, 1980.

Perry, E. K., Perry, R. H., Blessed, G., and Tomlinson, B. E. Neurotransmitter enzyme abnormalities in senile dementia—choline acetyltransferase and glutamic acid decarboxylase in necropsy brain tissue. *J. Neurol. Sci.* 34: 247–265, 1977a.

Perry, E. K., Perry, R. H., Gibson, P. H., Blessed, G., and Tomlinson, B. E. A cholinergic connection between normal aging and senile dementia in the human hippocampus. *Neurosci. Lett.* 6: 85–89, 1977b.

Pert, A., and Avis, H. Lack of cross dissociation between scopolamine and mecamylamine during fear conditioning in rats. *Physiol. Psych.* 2: 111–116, 1974.

Petersen, R. C., and Ghoneim, M. M. Diazepam and human memory: Influence on acquisition, retrieval, and state-dependent learning. *Prog. Neuro-Psychopharmacol.* 4: 81–89, 1980.

Pfeiffer, C. C., and Jenney, E. H. Effects of anti-AChE, physostigmine depressed pole-jump avoidance behavior. *Ann. N.Y. Acad. Sci.* 66: 753–760, 1957.

Phillips, K. C., and Lowe, G. The suppression of behaviors in rats by previous experience and electric shock and its antagonism by atropine. *Psychopharmacologia* 42: 99–103, 1975.

*Physician's Desk Reference,* 30th ed. Oradell, N.J.: Medical Economics Co., 1976.

Plas, R., and Naquet, R. Contribution to the neurophysiological study of imipramine. *Compt. Rend. Soc. Biol.* 155: 547–550, 1961.

Plenge, P., Mellerup, E. T., and Rafaelsen, O. J. Lithium action on the carbohydrate metabolism in rat brain, muscle, and liver. *Proc. 2nd International Meeting of the International Society for Neurochemistry,* 1969, p. 321.

Pletscher, A., and Gey, K. F. Pharmacological influence of 5-hydroxytryptamine metabolism in the brain and monoamine oxidase inhibition in vitro. *Helv. Physiol. Pharmacol. Acta* 17: C35, 1959.

Pletscher, A., and Gey, K. F. The effect of chlorpromazine on pharmacological changes in 5-hydroxytryptamine and noradrenaline content in the brain (in German). *Med. Exp.* 2: 259–265, 1960.

Pletscher, A., and Gey, K. F. Action of imipramine and amitriptyline on cerebral monoamines as compared with chlorpromazine. *Med. Exp.* 6: 165, 1962.

Pletscher, A., Shore, P. A., and Brodie, B. B. Serotonin release as a possible mechanism of reserpine action. *Science* 122: 374–375, 1955.

Plotnick, R., Mollenhauer, S., and Millberg, L. Scopolamine and food reinforced behavior in the rat. *Physiol. Psych. 4:* 443–446, 1976.

Plotnikoff, N. Magnesium pemoline: Enhancement of learning and memory of a conditioned avoidance response. *Science* 151: 703–705, 1966a.

Plotnikoff, N. Magnesium pemoline: Antagonism of retrograde amnesia in rats. *Fed. Proc.* 25: 262, 1966b.

Plotnikoff, N. Magnesium pemoline: Enhancement of memory after electroconvulsive shock in rats. *Life Sci.* 5: 1495–1598, 1966c.

Post, R. M., and Goodwin, F. K. Effect of amitriptyline and imipramine on amine metabolites in the cerebrospinal fluid of depressed patients. *Arch. Gen. Psychiat.* 30: 234–239, 1974.

Powell, T., Bullery, R., and Loman, W. A Quantitative study of the fornix-mammillothalamic system. *J. Anat.* 91: 419–432, 1957.

Pradhan, S. N., and Dutta, S. N. Behavioral effects of arecoline in rats. *Psychopharmacologia* 17: 49–58, 1970.

Predescu, V., Giureze, T., Tudorache, D., Nica, St., Ionescu, R., Nicolschi, L., Niturad, A., Popovici, E., and Curelaru, S. Hydergine-thioridazine combination in the treatment of psychopathological states in old age. *Activ. Nerv. Sup. (Praha)* 16: 237–238, 1974.

Preibisch-Effenberger, R., and Knothe, J. Der Einfluss zentralwirkender Pharmaka auf die Wortverständlichkeit des Normalhörenden bei binauraler Testsprache. *Z. Laryng. Rhinol. Otol. u. Grenzgeb.* 44: 619–630, 1965.

Pribam, K. *Languages of the Brain.* Englewood Cliffs, N.J.: Prentice Hall, 1971.

Prien, R. F., Wagner, M. J., Jr., and Kahn, S. Lack of facilitation in maze learning by picrotoxin and strychnine sulfate. *Am. J. Psychol.* 204: 448–492, 1963.

Pulver, R., Exer, B., and Herrmann, B. Einige Wirkungen des (γ-dimethylaminopropyl)iminobenzyl-HC1 und seiner Metabolite auf den Stoffwechsel von Neurohormonen. *Arzneimittel-Forsch.* 10: 530, 1960.

Quarton, G. C., and Talland, G. A. The effects of methamphetamine and pentobarbital on two measures of attention. *Psychopharmacologia* 3: 66–71, 1962.

Raisman, G., Cowen, W., and Powell, T. The extrinsic afferent, commissural, and association fibers of the hippocampus. *Brain* 88: 963–996, 1965.

Raisman, G., Cowen, W., and Powell, T. An experimental analysis of the efferent connections of the hippocampus. *Brain* 89: 83–108, 1966.

Rao, D. B., and Norris, J. R. A double-blind investigation of Hydergine in the treatment of cerebrovascular insufficiency in the elderly. *Johns Hopkins Med. J.* 130: 317–324, 1972.

Rasmusson, D., and Szerb, J. C. Cortical ACh release during operant behavior in rabbits. *Life Sci.* 16: 683–690, 1975.

Ray, D., and Nagy, M. Z. Emerging cholinergic mechanisms on ontogeny of response inhibition in the mouse. *J. Comp. Physiol. Psych.* 92: 335–349, 1978.

Regina, E. G., Smith, G. M., Keiper, C. G., and McKelvey, R. K. Effects of caffeine on alertness in simulated automobile driving. *J. Appl. Psychol.* 59: 483–489, 1974.

Reisine, T. D., Bird, E. D., Spokes, E., Enna, S. J., and Yamamura, H. I. Pre- and post-synaptic neurochemical alterations in Alzheimer's disease. *Trans. Am. Soc. Neurochem.* 9: 203, 1978.

Remington, G., and Anisman, H. Genetic and ontogenetic variations in locomotor activity following treatment with scopolamine or *d*-amphetamine. *Develop. Psychobiol.* 9: 579–585, 1976.

Rigter, H., van Riezen, H., and de Wied, D. The effects of ACTH- and vasopressin-analogues on $CO_2$-induced retrograde amnesia in rats. *Physiol. Behav.* 13: 381–388, 1974.

Ritter, R. M., Nail, H. R., Tatum, P., and Blazi, M. L. The effect of papaverine on patients with cerebral arteriosclerosis. *Clin. Med.* 78: 18–24, 1971.

Rizzoli, A. A., and Galzinga, L. Molecular mechanism of the unconscious state induced by butyrate. *Biochem. Pharmacol.* 19: 2727–2736, 1970.

Roberts, R. B., Flexner, J. B., and Flexner, L. B. Some evidence for the involvement of adrenergic sites in the memory trace. *Proc. Nat. Acad. Sci.* 66: 310–313, 1970.

Robinson, D. S., Nies, A., Davis, J. N., Bunney, W. E., Davis, J. M., Colburn, R. W., Bourne, H. R., Shaw, D. M., and Coppen, A. J. Aging monoamines, and monoamine-oxidase levels. *Lancet* 1: 290–291, 1972.

Robinson, D. S., Sourkes, T. L., Nies, A., Harris, L. S., Spector, S., Barlett, D. L., and Kaye, L. S. Monoamine metabolism in human brain. *Arch. Gen Psychiat.* 34: 89–92, 1977.

Robson, J. G., Burns, B. D., and Welt, P. J. L. The effect of inhaling dilute nitrous oxide upon recent memory and time estimation. *Can. Anesth. Soc. J.* 7: 399–410, 1960.

Robustelli, F. Azione della nicotina sul condizionamento di salvaguardia di ratti di un mese. *Rend. Classe Sci. Fisiche, Matemat. e Naturali* 40: 490–497, 1966.

Rosecrans, J., Dren, A., and Domino, E. Effects of physostigmine on rat brain acetylcholine, acetylcholinesterase and conditioned pole jumping. *Int. J. Neuropharm.* 7: 127–134, 1968.

Rosen, A. J., and Cohen, M. E. The effects of cinanserin, a potent serotonin antagonist, on the acquisition of a running response in the rat. *Neuropharmacol. (Oxford)* 12: 501–508, 1973.

Rosen, H. J. Mental decline in the elderly: Pharmacotherapy (Ergot alkaloids versus paperverine). *J. Am. Geriatr. Soc.* 23: 169–174, 1975.

Rosenzweig, M. R., Krech, D., and Bennett, E. L. A search for relationship between brain chemicals and behavior. *Psychol. Bull.* 57: 476–492, 1960.

Ross, J. F., and Grossman, S. P. Intrahippocampal application of cholinergic agents and blockers. *J. Comp. Physiol. Psych.* 86: 590–600, 1974.

Ross, J., McDermott, L., and Grossman, S. Disinhibitory effects of intrahippocampal or intrahypothalamic injections of anticholinergic compounds in the rat. *Pharmacol. Biochem. Behav.* 3: 631–639, 1975.

Roth, J. A., and Gillis, C. N. Inhibition of lung, liver and brain monoamine oxidase by imipramine and desipramine. *Biochem. Pharmacol.* 23: 1138–1140, 1974.

Roth, J. A., Whitemore, R. M., Shakarjian, M. P., and Eddy, B. J. Inhibition of human brain type A and B monoamine oxidase by chlorpromazine and metabolites. *Commun. Psychopharm.* 3: 235–243, 1979.

Rubio-Chevannier, H., Bach-E-Rita, G., Penaloza-Rojas, J., and Hernandez-Peon, R. Potentiating action of imipramine upon "reticular arousal." *Exp. Neurol.* 4: 214, 1961.

Russell, R. W., and Warburton, D. M. Acquisition of new responses by rats during chronic depression of acetylcholinesterase activity. *J. Comp. Physiol. Psych.* 77: 228–233, 1971.

Ryback, R. State-dependent or "dissociated" learning with alcohol in the goldfish. *Quart. J. Stud. Alcohol.* 30: 598–608, 1969a.

Ryback, R. The use of goldfish as a model for alcohol amnesia in man. *Quart. J. Stud. Alcohol.* 30: 877–882, 1969b.

Ryback, R. S. Alcohol amnesia. *J. Am. Med. Assoc.* 212: 1524, 1970.

Sakalis, G., Oh, D., Gershon, S., and Shopsin, B. A trial of Gerovital H-3 in depression during senility. *Curr. Ther. Res.* 16: 59–63, 1974.

Samanin, R., Gumulka, W., and Valzelli, L. Reduced effect of morphine in midbrain raphe lesioned rats. *Eur. J. Pharmacol.* 10: 339–343, 1970.

Sandberg, F. A comparative quantitative study of the central depressant effect of seven clinical used phenothiazine derivatives. *Arzneimitt. Forsch.* 9: 203–206, 1959.

Sanders, H. L., and Warrington, E. K. Memory for remote events in amnesic patients. *Brain* 94: 661–668, 1971.

Sandman, C. A., George, J. M., Nolan, J. D., Van Riezen, H., and Kastin, A. J. Enhancement of attention in man with ACTH/MSH 4–10. *Physiol. Behav.* 15: 427–431, 1975.

Schaaf, M., and Payne, C. A. Dystonic reactions to prochlorperazine in hypoparathyroidism. *N. Engl. J. Med.* 282: 991–995, 1971.

Schaefer, G. L., Buchanan, D. C., and Ray, O. S. Effects of neonatal strychnine administration on active avoidance in rats. *Behav. Biol.* 10: 253–258, 1974.

Schallek, W., Kuehn, A., and Seppelin, D. K. Central depressant effects of methylprylon. *J. Pharmacol. Exp. Therap.* 118: 139–147, 1956.

Schanberg, S., Schildkraut, J. J., and Kopin, I. J. The effects of psychoactive drugs on norepinephrine-$H^3$ metabolism in brain. *Biochem. Pharmacol.* 16: 393–399, 1967.

Scheckel, C. L., and Boff, E. Behavioral effects of interacting imipramine and other drugs with 3-amphetamine, cocaine, and tetrabenazine. *Psychopharmacologia* 5: 198–208, 1964.

Schmidt, M. J., and Davenport, J. W. TZAP: Facilitation of learning in hypothyroid rats. *Psychonom. Sci.* 7: 185–186, 1967.

Schneider, R. A., and Costiloe, J. P. Inhibition and facilitation of the conditioned galvanic skin reflex by centrally acting drugs (chlorpromazine, amobarbital and methylphenidylacetate). *Clin. Res. Proc.* 4: 45, 1956.

Schou, M. Normothymoleptics "mood normalizers." Are lithium and imipramine drugs specific for affective disorders? *Br. J. Psychiat.* 109: 803, 1963.

Schou, M. Lithium, sodium and manic depressive psychosis. In: Walaas, O. (Ed.) *Molecular Basis of Some Aspects of Mental Activity, vol. 2.* New York: Academic Press, 1967, p. 457.

Schulenberg, O. J., Riccio, D. L., and Stikes, E. R. Acquisition and retention of a passive avoidance response as a function of age in rats. *J. Comp. Physiol. Psych.* 74: 75–83, 1971.

Schulz, R., Wuster, M., Duka, T., and Herz, A. Acute and chronic ethanol treatment changes endorphin levels in brain and pituitary. *Psychopharmacology* 68: 221–227, 1980.

Schwartzkrain, P., and Anderson, P. Glutamic acid sensitivity of dendrites in hippocampal slices in vitro. In: Kreuzberg, G. (Ed.) *Properties of Dendrites.* New York: Raven Press, 1975.

Scovell, W. B., and Milner, B. Loss of recent memory after bilateral hippocampal lesions. *J. Neurol. Neurosurg. Psychiat.* 20: 11–25, 1957.

Sellers, E. M., and Koch-Weser, J. Potentiation of warfarin induced hypoprothrombinemia by chloral hydrate. *New Engl. J. Med.* 283: 827–831, 1970.

Shchelkunov, Ye. 1. Usiliniye tofranilom i khloratsizinom antirezerpinovogo deystviya fenamina v apytakh na krysakh s uslovnymi refleksami. *Activitas Nervosa Superior* 5: 4–12, 1963.

Shin, K. C. L., and Cheon, Y. S. Influences of reserpine and chlorpromazine on the analgesic and metabolic effects of morphine. *Korean U. Med. J. (Seoul)* 10: 653–661, 1973.

Shute, C. C. Chemical transmitter system in the brain. *Mod. Trends Neurol.* 6: 183–203, 1975.

Shute, C., and Lewis, P. Cholinesterase containing systems of the brain of the rat. *Nature* 199: 1160–1164, 1963.

Sigg, E. B. Pharmacological studies with Tofranil. *Can. Psychiat. Assoc. J.* 4: 75, 1959.

Signorelli, A. Influence of physostigmine upon consolidation of memory in mice. *J. Comp. Physiol. Psych.* 90: 658–664, 1976.

Signoret, J., Whiteley, A., and Lhermitte, F. Influence of choline on amnesia in early Alzheimer's disease. *Lancet* 2: 837, 1978.

Singer, G., Ho, A., and Gershon, S. Changes in activity of choline acetylase in central nervous system of rat after intraventricular administration of noradrenalin. *Nature (London) New Biol.* 230: 152–153, 1971.

Singh, H. K., Ott, T., and Matthies, H. Effect of intrahippocampal injections of atropine on different phases of a learning experiment. *Psychopharmacologia* 38: 247–258, 1974.

Sitarem, N., Weingartner, H., Caine, E. D., and Gillin, J. C. Choline: Selective enhancement of serial learning and encoding of low imagery words in man. *Life Sci.* 22: 1555–1560, 1978.

Small, I. F., Sharpley, P., and Small, J. G. Influence of cylert upon memory changes with ECT. *Am. J. Psychiat.* 125: 837–840, 1968.

Small, J. G., and Small, I. F. EEG spikes in non-epileptic psychiatric patients. *Dis. Nerv. Syst.* 28: 523–525, 1967.

Smigel, J. O., Piller, J., Murphy, C., Lowe, D., and Gibson, J. H-3 procaine hydrochloride therapy in aging institutionalized patients. *J. Am. Gerontol. Soc.* 8: 785–794, 1960.

Smith, C. M., Swash, M., Exton-Smith, A. N., Phillips, M. J., Overstall, P. W., Piper, M. E., and Bailey, M. R. Choline in Alzheimer's disease. *Lancet 2:* 318, 1978.

Smith, G., and Shirley, A. W. Failure to demonstrate effect of trace concentrations of nitrous oxide and halothane on psychomotor performance. *Br. J. Anaesth.* 49: 65–70, 1977.

Smith, R. G. Magnesium pemoline: Lack of facilitation in human learning memory and performance tests. *Science* 155: 603–605, 1967.

Smith, W. L., Philippus, M. J., and Lowrey, J. B. A comparison of psychological and psychophysical test patterns before and after receiving papaverine HCl. *Curr. Therap. Res.* 10: 428–431, 1968.

Solyom, L., and Galley, H. M. Effect of malononitrile dimer on operant and classical conditioning of aged white rats. *Int. J. Neuropsychiat.* 2: 577–584, 1966.

Soubrie, P., and Boissier, J. R. An amnesic effect of benzodiazepines in rats. *Experientia* 32: 359–360, 1976.

Sourkes, T. L., and Missala, K. Metabolism of dihydroxyphenylalanine and tryptophan in pyridoxine-deficient rats. *Ann. N.Y. Acad. Sci.* 166: 235–245, 1969.

Spillane, J. A., White, P., Goodhardt, M. J., Flack, R. H. A., Bowen, D. M., and Davison, A. N. Selective vulnerability of neurons in organic dementia. *Nature* 266: 558–559, 1977.

Stanes, M. D., and Brown, C. P. Effect of physostigmine on Y-maze discrimination retention in the rat. *Psychopharmacologia* 46: 269–276, 1976.

Stein, D. G. The effects of early saline injections and pentylenetetrazol on Hebb-Williams maze performance in the adult rat. *Behav. Biol.* 1: 415–422, 1974.

Stein, D. G., and Brink, J. J. Prevention of retrograde amnesia by injection of magnesium pemoline in dimethylsulfoxide. *Psychopharmacologia* 14: 240–247, 1969.

Stein, L. Reserpine and the learning of fear. *Science 124: 1082*–1083, 1956.

Steinberg, H., and Summerfield, A. Influence of a depressant drug on acquisition in rote learning. *Quart. J. Exp. Psychol.* 9: 138–145, 1957.

Steinberg, H., and Watson, R. H. J. Chlorpromazine inhibition of reactions of rats to unfamiliar surroundings. *J. Physiol. (London)* 147: 20P, 1959.

Stern, F. H. Management of chronic brain syndrome secondary to cerebral arteriosclerosis with special reference to papaverine hydrochloride. *J. Am. Geriatr. Soc.* 18: 507–512, 1970.

Stern, W. C., and Heise, G. A. Failure of TCAP to facilitate acquisition of double alternation in rats. *Physiol. Behav.* 5: 449–452, 1970.

Stevens, D. A., Resnick, O., and Krus, D. M. The effects of *p*-chlorophenylalanine, a deplector of brain serotonin on behavior. Ɩ. Facilitation of discrimination learning. *Life Sci.* 6: 2215–2220, 1967.

Stewart, J. Differential response based on the physiological consequences of pharmacological agents. *Psychopharmacologia* 3: 132–138, 1962.

Stewart, W. J. Effect of experience in the test environment on scopolamine induced changes in activity in an exploration box. *Psychol. Rep.* 40: 215–254, 1977.

Stewart, W. J., and Blain, S. Dose-response effects of scopolamine on activity in an open field. *Psychopharmacologia* 44: 291–295, 1975.

Stewart, W. J., Blampied, N. M., and Hughes, R. N. The effect of scopolamine on a geometric progressive ratio schedule. *Psychopharmacologia* 38: 55–66, 1974.

Stewart, W., and Stewart, N. Habituation should be measured directly: Effects of physostigmine on activity. *Psychol. Rep.* 40: 1223–1226, 1977.

Stolerman, I. P., Fink, R., and Jarvik, M. E. Acute and chronic tolerance to nicotine measured by activity in rats. *Psychopharmacologia (Berlin)* 30: 329–342, 1973.

Stone, G. C., Bernstein, B. M., Hambourger, W. E., and Drill, V. A. Behavioral and pharmacological studies of thiopropazate, a potent tranquilising agent. *Arch. Int. Pharmacodyn. Therap.* 127: 85–103, 1960.

Storm, T., and Caird, W. K. The effects of alcohol of serial verbal learning in chronic alcoholics. *Psychonom. Sci.* 9: 43–44, 1967.

Stratton, L. O., and Kastin, A. J. Avoidance learning at two levels of shock in rats receiving MSH. *Horm. Behav.* 5: 149–155, 1974.

Stratton, L. O., and Kastin, A. J. Increased acquisition of a complex appetitive task after MSH and MIF. *Pharmacol. Biochem. Behav.* 3: 901–904, 1975.

Strickland, K. P., and Noble, D. M. The in vitro incorporation of inorganic $P^{32}$ into the phosphatides of different areas of brain. The effect of chlorpromazine administered in vitro and in vovo. In: Kety, S. S., and Elkes, J. (Eds.) *Regional Neurochemistry* London: Pergamon, 1961, p. 489.

Stripling, J. W., and Alpern, H. P. Nicotine and caffeine disruption of the long-term store memory and proactive facilitation of learning in mice. *Psychopharmacologia (Berlin)* 38: 187–200, 1974.

Stripline, J. W., and Alpern, H. J. Sensory input and cholinergic agents: Effects on STM in the mouse. *Physiol. Psych.* 4: 69–75, 1976.

Sulser, F., Bickel, M.. H., and Brodie, B. B. The action of desmethylimipramine in counteracting sedation and cholinergic effects of reserpine-like drugs. *J. Pharmacol. Exp. Therap.* 144: 321–330, 1964.

Sulser, F., Watts, J., and Brodie, B. B. On the mechanism of antidepressant action of imipraminelike drugs. *Ann. N.Y. Acad. Sci.* 96: 279–288, 1962.

Swonger, A. K., and Rech, R. H. Serotonergic and cholinergic involvement in habituation of activity and spontaneous alternation of rats in a Y-maze. *J. Comp. Physiol. Psych.* 81: 509–522, 1972.

Taeschler, M., and Cerletti, A. Differential analysis of the effects of phenothiazine-tranquilizers on emotional and motor behavior in experimental animals. *Nature* 184: 823, 1959.

Tagliente, T. *Regional effects of barbiturates on monoamine oxidase type A and type B activity in the mouse brain.* Ph.D. Dissertation, City University of New York, 1979.

Talland, G. A., Mendleson, J. W., Koz, G., and Aaron, R. Experimental studies of the effects of tricyano-aminopropene on the memory and learning capacities of geriatric patients. *J. Psychiat. Res.* 3: 171–179, 1965.

Talland, G. A., and Quarton, G. C. The effects of methamphetamine and pentobarbital on the running memory span. *Psychopharmacologia* 7: 379–382, 1965.

Tannen, R. L., Regal, E. M., Dunn, M. J., and Schrier, R. W. Vasopressin resistant hyposthenuria in advanced chronic renal disease. *Engl. J. Med.* 280: 1135–1141, 1969.

Teitelbaum, H. A., Newtron, J. E. O., Gliedman, L. H., and Gantt, W. H. Conditioned reflex formation under pentobarbital. *Psychosom. Med.* 23: 446, 1961.

Tenen, S. S. The effects of *p*-chloropenylalanine, a serotonin depletor, on avoidance acquisition, pain sensitivity and related behavior in the rat. *Psychopharmacologia* 10: 204–219, 1967.

Teoh, P. C., and Cheah, J. S. Electrocardiographic changes in hyperthyroidism after adrenergic blockade with reserpine and propranalol. *Med. J. Australia (Sydney)* 2: 116–118, 1973.

Theobald, W. The course of a conditioned avoidance response in rats after treatment with Tofranil and reserpine combined. *Med. Exp.* 1: 102–108, 1959.

Theobald, W., Buch, O., King, H. A., Morpurgo, C., Wilhelmi, G., and Stengar, E. G. Comparative pharmacological investigations with Tofranil, Pertofane, and Ensidon. *Arch. Int. Pharmacodyn.* 148: 560, 1964.

Tissari, A. H., and Suurhasko, B. V. A. Effect of imipramine on the turnover of brain 5-HT in post-natal rats. *Acta Pharmacol. Toxicol. (Kobenhavn)* 31 (Suppl. 1): 29, 1972.

Tolman, E. C. Retroactive inhibition as affected by conditions of learning. *Psychol. Monogr.* 18: no. 107, 1917.

Torack, R. M. Adult dementia: History, biopsy, pathology. *Neurosurg.* 4: 434–442, 1979.

Trautner, E. M., Morris, R., Noack, C. H., and Gershon, S. The excretion and retention of ingested lithium and its effect on the ionic balance of man. *Med. J. Australia* 2: 280–291, 1955.

Turner, D. J., and Wilson, J. Effect of diazepam on awareness during caesarean section under general anaesthesia. *Br. Med. J.* 2: 736–737, 1969.

Valenstein, F., and Nauta, W. A comparison of the distribution of the fornix system in the rat, guinea pig, and monkey. *J. Comp. Neurol.* 113: 337–363, 1959.

Valliant, G. E. A comparison of physostigmine induced suppression of behavior. *J. Pharmacol. Exp. Therap.* 157: 636–648, 1967.

Van der Poel, A. M. The effects of some cholinolytic drugs on a number of behavior parameters in the T-maze. *Psychologia* 37: 45–58, 1974.

Van Wimersma Greidanus, T. j. B. Bohus, B., and de Wied, D. Effects of peptide hormones on behavior. In: *Progress in Endocrinology (Proce. 4th International Congress on Endocrinology,* Washington, D. C.), Amsterdam. Excerpta Medica I. C. S., no. 273. 1971, Excerpta Medica, pp. 197-201.

Van Wimersma Greidanus, T. j. B., and de Wied, D. The physiology of the neurohypophyseal system and its relation to memory processes. In: Davidson, A. N. (ed.) *Biochemical Correlates of Brain Function.* London: Academic Press, 1977, pp. 284–289.

Vernier, V. G. The pharmacology of antidepressant agents. *Dis. Nerv. Syst.* 22: 7–13, 1961.

Veronin, L. G., and Napalkov, A. V. Complex systems of conditioned reflexes in the analysis of drug effects. In: Votava, Z., Horvath, M., and Vinar O. (Eds.) *Psychopharmacological Methods.* New York: Macmillan, 1963, p. 182.

Victor, M., Adams, R., and Collins, G. *The Wernicke–Korsakoff Syndrome.* Oxford: Blackwell, 1971.

Vinogradov, V. V. Ismenenie oboronitel' no dvigatel' mykh uslovnykh refleksov u kotov pod vluyaniem damilena (amitriptilina) i imipramina. *Farmakol. Toksikol.* 32: 259–261. 1969.

Waddington, J. L., and Olley, J. F. Dissociation of the antipunishment activities of chlordiazepoxide and atropine using two heterogenous passive avoidance tasks. *Psychopharmacology* 52: 93–96, 1977.

Walk, R. D., Owens, J. W. M., and Davidson, B. S. Influence of reserpine on avoidance conditioning, exploratory behavior, and discrimination learning in the rat. *Psychol. Rep.* 8: 251–258, 1961.

Walker, D. O., and Schenker, S. Pathogenesis of hepatic encephalopathy. *Am. J. Clin. Nutrition* 23: 619–632, 1970.

Walsh, F. B. *Clinical Neuro-Ophthalmology.* Baltimore: Williams and Wilkins, 1947.

Warburton, D. M., and Brown, K. Attenuation of stimulus sensitivity by scopolamine. *Nature* 230: 1126–1167, 1971.

Warburton, D. M., and Brown, K. The facilitation of discrimination performance by physostigmine sulfate. *Psychopharmacologia* 27: 275–284, 1972.

Warburton, D. M., and Brown, K. Effects of scopolamine on a double stimulus discrimination. *Neuropharmacology* 15: 659–663, 1976.

Warburton, D. M., and Groves, P. M. The effects of scopolamine on habituation of acoustic startle response in rats. *Behav. Biol.* 3: 289–293, 1969.

Wechsler, H., Grosser, G. H., and Greenblatt, M. Research evaluating antidepressant medications on hospitalized mental patients. A survey of published reports during a five-year period. *J. Nerv. Ment. Dis.* 151: 231–239, 1965.

Weckowicz, T. E., Nutter, R., and Gibbs, J. T. The effect of tranylcypromine (Parnate) on eyelid conditioning and paired associate learning in depressed patients. *Pavlovian J. Biol. Sci.* 9: 122–123, 1974.

Weiner, N., and Deutsch, J. Temporal aspects of anticholinergic and anticholinesterase induced amnesia for an appetitive habit. *J. Comp. Physiol. Psych.* 66: 613–617, 1968.

Weiss, B., and Laties, V. G. Enhancement of human performance by caffeine and the amphetamines. *Pharmacol. Rev.* 14: 1–36, 1962.

Weiss, B., and Laties, V. G. Behavioral pharmacology and toxicology. *Ann. Rev. Pharmacol.* 9: 297–326, 1969.

Weissman, A. Interaction effects of impramine and *d*-amphetamine on non-discriminated avoidance. *Pharmacologia* 3: 60, 1961.

Wenzel, D. C., and Davis, P. W. The effect of caffeine and nicotine as tension-inducing agents and the ability of meprobamate to counteract such effects upon performance. *Tech. Rep., Office of Naval Research Armed Services Tech. Inf. Agency,* 1961, pp. 1–11.

White, P., Goodhardt, M. J., Keet, J. P., Hiley, C. R., Carrasco, L. H., Williams, I. E. I., and Bowen, D. M. Neocortical cholinergic neurones in elderly people. *Lancet* 1: 668–670, 1977.

White, S. Atropine, scopolamine and hippocampal lesions. Effects on alternation performance of rats. *Pharmacol. Biochem. Behav.* 2: 297–307, 1974.

Will, B. E. Neurochemical correlates of individual differences in animal learning capacity. *Behav. Biol.* 19: 143–171, 1977.

Williams, J. M., Hamilton, L. W., and Carlton, P. Pharmacological and anatomical dissociation of two types of habituations. *J. Comp. Physiol. Psych.* 27: 724–732, 1974.

Williams, J. M., Hamilton, L. W., and Carlton, P. Ontogenetic dissociation of two classes of habituation. *J. Comp. Physiol. Psych.* 89: 733–737, 1975.

Wilson, J., and Turner, D. J. Awareness during caesarean section under general anaesthesia. *Br. Med. J.* 1: 280–283, 1969.

Wilson, L. M., and Riccio, D. C. CS familiarization and conditioned suppression in weanling and adult albino rats. *Bull. Psychonom. Soc.* 1: 184–186, 1973.

Wilson, L. M., and Riccio, D. C. Scopolamine's effects on passive avoidance behavior in immature rats. *Develop. Psychobiol.* 9: 245–254, 1976.

Wilson, W. A., and Escueta, A. V. Common synaptic effects of pentylenetetrazol and penicillin. *Brain Res. (Amsterdam)* 72: 168–171, 1974.

Winblad, B., Adolfsson, R., Gottfries, C. G., Oreland, L., and Roos, B. E. Brain monoamines, monoamine metabolites and enzymes in physiological ageing and senile dementia. In: Frigerio, A. (Ed.) *Recent Developments in Mass Spectrometry in Biochemistry and Medicine,* vol. 1. New York: Plenum, 1978, pp. 253–267.

Winson, J. Loss of hippocampal theta activity results in spatial memory deficit in rats. *Science* 201: 160–163, 1978.

Wiśniewski, H. M., Ghetti, B., and Terry, R. D. Neuritic (senile) plaques and filamentous changes in aged rhesus monkeys. *J. Neuropathol. Exp. Neurol.* 32: 566–584, 1973.

Wiśniewski, H. M., Narang, H. K., and Terry, R. D. Neurofibrillary tangles of paired helical filaments. *J. Neurol. Sci.* 27: 173–181, 1976.

Witt, P. N. Die Wirkung einer einmaligen Gabe von Largachtil auf den Netzbau der Spinne Zilla-x-notata. *Monatsschr. Psychiat. Neurol.* 129: 123–128, 1955.

Wolff, K. Treatment of the confused geriatric patient. *Dis Nerv. Syst.* 23: 199–203, 1962.

Woolley, D. W. A method for demonstration of the effects of serotonin of learning ability. In: Mikhel'son, M. Ya., and Longo, V. G. (Eds.) *Pharmacology of Conditioning, Learning and Retention.* Oxford: Pergamon Press, 1965, pp. 231–236.

Worsham, E., and Hamilton, L. W. The effects of septal lesions or scopolamine injections on retention of habituation to a novel environment. *Bull. Psychonom. Soc.* 7: 193–195, 1976.

Wurtman, R. Memory disorders. *Trends in Neurosciences,* Mar. 1980, pp. VII–X.

Wurtmen, R. J., Hirsch, M. I., and Growdon, J. H. Lecithin consumption raises serum-tree-choline levels. *Lancet* 1: 68–69, 1977.

Zieve, L. Pathogenesis of hepatic coma. *Arch. Intern. Med.* 118: 211–223, 1966.

# Index